TRINITY AND MINISTRY

PETER DRILLING

TRINITY AND MINISTRY

Fortress Press • Minneapolis

TRINITY AND MINISTRY

Scripture quotations unless otherwise noted are from the Revised Standard Version of the Bible, copyright © 1946, 1952, and 1971 by the Division of Christian Education of the National Council of Churches.

Excerpt from "You, Neighbor God," from *Poems from the Book of Hours* by Rainer Maria Rilke, translated by Babette Deutsch is copyright © 1941 New Directions Publishing Corporation and reprinted by permission of the publisher.

Cover design: Brian Preuss

Library of Congress Cataloging-in-Publication Data

Drilling, Peter. 1942–
    Trinity and ministry / Peter Drilling.
        p.   cm.
    Includes bibliographical references and index.
    ISBN 0-8006-2490-4
    1. Pastoral theology—Catholic Church.   2. Lay ministry—Catholic Church.   3.
Women clergy.   4. Catholic Church—Doctrines.
    I. Title.
BX1913.D75   1991
253—dc20   91-31974
                                                                                            CIP

Manufactured in the U.S.A.   AF 1-2490
95   94   93   92   91   1   2   3   4   5   6   7   8   9   10

CONTENTS

PREFACE

THIS BOOK HAS BEEN GERMINATING FOR MANY YEARS. THE
issues addressed—the relationship between the ministries of the baptized
and of the ordained, the role of women in ministry, mutual recognition of
ministry by the many Christian communions, the inculturation of ministry,
and the interior formation of Christians for ministry—challenged me regularly, in their practical dimensions, through twelve years as a parish priest.
For the last eight years I have been wrestling with them in the manner of
the systematic theologian. Happily, practical and theoretical reflection have
come together into a common conclusion.

Still, I bring this book to publication with some hesitation, for, in these
days, systematic theologians who publish are almost certain to be labeled
either conservative or liberal. Such labels seem to me to be singularly un-
productive of healthy theological dialogue, because they become an excuse
to dismiss authors who do not share one's own bias.

Is not all theology, first and finally, an effort to articulate some understanding of faith in God? Thus, the theological reflections of this book
combine to suggest that contemporary ministerial issues admit of intelligent, reasonable, responsible resolution if they are studied in their connection with Christian trinitarian doctrine and theology. I present my conclusions as one more voice in the dialogue, eager for criticism.

My perspective is unabashedly Roman Catholic. But I write with full
awareness and unhesitating acceptance of the ecumenical quest for Christian unity. I believe that it is an evangelical mandate that Christians seek
unity within the community of disciples. In my view, a theology of ministry
that does not engage in ecumenical dialogue is not of much use today.

While chapter 5 takes up the specifically ecumenical issue of mutual recognition of ministries, I am conscious throughout each chapter of the several ecclesial communities and individual Christians of every sort as dialogue partners. Of course, I cannot answer for them, so I am only able to present my side of the dialogue.[1]

Although ecumenical considerations are prominent, agitation over ministry within the Roman Catholic communion cannot be ignored. Contributing in some measure to the resolution of difficult ministerial issues on the part of Roman Catholics motivates much of this book as well. Here, too, I do not imagine myself offering the last word in the discussion, but rather participating with a careful voice in the dialogue.

I am grateful to many classes of students whose discussion of these issues has assisted my reflection, to colleagues and friends who have reviewed parts of the manuscript and offered useful criticism, and to J. Michael West and David Lott, editors at Fortress Press, for their guidance through the process to publication.

—*Peter Drilling*

---

1. The present work might be compared to Carl E. Braaten, *The Apostolic Imperative: Nature and Aim of the Church's Mission and Ministry* (Minneapolis: Augsburg, 1985), in which Braaten takes up the ecumenical issues from a Lutheran perspective.

Chapter One

CONSTRUCTING A MINISTERIAL THEOLOGY

CHRISTIAN MINISTRY IS ROOTED IN THE GOSPEL OF JESUS Christ. This proposition is so commonplace as to be banal, except for the fact that there is no end to the controversy among Christians about what is of Jesus and what is not. Most Christians would agree that Jesus was a Palestinian Jew of the first century of the common era sent from God to announce the imminence of God's kingdom. He did this by means of a ministry of teaching and healing in Galilee and Judea. His endurance of execution at the instigation of the leaders of his own people and at the hands of the Roman authorities was the ultimate self-gift, a ministry in its own right because it effected freedom from enslavement to sin and communion with the living God for all humanity. Rising from the dead the Lord sends his Spirit to animate his followers. In imitation of their Lord the followers of Jesus take up ministry on their own, acting in the name of Jesus and by the power of his Spirit.

Having accepted these affirmations about Jesus and about discipleship, there is, nevertheless, no agreement among Christians about the structure of the church, the forms ministry ought to and might take, and the lines of authority within the church for ministerial activity.

Administration of the Gospel of Jesus has taken shape in various traditions. The tradition to which I adhere is the Roman Catholic; its significance will be clear throughout the present work. Roman Catholicism takes seriously the Scriptures of the Hebrew and Christian Testaments together with the ongoing tradition that both created and is derived from and interprets the Scriptures. For a Roman Catholic, the tradition includes theology and practice, but also doctrinal statements of belief formulated and taught

1

by the church. Some doctrines are considered to be permanent achievements, while others are positions taught at a particular time which may be
confirmed or revised at a later time. The theology of Christian ministry
proposed in these pages respects the normative character of the church's
tradition from the Bible through to the present as the Roman Catholic
Church understands its normativity.

Still, this is an ecumenical age, and dialogue among the several Christian
traditions cannot be given short shrift in a contemporary theology of ministry. The present reflection keeps in mind the conversations about ministry
that have been conducted among the Christian communions since the Second Vatican Council. These will be given particular attention in chapter 5,
but throughout my text I am conscious of the dialogue and hope to be
making a contribution to it. At this point it is noteworthy that some Christians of different denominations who are involved in ministry share their
concerns and quite readily share their ministry in certain areas. It is common for Christians of several denominations to join forces in establishing
and maintaining soup kitchens and shelters for the homeless. Bread for the
World and Pax Christi are ecumenical social ministries. When the corpora-
tions were closing the steel mills in Youngstown, Ohio, in the 1970s, the
churches formed an ecumenical coalition to keep the industry going and
save jobs.

Simultaneously, the same Christians who willingly collaborate together
on some projects find that in other areas of ministry they are quite divided.
While the role of baptism is sometimes at issue, especially on the part of
some of the Free churches, generally the division centers on the issue of
ordained ministry. Is there a sacrament of order and an ordained priesthood? Can the ordained ministries of the several Christian churches be
acknowledged as valid by the other Christian communions? What is the
basis for such acknowledgment? Related to this question is that of apostol-
icity in succession and in doctrine. Also significant is the role of the bishop
of Rome within the worldwide church.

Nor is ministry unaffected by interreligious dialogue. In a world where
the fragile peace that exists is constantly under threat, and where so much
injustice holds sway, enough members of the world's many religions feel
themselves compelled to push outside the confines of their own religion's
mediation of the true and the good to find a common meeting-ground with
the adherents of other religions. There is no intent to deny the truth and
value achieved in one's own religion. It is more a matter of recognizing the
points of convergence. So Jews and Muslims share a kibbutz on the Sea of
Galilee, leaders of a whole array of quite different religions accept Pope
John Paul's invitation to pray for peace at Assisi, and Buddhists and Chris-

tians form a community of peace in Massachusetts. The Christian churches are part of the growing interreligious dialogue. Ministry can no longer be carried on as if one's own religion, or one's own church, were the only one. Ministry is action on behalf of the world's conversion to truth and goodness. It includes cooperation with others sharing the goal in common and convinced that the goal and its achievement include a transcendental dimension.

The late twentieth century is also characterized by the contribution of the post-Kantian turn to the subject, and no adequate theology can be articulated nor reflective ministry performed without taking that turn into account. What that turn means specifically in the pages that follow is the adoption of transcendental method, a Thomistically informed but post-Kantian rational psychology, epistemology, and ontology derived from a study of the intentionality of the human subject. Included in the turn to the subject is an appreciation of the historicity of every human creation, including theology and ministry; so, the present theology attempts to discern both the universal and the particular, the transcultural and the cultural elements of a ministry that is both transcendentally and historically based.

Interpreting the Place of Christ in a Theology of Ministry

An examination of the meaning of these presuppositions begins best at the heart of it all: the saving good news of Jesus Christ. Jesus, who was an itinerant holy man of first-century Palestine and the Christ, and who continues to live as the cosmic Lord of the universe, is the originator and guide of Christian ministry. Thus, we must appropriate something of this first-century figure. We attend to the biblical data on Christ and to subsequent Christian tradition. Our attention will uncover culturally conditioned data. Some of that data will be interpreted as relevant only to Jesus' culture; other data to additional cultures besides the specific culture of Jesus; and other data still to all cultures of every time and place.

We can state as a conviction of faith that the triune God communicates truth and love for humanity in Jesus. Both in his earthly and in his risen existence Jesus communicates in specific human events, gestures, and words, then temporally, now sacramentally. However, God's communication cannot be contained within human lives with their events, gestures, and words, even within the humanity of Jesus. God's meaning always exceeds the human vesture in which it is clothed. How is that excess of meaning to be recognized? Is there a method by which we can discover where human and divine meaning intersect in Jesus?

Christian faith maintains that the triune God, through the power of the Holy Spirit, enlightens the minds of believers with truth and persuades their hearts by love so that they discern in Christ's life, death, and resurrection the guide in human history to fullness of life with God. This conviction is often expressed in terms of the divine missions. God is said to send the Holy Spirit to touch the spirits of believers (one of the divine missions) so that they are enabled to recognize in Jesus Christ God's personal entrance into human history through the Word made flesh (the other divine mission) for the purpose of establishing new interpersonal relationships between human persons and the divine persons.

Roman Catholics believe further that the community of believers, the church, is privileged to be endowed with the resources for interpreting the Spirit's enlightenment and persuasion and the risen Lord's guidance at each time and place. The church continues the incarnation of Christ in the world as the sacrament of the Lord's presence and of the action of the Holy Spirit. Both the divine missions and the church established and maintained by their power have their source and, finally, their goal in the first person of the Trinity, whom the tradition has most frequently named Father. The church lives by the life-giving power of the Trinity. It is in and through the church alive in history that believers come to glimpse and conduct their lives by the excess of meaning that is God at work in the human world.

What is ultimately simple enough because it is grounded in the simplicity of God, is in the present order of things complicated by several factors that need to be taken into account in every attempt to discern what truth for human being God is communicating through Jesus and his Holy Spirit in the church. A first factor is the relation between human realities and God's use of them to communicate the more-than-human, divine message. It is a matter of the limits of human experiences. Some experiences have an uncanny quality to them; they put us in touch with something more than what seems at face value to be the case.

Not only experiences, but language, too, is limited, and yet the languages of the Scriptures, doctrine, and theology communicate something more in their very limitations. The action of ministry is quite human, too, and yet it puts its agents and recipients in touch with the transcendent.[1] How does human experience, language, and action lead into the mystery of God?

---

1. See David Tracy's discussion of the meaning of *limit* in religion and theology throughout *Blessed Rage for Order: The New Pluralism in Theology* (New York: Seabury, 1975), and in idem, *The Analogical Imagination: Christian Theology and the Culture of Pluralism* (New York: Crossroad, 1981), 160–64, 172–78. Tracy continues his discussion of language and discourse in *Plurality and Ambiguity: Hermeneutics, Religion, Hope* (San Francisco: Harper & Row, 1987).

To take a ministerial example, newly debated again as the many Christian denominations receive the study paper of the Faith and Order Commission, *Baptism, Eucharist and Ministry,* we can ask how Christians are to determine whether bishops are leaders of the church by divine ordinance.[2] Does the name *episcopos* (overseer, bishop) to designate church leaders in some New Testament writings suffice to ensure that bishops are of divine ordinance? Or is there some New Testament data, not so specific, which connects with the specific data to communicate divine ordinance? Or does their gradual establishment as leaders of local churches during the first centuries of the church's formation, even before canonical lists of the New Testament Scriptures were finally established, ensure that bishops are of divine ordinance? Or is explicit endorsement by those who exercise leadership in the contemporary church together with reception by the larger body of the faithful what ensures that a practice is of divine ordinance? The Roman Catholic position maintains that the divine will is most evident in the fact of continuity, but there is disagreement whether continuity means identity (in the sense of Vincent of Lérins's canon: "What has been believed everywhere, always, and by all") or organic development.

Then there is the question of fidelity to the divine will not only in transcultural (continuous) but also in cultural (possibly discontinuous) determinations of Christian belief and practice. Could something that might be divinely willed at one stage of the church's history be left aside or transformed in favor of another divinely willed position at another period of time and/or in another sociocultural situation? In short, how are we in concrete instances to determine the divine meaning in the human mediations? It is, again, a matter of recognizing the "something more" communicated in the human meaning.

A second factor is that of historicity. Jesus was a first-century Palestinian Jew, who thought, talked, and acted as such. Are all Jesus' actions and words normative in themselves, in detail, for all later Christian practice? If so, then first-century Palestinian Judaism is normative for later Christianity.

Some early Christians did not think that the gospel of Jesus should be so narrowly circumscribed, for shortly after the death and resurrection of Jesus they determined that converts to Christianity from among the Gentiles did not have to submit to circumcision, thus adjusting beliefs and practices that had been supposed to express, or at least be related to, the meaning of

---

2. Faith and Order Paper No. 111, *Baptism, Eucharist and Ministry* (Geneva: World Council of Churches, 1982). Six volumes of reception documents have been published by the World Council of Churches, Max Thurian, ed., *Churches Respond to BEM* (Geneva: WCC, 1986–88). They include responses from many of the member churches of the council as well as the official response of the Roman Catholic church, vol. 6, pp. 1–40.

salvation in Christ. How could Jesus' followers make decisions in new situations? A partial answer is that just as Jesus is situated in a particular sociohistorical milieu, so is every other phase of the history of the Christian church. What is faithful to the divine will in one culture may become unfaithful in another, not because the divine will changes, but because the human situation approximates differently to the divine will as circumstances change. In other words, some human realities never change; others do. When the divine will is brought to bear upon the former, it may be expected to endure permanently; when it is brought to bear upon the latter, changing circumstances may mean that fidelity to God's will requires changes in personal living or church order.

Often it is necessary to ask not what Jesus did, but what Jesus might do if he were deciding in the present sociocultural context. In asking the question, however, we must keep in mind that worldviews change from culture to culture. So we try to determine how Jesus and his early followers are thinking and deciding within the particular worldview of their culture and where they break out of it into the transculturally significant worldview of the kingdom of God. We also try to distinguish between Jesus and his followers. For example, did Jesus in his own time or did his followers later raise the issue of a gentile mission? That is to say, did the Christians who made a decision about a gentile mission do so on the basis of specific words or actions of Jesus or on the basis of what seemed most faithful to the spirit of the Lord? The decisions and actions of early ecclesial communities, including even the canonical composition of the New Testament Scriptures, are the product of particular men and women imaging a worldview out of their particular interests, concerns, understandings, judgments, and values. We may reasonably assume, therefore, that their memory of Jesus is selective, not total, and in some instances perhaps unrelated to worldviews either of Jesus who came before them or of Christians who would follow them.

In turn, for present-day believers to make determinations of what is Christian is risky but necessary business, involving estimation of the spirit of Jesus, listening with religious attentiveness (*obsequium religiosum*) to the entire previous tradition of the church, and assessing all these by implementing the dynamically related operations of consciousness. People willing to risk such determinations, even after having arrived at them with care, have to be prepared to be corrected.

Both the factor of divine meaning within human limitations and the factor of historicity exercise their influence on the place of Christ in a theology of ministry. Relating to the first factor is the issue of Jesus' humanity. Jesus is the second person of the Trinity become human. In and through his true humanity Jesus communicates the divine meaning which exceeds all its finite vesture and boundaries. But how much divine meaning does Jesus in his human nature communicate, for example, with regard to forming a church and commissioning its ministers? Christians believe that to a great extent the work of the establishment of the church and the commissioning of its ministers is the fruit of the dying and rising Jesus, accomplished in the Pentecostal outpouring of his Spirit. Such a presupposition, I take it, leaves to the community of the Christian faithful the possibility of continuing to write the story of Christian meaning in fresh decisions about beliefs and practices. Moreover, just as Jesus' own life, so these decisions will be made and articulated within the confines of humanity, determining that the transcendent meaning embodied in them will never be separate from the finity of human words, gestures, and events. As a result, Christians of each age must reappropriate the divine meaning revealed in Jesus and the apostolic age and interpreted in subsequent historical periods.

Relating to the second factor, that of historicity, there is the issue of what Jesus intended. Scripture scholars seem to be in agreement that within the New Testament writings three levels of tradition come together. There is the level of Jesus' life, with its actions and words, then a level of oral traditions about Jesus and his meaning, and finally several layers of written testimony and reflection. With such variety in the New Testament how is the later church accurately to determine the intentions of Jesus?

Lately, the noted biblical scholar John Meier has proposed that theologians not base their reflection on what they suppose the *ipsissima verba et gesta* ("very words and deeds") of Jesus to have been. Meier notes that it is not possible to discover by studying the data of the New Testament precisely what Jesus said or did. Theologians who rely on what biblical scholarship is thus far able to determine about the so-called historical Jesus paint themselves into a corner unnecessarily and in a way detrimental to their theology. Rather, Meier suggests, theologians should take "the whole Bible's witness to the whole Christ" as a source for theology.[3] In addition to Meier's biblically based concerns, we can recall what has been stated above, namely, that Catholic theology has never considered itself bound solely to the findings of historical criticism of the Bible, relying as the church does on Jesus as interpreted by the ongoing developments of the christological tradition. The point is not to ignore the biblical text except when it is more convenient to attend to it, but rather to place the biblical text within the history of the church's faith.[4]

3. John P. Meier, "The Bible as a Source for Theology," *Proceedings of the Catholic Theological Society of America* 43 (1988): 1–14, see esp. 6, 13–14.
4. Joseph Ratzinger stated all this differently, but making the same point, in a lecture he delivered in New York City at a Lutheran-sponsored symposium on contemporary biblical

The issue of the Holy Spirit also figures in the factor of historicity, for the Spirit is ever renewing the church in each new age and each new place where the church takes root. Could the Spirit guide the church beyond the socially and historically conditioned intentions of Jesus and beyond the intentions of the New Testament canonical writings? Christians seem to say yes when they acknowledge that some New Testament demands, such as Paul's call for women to keep their heads covered at liturgy, are culturally conditioned commands that can, in another cultural situation, be abandoned. But then how does the foundational revelation of the apostolic age serve as foundation? And what are the criteria for discerning when the Spirit is leading the church to a new stage of development? We are back again at the need to keep in mind and weigh a multiplicity of factors; we shall suggest an epistemologically normative method, that is, a transcendental method, to assist with this task in the next section.

Besides the reasons given by John Meier for abandoning the quest to ground all later church life and theology on the specific words and deeds of the historical Jesus, there is another reason not to attempt to hearken back to Jesus and the apostolic age in a literal way in every instance: significant developments that have become part of the church's heritage were only hinted at in the apostolic age. Unless, then, we are prepared to cast aside some revered beliefs, practices, and theological conclusions, we cannot be restrictively rooted in the apostolic age. Some developments came later and, while each must be submitted to criticism, they cannot be considered illegitimate simply because they are not explicitly included in the New Testament canon or in the nonwritten tradition of the apostolic age, if the latter is ever possible to determine securely. For examples, the establishment of bishops as leaders of local churches can be cited, along with the sacrificial meaning of the eucharistic meal, and the acknowledgment of a triune God. Catholic theology certainly recognizes continuity in the tradition from the apostolic age to the later determinations, but that very affirmation of continuity confirms the presuppositions I have been expressing, for the later development often interprets the meaning of the earlier stage as much as interpretations of the earlier stages lead to both confirmations and revisions of later developments. Thus, while we continually look back to and

---

exegesis: "Certainly texts must first of all be traced back to their historical origins and interpreted in their proper historical context. But then, in a second exegetical operation, one must look at them also in light of the total movement of history and in light of history's central event, Jesus Christ. Only the combination of both these methods will yield understanding of the Bible." See Joseph Ratzinger, "Biblical Interpretation in Crisis: On the Question of the Foundations and Approaches of Exegesis Today," in Richard John Neuhaus, ed., *Biblical Interpretation in Crisis: The Ratzinger Conference on Bible and Church* (Grand Rapids: Wm. B. Eerdmans, 1989), 20–21.

rely upon foundational revelation in Jesus and the apostolic age, respecting its privileged place in the tradition, we also count on the ongoing guidance of the Holy Spirit.

Just as it would be unfaithful to the spirit of Jesus to rely too literally upon the expressions of Christianity that appeared in the first century, we cannot assume that later expressions are superior or inferior to the earlier simply because they are later. Christians have fallen into both traps at times.[5] It is a matter of critical assessment by means of raising and answering the questions of intelligibility, truth, and value. Again, transcendental method makes its contribution.

While there is no uncomplicated way to interpret the gospel's meaning and the implementation of that meaning in the church as it makes its pilgrim way from era to era, nevertheless the church is not stranded in history. Intelligent, reasonable, loving, faithful determinations of what to believe and what to do are possible. The experience and reflection of all the faithful who are sincerely interested can be consulted. Carefully constructed hypotheses and theories of theologians make a contribution. The bishops of local churches, individually and in their national conferences, assess both the experience of the living church of their region and the theories of theologians. The bishops consult their fellow bishops informally and also formally at synods and councils. Ultimately, the bishop of Rome confirms definitive interpretations of Christian meaning and makes decisions about definitive Christian practice. Moreover, as the point of unity in the church the Pope actively involves himself in the discussion of issues of faith and practice.[6]

In the present situation of a divided Christian church it is also necessary for Catholic theology and for all other Christian theologies, when attempting to discern the guidance of Christ in his Spirit in matters of belief and practice, to observe and appreciate in a respectful way the experience, convictions, practices, and interpretations of the other Christian communities, including both mainline denominations and Free churches.

Guiding the Theology of Christian Ministry by Transcendental Method

There is no single norm, or even group of norms, external to human subjects who are in search of what is intelligible, true, and good, that exists as

---

5. Ratzinger cautions against a "simplistic transferral of science's evolutionary model to spiritual history. Spiritual processes do not follow the rule of zoological genealogies" (ibid., p. 10).

6. For a more complete development of these points on the involvement of the whole church in achieving Christian beliefs and practices, see the essay by Ladislas Örsy, *The Church: Learning and Teaching* (Wilmington, Del.: Michael Glazier, 1987).

pure and simple criterion to assure the success of the search. Foundational revelation, as well as the tradition of doctrine, practice, and theology, and ecumenical respect are sufficient only when they are elements of a dialogical process of reflection guided by dynamic, self-transcending subjectivity. For the same God who is primary source and guide of the revelation and tradition that precede any generation of Christians is also primary agent in the current generation's interpretations of and decisions in faith. And just as in the past God's self-communication has been through human subjects, both individuals and communities, so it is the same in the present. By the interplay of the criteria that are both external and internal to the human subject, two false extremes are avoided: extrinsicism and intrinsicism, objectivism and subjectivism.

The insufficiency of the external criteria can be illustrated positively and negatively. On the negative side, New Testament data include the acceptance of ways of life that later came universally to be recognized as evil. I am thinking of the social system of slavery. Whatever God might have been communicating and despite the statement of Gal. 3:28, the human interpreters who guided the Christian community and authored the Christian Scriptures never thought seriously to call the social system of slavery radically into question. The household codes do not call into question the status quo; they endorse it.[7] In such an instance it would be unfortunate to build Christian doctrine or practice upon data derived from the apostolic age alone. Later achievements of social truth, under the impetus of external factors and the human dynamism toward reasonable and responsible living, have also contributed to the development of Christian doctrine and practice. Thus, the church now condemns slavery.

On the positive side, as we have already noted with regard to bishops, the Eucharist as sacrifice, and trinitarian dogma, every new flowering of life within the church is not explicitly endorsed in the Scriptures or the apostolic age. Christianity can build on hints as the criteria for faithful expressions of Christian meaning. The Scriptures, the apostolic tradition, the teaching church, the experience of the faithful, all function as instances of the ongoing dynamism of human subjects seeking the intelligible, the true, and the good.

Our assessment of all that precedes us, from the apostolic age to the present, and our response to the contemporary challenge to live by the Gospel of Jesus requires more than simply receiving the past or doing what

---

7. New Testament data indicate that early Christian communities were not concerned to influence relationships in the wider society but only within the church. See Karl Heinrich Rengstorf's comments on the complex relationship of religious conviction and the social situation in his article on δοῦλος in Gerhard Kittel, ed., *Theological Dictionary of the New Testament* (Grand Rapids: Wm. B. Eerdmans, 1964), 2:272–73.

appears best for the present. What is required is critical reception of the past and critical decisions for the present. Bernard Lonergan remarks that "to be practical is to do the intelligent thing."[8] Intelligent practicality has a better chance of happening when human subjects who are making the judgments and decisions about living know how intelligent practicality is implemented. It is a matter of coming into possession of human interiority that has come under the tutelage of the Word of God.

But what exactly is the inner motor that operates in the situation to keep the whole church faithful to the incarnate Word in each new historical moment? How, concretely, does the Spirit of Jesus touch human spirits? Is it all a matter of intuition?

Before answering these questions directly by recalling Bernard Lonergan's development of transcendental method, I offer Karl Rahner's theology of symbol as background. In his well-known essay sketching out both the philosophical and the theological centrality of symbol, Rahner reflects on the necessary bond, even the identity, between the simple form of every reality and the multiplicity of its expression.[9] The utterly simple God intrinsically expresses itself in three divine persons, which are really distinct from each other though only notionally distinct from the Godhead. Human beings are also expressions of the divine self, though really distinct from the Godhead. Indeed, according to Rahner, the whole world is somehow expressive of the divine self, somehow the body of God, because every creature bears the imprint of the creator. As Rahner himself notes, the symbolic character intrinsic to all being is of considerable significance for ministry, but we will put off discussion of that aspect of Rahner's theology of symbol until the next chapter.[10] The point of this present brief reference to Rahner's notion of symbol is to emphasize how all reality, beginning with God the creator, becomes known in the multiplicity of its expressions. As the creator, so creation. Herein lies the theological significance of transcendental method.

Transcendental method, of which Rahner is a proponent along with Lonergan, makes practical the theologically and philosophically grounded view that the human subject is a unity expressed in plurality, a symbolic animal, to use Ernst Cassirer's phrase.[11] Each human subject can only know itself through its actions. Human communities, including the church, can

8. Bernard Lonergan, *Insight: A Study of Human Understanding* (London: Longmans, Green, 1957), xiii–xiv.

9. Karl Rahner, "The Theology of the Symbol," in *Theological Investigations* (New York: Seabury, 1974), 4:221–52.

10. Ibid., 242.

11. Care must be taken not to lump together the proponents of transcendental method in an uncritical manner. See Bernard Lonergan's caution in his *Method in Theology* (New York: Herder & Herder, 1972), 13–14 n. 4.

only know themselves in the same way. [12] Rahner recognizes that it is in the activities of knowledge and love that the subject really becomes itself. It realizes or takes possession of itself as it advances in knowing and loving. [13] In continuity with this line of thought, we can add that individuals and communities of subjects acting under the tutelage of the Word of God have a much better possibility of monitoring their fidelity to the Word to the extent that they come to understand their activities of knowing and loving.

Guiding the present theology of ministry are the explicitly distinguished activities of knowing and loving, the operations of human consciousness, as they combine into the dynamism of self-transcendent subjectivity. Bernard Lonergan has demonstrated how these operations and their combinations, normative for critically grounded thought, can be discovered by each of us as we investigate human interiority in the theoretical and practical achievements of ourselves and one another. [14] What appropriation of the operations of consciousness and their dynamic combination yields is a grasp of objectivity as the fruit of authentic subjectivity. [15] The recognition dawns that there is a right way (a sort of orthodoxy) to go about the search for intelligibility, reality, and goodness, and it is a way not reserved for an elite corps of superintellects but is accessible to ordinary human beings willing to take the trouble to discover why the way is normative and how to go about implementing it.

The requirement for dynamic human subjectivity to serve successfully as a norm that accompanies the normativity of the Christian Scriptures and the interpreting tradition is that each individual continually be about the business of appropriating her or his own subjectivity, and that the process of learning and teaching within the church be the activity of Christians who are appropriating themselves as self-transcending subjects.

The first reality of human interiority to which to attend when doing theology is conversion. Conversion refers to a radical shift in the orientation of human interiority. It assumes that human subjects are not automatically authentic; effort is necessary to become authentic. More specifically, human authenticity is a matter of self-consciousness. The subject comes to

12. Picking up on both Rahner and Lonergan, Joseph Komonchak has been developing a self-conscious ecclesiology. See, as just two examples, Joseph Komonchak, "Clergy, Laity, and the Church's Mission in the World," *The Jurist* 41(1981): 422–47, and idem, "Towards a Theology of the Local Church," *FABC Papers*, No. 42 of Federation of Asian Bishops' Conferences Papers (Hong Kong: Federation of Asian Bishops' Conferences, 1986).

13. Rahner, "Theology of the Symbol," 229–30.

14. Bernard Lonergan's entire literary corpus, even the treatises of dogmatic and systematic theology, deals with human subjectivity and its authentic activity, but the most common references are to *Insight: A Study of Human Understanding* and *Method in Theology*.

15. Lonergan, *Method in Theology*, 292; see also 265.

grasp not only what the operations of consciousness are and how they function, but also the orientations within which the subject must function if one is to achieve intelligibility, truth, and goodness. The basic orientations, each with its own particular mode of conversion, are religious and Christian, intellectual and moral.

In its first instance conversion is religious. Religious refers to that shift of orientation by which the subject is dislodged from seeking life's meaning wholly within the boundaries of the here and now and turns to the realm of mystery for life's deeper meanings. The shift in orientation takes place as the subject becomes attuned to the Spirit of God (though a person so converted is not always able to articulate the process of her or his conversion so precisely). This is what Lonergan names religious conversion. What a subject experiences in religious conversion is being caught up in something far greater than itself. The mundane explanations of things and events and the values that more immediately respond to needs are no longer adequate; a person becomes disenchanted with business as usual. Eventually the subject may come to recognize that this something taking hold of its interest is infinitely greater. The subject of religious conversion also notices that the Spirit attracting it is the object of a penetrating love. [16] It knows it must yield to this love. To the extent that it does so, religious conversion has taken place. As the subject yields there is a new, other-worldly orientation for one's interior operations.

Why distinguish religious from Christian conversion? By identifying the basic meaning of religious conversion, Christians are enabled to identify the Spirit of God guiding and directing human persons in their life's efforts. Christian faith is not concerned only with specifically Christian faith and practice. No human endeavor remains unrelated to the promotion of the kingdom of God, for nothing human lies outside the subject's being gathered up by the Spirit. Human endeavors can, then, be criticized regarding their fidelity to the influence of the Spirit of God. The religiously converted subject functions within a horizon that enables such criticism.

Distinguishing religious conversion from Christian conversion serves another purpose. It promotes the judgment that women and men of religious faiths other than Christian also experience religious conversion, for the orientation of religious conversion undergirds all authentic religious faith. It must, since authentic religion, however one evaluates the adequacy of its expressions, can only be the product of the one Spirit of God acting within human interiority and in the world through human subjects. The need for

16. While scholars of comparative religion dispute whether religious experience is ultimately a matter of love of God, Lonergan contends that it is. See *Method in Theology*, 108–09.

interreligious ministry was adverted to several paragraphs above. Now the basis for genuine interreligious dialogue and ministry is identified to be religious conversion.

Some persons among all those who are attracted by the infinitely greater reality and who yield to the attraction so that their orientation is changed in an instance of religious conversion go on to recognize that the Spirit they love is indeed the triune God inviting them to interpersonal communion and conversation. In fact, while we distinguish religious conversion from more specific Christian conversion, in Christians the two most often take place simultaneously. The distinction is made when we reflect on the components of what has taken place. Then we appreciate that the human person who recognizes that it is the Father and Spirit and Jesus the Logos who are intersubjectively interacting with him or her has undergone a specifically Christian religious conversion. In that case, the subject comes to know the Logos in Jesus the Christ, who in turn reveals the Father and the Spirit. The stories of men and women who can detail the events of their first attraction and eventual commitment to God through Christ fill the annals of Christianity. Besides the few whose Christian conversion is publicly reported, there are countless others of Christian conviction in whom the conversion seems to have happened so normally, beginning as a faith handed on by their parents, that they would be hard-pressed to identify a remarkable event connected with their faith.[17] But their orientation is just as firm.

The response to these transcendent events by the person who accepts them for what they are is the attitude of Christian faith. From being attracted by the pull of the transcendent, even as one experiences tension between the pull and the demands of getting by in daily living, a person moves to the surrender of love and through love comes to the act of faith. Faith is knowledge drawn from affective encounter with the risen Lord Jesus within one's subjectivity and illumined by the data of Scripture and the Christian tradition. Such faith is always active in genuine Christian theology. There is no possibility of dealing with foundational revelation and the interpretative Christian tradition from the standpoint of Christian theology without acquiescence to conversion by faith. Without faith the data of Scripture and the Christian tradition lose their religious value.

There are more dimensions to conversion, however, than the religious

---

17. See, e.g., the autobiographical accounts of their conversion by fifty prominent and diverse Christians in Hugh T. Kerr and John M. Mulder, eds., *Conversion: The Christian Experience* (Grand Rapids: Wm. B. Eerdmans, 1983).

and Christian. Apprehending the importance of the dynamism of the subject's search for intelligibility and truth, making the effort to grasp the moments of the dynamism, and understanding how the fully implemented dynamism actually achieves intelligibility and truth: this process is so radical and so significant that Lonergan uses the religiously suggestive term *conversion* for this dimension of human subjectivity as well. More precisely, he names it intellectual conversion.

A subject embarks on the journey of intellectual conversion with the recognition that careful thinking is not an automatic human activity. There is a method to be implemented. One is doing one's self, one's society, one's religious tradition a favor by coming to know and abiding by the method. Moreover, getting to know the method is not some arcane activity, a project only for those initiated into the mysteries. It is a possibility for any reasonably educated and moderately interested adult.

One need only draw up a list of instances from one's academic career or practical living in which she or he was sufficiently attentive to the data that required understanding, experienced the freedom of insight into the meaning of the data, and devised some way to verify the accuracy of the experienced insight. In each instance what has been achieved, with greater or less degrees of probability, is intelligibility and truth. A neophyte biologist in the second year of high school dissects a frog. By sight she experiences the system of blood vessels, examines the various body tissues and the arteries and veins connecting them with the heart, experiences the insight of the cardiovascular system, works out her understanding by writing up the set of discoveries she has made, and then checks out her findings by sight and touch. The student's process of learning shows itself to have a certain normativity; if each step is executed with care, she learns something about reality, namely, how the cardiovascular system functions in a frog, and perhaps in other animals as well.

A man and a woman fall in love, spend some time in courtship, marry, and start to raise a family. Gradually one, and then the other, begins to sense that something is amiss in the relationship. Decisions are made one-sidedly. Moodiness taints the couple's time together. The relationship loses some of its joy. The couple questions what might be wrong. After reflection, discussion, and perhaps consultation with trustworthy friends, the insight dawns that communication between husband and wife is too superficial for the demands of the relationship. The couple checks out the sufficiency of the insight to explain the one-sided decisions, the moodiness, the loss of joy in the relationship. It seems to make sense. So they make new efforts to deepen their communication. If the relationship improves, chances are they understood the cause of their problems; if not, the effort turns out to be an experiment that heads toward but has not reached the intelligibility of the situation.

In the two examples, the operations of intellectual consciousness, while many and discrete, can be conveniently divided into three types: attentiveness to the data to be understood, the act of understanding, and reasoning to ascertain that the act of understanding is in fact understanding the data to be understood. These three types of operation combine to reinforce each other in each instance in which a subject or subjects come to know. Sometimes, in instances where one can be a cool observer, such as in a biology experiment, the dynamic process begins with attentiveness to the data, moves on to understanding, and then to verification. At other times, especially when the intelligibility and truth are matters of affective intersubjectivity, that is to say, when love is the motivating force, as in appreciating the dynamics of a marriage relationship or in religious and Christian conversion, a person is moved by love to an affirmation of the truth, and goes on afterward to sort out one's attentiveness to the data and determine intelligibility. In both types of combination of the operations of consciousness, the normativity of the intellectual conversion is that, at least in the long run, it provides a self-correcting process of learning.

If one is beginning simply from the starting point of intellectual curiosity, with one sort or another of a puzzle to be solved, the basic nest of questions follows the order: Am I attending to all the data relevant to solving my puzzle? Am I asking all the relevant questions for understanding the meaning of this data? Am I asking all the relevant questions to determine whether the meanings I have come up with can in some way be shown to be reasonable? If one is beginning from an experience of love or commitment, the questions follow the reverse order: Is my love or my commitment mature and therefore to be endorsed and pursued, or is it fatuous and ill-chosen? What affirmations (statements of belief) are entailed by my love of this person or my commitment to this project (such as the Christian gospel)? Is there some way these affirmations can be coherently related to each other and to the rest of life's meanings? What impact do these affirmations and their intelligibility have upon the arrangements of daily living? Asking the questions honestly and rigorously from either direction provides persons and communities with a method that heads toward objectivity.

Besides the religious and intellectual dimensions of conversion, there is also the moral dimension. Moral conversion shifts the orientation of a subject to the choice of the good option in each instance in which a decision is to be made. The shift may be away from selfishness as the horizon of one's values or from a well-intentioned but ill-conceived priority of values, as on the part of people who are convinced that nothing good can come out of Nazareth, thus placing tribal identity above respect for persons. Moral conversion begins with apprehension that the good is to be chosen in each instance where a choice is to be made. It moves on to an effort to come to know the operations of consciousness that are implemented each time a decision is made. It is achieved when the subject dedicates her- or himself to making that choice in every decision.

The operations that are implemented in deliberation about values include attention to and assessment of those feelings that attract a person to or repel a person from values, with all the nuances of both types of feeling. The values are attached to a possible object of choice. Depending upon the way in which one's feelings have been educated or socialized, one assesses the value of her or his object of possible choice. The person in the process of moral conversion is making the effort to educate his or her feelings according to an order of values, ranging from physical or emotional health individually and socially, to the human products of ecology, education, law, economy, politics, art, to the primary dignity of each human person as created by God, to the overriding value of the creating, redeeming, and sanctifying three divine persons. Each set of values has its place within an integrated perspective of the value of human life, but for the morally converted subject all objects of possible choice finally derive their value from the ultimate good which is God. Each possible object of choice comes to be understood by its place within the order of the human good discerned to be derived from the divine Creator, and to be chosen accordingly.

By developing the theology of Christian ministry in the pages that follow according to the demands of attentiveness to the data, inquiry, insight, reflection, judgment, deliberation, and responsible choice as operations of religiously, intellectually, and morally converted subjects, we do much to avoid an arbitrary use of biblical and historical data, of doctrines and legislation proposed by the church, and of communal faith in this ecumenical age.

Historicity and Cultural Particularity

Besides the revelation of God in Jesus, which is handed on from generation to generation, and the active place of human subjectivity, a contemporary theology of ministry also needs to be concerned with the cultural context of ministry. For just as the historicity of Jesus cannot be ignored when the church tries to determine how it might be the community of faithful disciples of the Lord, so the cultural particularity of each setting in which the church takes shape must be acknowledged as well.

While the Word made flesh transcends each time and place and holds
for every time and place, still the cultural particularities of Jesus do not hold
transcultural validity. So it is with the church and the church's ministry.
Every embodiment of the church and its ministry within particular cultures
is not of universal significance nor lasting value, though some embodiments
do have transcultural validity. Indeed, every attempted embodiment of the
gospel is not even valid temporarily, as surely every Christian will agree. On
this matter it is useful to recall the words of R. McL. Wilson in *Gnosis and
the New Testament*:

> On its entry upon the stage of the wider world Christianity had to be "trans-
> lated" from its original Palestinian thought-forms and terms of reference into
> those comprehensible in its new environment. It is not in the least surprising
> that there should have been some people who in the process lost the essence
> of the Gospel in "the maelstrom of Hellenistic syncretism." For convenience
> in study and analysis, we have to talk in terms of ideas, trends and currents of
> thought; but in fact we are dealing with ideas in the minds of *people*, which
> introduces a highly complicating factor into all our investigations.[18]

Inculturation is the name currently given to the insertion of the good
news of the life, death, and resurrection of Jesus of Nazareth into each
culture that it encounters and enters. The theological meaning of inculturation is that church and ministry are an extension of the incarnation of the
divine Logos. Incarnation is at the heart of salvation in Christ Jesus. As the
second preface to the eucharistic liturgy for Christmas puts it: "Today you
fill our hearts with joy as we recognize in Christ the revelation of your love.
No eye can see his glory as our God, yet now he is seen as one like us.
Christ is your Son before all ages, yet now he is born in time. He has come
to lift up all things to himself, to restore unity to creation, and to lead
humankind from exile into your heavenly kingdom."

The Logos of God became incarnate in the only way that it is possible
to become human, as a member of a particular culture. Inculturation brings
to bear what Jesus accomplished once and for all not only upon the culture
of Palestinian Jews of the first years of the common era but upon diverse
cultures of peoples inhabiting every part of the globe and in every time.

The Logos, however, became human in order to offer a universally desirable gift of divine salvation and make it universally accessible. For people of
cultures other than the culture of Jesus of Nazareth to receive and accept
the salvation God offers in Jesus, the message of this salvation has to be
transposed from the culture of first-century Palestinian Judaism into the

18. R. McL. Wilson, *Gnosis and the New Testament* (Philadelphia: Fortress Press, 1968), 51.

languages, worldviews, thought patterns, and customs of other cultures. In the process the culture encountered by the gospel is challenged in many ways to be transformed. In the process, too, the gospel is variously expressed according to the peculiarities of each culture. [19] The gospel does not look exactly the same as it takes root in diverse cultures.

It also happens that universally valid truths and values that belong to the gift of salvation only become apparent in their contact with particular cultures. This, too, is an element of inculturation. The triune character of the one God, for example, became explicit only when it entered into the culture of Hellenism; the character of marriage as a sacrament became explicit within the culture of medieval scholasticism.

Official documentation of the Catholic church since the Second Vatican Council affirms not only the fact of inculturation but also teaches that inculturation of the gospel is a value to be respected and indeed pursued. The Second Vatican Council's *Pastoral Constitution on the Church in the Modern World* and its *Decree on the Church's Missionary Activity* brought the issue to center stage. [20] In 1975 Pope Paul VI followed up a meeting of the World Synod of Bishops on the topic of evangelization with an apostolic exhortation in which he addresses the matter of inculturation. [21] Presently, Pope John Paul II recurrently returns to the topic in his speeches. [22]

The Roman documentation asserts that the first result of the authentic implantation of the gospel in a particular culture is that the people of the culture who accept the gospel are freed from enslaving myths and mores that are carried by the culture. It is the transcultural good news of the message of Jesus as Savior and Lord that frees people in this way. The gospel empowers people to purge themselves of hindrances to human living and opens them up to enrich their cultures with more objectively valid and valuable myths and mores.

The result of the implantation of the gospel in different cultures does not lead, however, to a single Christian culture, a monolithic superculture. While at one time it was presumed that there was only one normative culture, usually European, now it is generally recognized that variety is here to stay. Rather than resign ourselves to an unfortunate fact, rejoicing in a

19. An insightful study of the ways in which Western cultures and the gospel have related to each other is offered by H. Richard Niebuhr, *Christ and Culture* (New York: Harper & Row, 1951).

20. See *The Church in the Modern World*, art. 58, and the *Decree on the Church's Missionary Activity*, art. 11, 15.

21. See *Evangelization in the Modern World* (Washington: United States Catholic Conference, 1976), art. 19, 20, 63, 65, 73.

22. See, for example, John Paul II's address, "Father Matteo Ricci: Bridge to China," *The Pope Speaks* 28.2 (1983): 97–103. See also, "Faith and Inculturation," (a document of the International Theological Commission), *Origins* 18 (May 4, 1989): 800–07.

happy gift is in order. However, it may not be so easy to rejoice in a fact
that has often not been acknowledged at all—classical culture considered
itself to be the normative culture. When cultural variety has been acknowledged as a fact, it has sometimes seemed to be an expression of aberration
rather than development—in the eighteenth and nineteenth centuries, anthropology and ethnology considered cultures that had not taken the shape
of European culture primitive. However, taking cultural variety as a methodological presupposition of a theology of ministry puts inculturation in
just the opposite light, making it a positive element of the ongoing life of
the gospel in new historical moments.

Transposing the theological meaning of historicity and cultural particularity into a methodological presupposition of this study of Christian ministry, it can be asserted that gospel ministry will not take shape in exactly
the same way in varying cultures. We are not surprised or dismayed to discover different forms of Christian ministry activated at different times
within a single culture or among different peoples at the same time. On the
other hand, because the one gospel of Jesus Christ is being inculturated in
the many different cultures, we can expect that, once we have become educated and acclimated to the differing cultural embodiments, we are going
to discern that Christians have embraced the same gospel everywhere and
in every time. Indeed, each Christian, as well as the worldwide church, may
well learn from those inculturations of the gospel that are foreign to our
peculiar sensitivities something about the transculturally meaningful gift of
salvation to which we had previously never adverted.

By claiming that inculturation is a methodological presupposition, we
return once more to the importance of transcendental method. It is not
theologically acceptable simply to acknowledge and observe that the gospel influences cultures and that cultures influence the gospel. It is required
that the mutual influence be critically examined. For since inculturation is a
joint endeavor of the living Spirit of Jesus and human members of the
church who are limited in their abilities and truncated by their sin, mistakes
will accompany the enterprise of rooting the gospel in a culture. Sometimes
it happens that the culture co-opts the gospel and reduces its transforming
power to accommodation, and sometimes those who preach the gospel fail
to respect what is true and good in the culture.

Critical Christians, then, make every effort to accept and to be absorbed
by the love of God who is always seeking to engage them. They spend
themselves in prayerful faith in pursuit of deeply felt knowledge of Jesus.[23]

---

23. "Deeply felt knowledge of Jesus" is the product of study of scholarly investigation of
biblical data, educated affirmation of church doctrine that has developed, and affective engagement with the person of Jesus who is revealed in prayer to be living in our interiority through
his Spirit.

A theology developed apart from the love and faith of the theologian and of the theologian's Christian community is out of touch with the God whose church and ministry are theology's concern. Transcendental method means that within the context of self-consciously appropriated love and faith, theologians pay attention to all the relevant data, raise questions in order to gain understanding, reflect critically upon their understandings in order to determine their accuracy, and responsibly evaluate each instance of inculturation to assess both fidelity to the gospel and respect for authentic cultural values.

Inculturation will be active as a methodological presupposition as often as the present study examines the theological meaning of specific biblical data and historical developments within baptized as well as ordained ministry, since there is no abstract, simply universal, development of ministry from the apostolic age to the present. Critical investigation from the methodological perspective of inculturation yields transcultural, as well as more limited cultural, truth in ministry, its practice, doctrine, and theology. It also uncovers mistakes.

Chapter Two

THE MINISTRY OF ALL
THE BAPTIZED

CAUTION WAS COUNSELED AT THE WORLD SYNOD OF bishops on the laity in 1987 against too wide a use of the term *ministry*. While acknowledging that all the baptized bear responsibility for service within the church and to the world, it was suggested that the title ministry be reserved for "those who occupy some formal position in church service."[1] Admirably, the intent of the caution was to avoid that night where all cats are black, but it seems to be too narrow a use of the term ministry to reserve it for those who occupy a formal position in church service. For while ministry can be distinguished from nonministerial activity, still the proper use of the term extends beyond formally designated church service. The concern of the present chapter is to examine the theological content of the reality that is designated by the term *Christian ministry*, and to discuss how the term applies to baptized Christians.

The meaning of ministry is intimately connected with the Greek word that denotes service, *diakonia*. In the New Testament such service is instrumental of God's activity. People who choose to walk the way of Jesus as his disciples are disposed constantly to serve in the name and spirit of Jesus. *Diakonia* is an attitude inherent in acceptance of the gospel of Jesus; it is expressed in a wide range of activities; neither the attitude nor the activities is optional for the Christian. The route of the translation of *diakonia* into

---

1. Abp. Roger Mahony, "The Relationship of Priests and Laity," *Origins* 17 (Oct. 22, 1987): 350. In his postsynodal apostolic exhortation, *Christifideles Laici* (Christian Laity), Pope John Paul II acknowledges this criticism, but he does not suggest a resolution except to indicate that a distinction may be made between ministry and charism (art. 23, 24). For the complete text of the exhortation, see *Origins* 18 (Feb. 9, 1989), 561–95.

the English word *ministry* is through the Latin *ministerium*, referring to the activity of those who are or who choose to be less (*minus*).

Ministry is the action of service on behalf of the common good, whether of the church or of wider society. St. Paul proposes this meaning in 1 Corinthians 12, where he makes use of three terms indiscriminately, *diakonia* (ministry), *charisma* (charism), and *energema* (work). In chapter twelve and elsewhere Paul includes lists of ministries. [2] Ranging from encouraging others by the strength of one's own faith to starting a new local church as an apostle to pastoring a local congregation to giving alms, the Pauline lists of ministries are functions inspired by God to be performed primarily for the sake of benefiting others who are either actual or potential members of the ecclesial community.

What, Then, Is Ministry?

The ultimate goal of the various ministerial actions, which Paul expresses vaguely in 1 Corinthians to be "the common good" (12:7), and metaphorically in Ephesians to be "for building up the body of Christ" (4:12), can be expressed with greater theological precision. Consistent with the pattern of all ministry as priestly, prophetic, and pastoral, a pattern that will receive attention later in this chapter, ministry can be appreciated as fostering communion and/or conversation between human communities or individuals and the divine community. In some instances ministry directly promotes communion and conversation, and in some instances it is an effort to set up the conditions for communion and conversation.

Communion is participation in a common life. Ministry's noble goal is to serve human communion with the divine community. Ministers are instruments of the gracious invitation of the triune God to every human person, individually and in the human communities to which each belongs, to enter into a mutual exchange of life and love with God. It is a matter of incorporation into a communal life with the divine Trinity and with one's fellow human beings, especially the baptized. Incorporation includes a feeling of belonging, a sense of intimacy. No longer isolated or ruggedly individualist, but with no affront to personal integrity or individuality, dependence upon God and interdependence with other human persons become characteristics of daily living.

While all ministry serves communion in a general way, some ministries

---

2. See 1 Cor. 12:8-10, 28, as well as Rom. 12:4-8 and Eph. 4:11 (I assume that, if it is not of direct Pauline authorship, Ephesians is the product of a Pauline community, probably of the early 60s C.E. See Helmut Merklein, *Das kirchliche Amt nach dem Epheserbrief* [Munich: Kösel, 1973]).

promote communion explicitly. Sacramental ministries promote incorporation into the divine community (baptism and confirmation), or nourishment of one's life in the divine community (Eucharist), or healing for alienation that intrudes upon human relationship with the divine community
(penance and reconciliation). Married couples who give of themselves self-
lessly to create a common life in their marriage provide a sign and therefore
an encouragement of the common life of God's kingdom. Similarly, the effort of the local churches within the universal church to live every aspect of
ecclesial life as a communion in total justice and charity serves the ultimate
communion by anticipating it. Christians who teach prayer or guide prayer
groups, and thus foster intimacy with the divine persons, are also rendering
ministry of communion.

Whereas communion offers the security of belonging, conversation offers the stimulation of dialogue. Ministry serves the ongoing dialogue between the divine community and humanity initiated when the world was
created through the Word of God.[3] Divine-human dialogue is not tedious
chatter to pass the time of day; however, it can be like light conversation
over dinner with friends. Chiefly, it is the divine self-communication of
truth and the human response of lives lived in authentic fidelity to the truth.
Conversation that is self-communicative is not easy. It requires trust, for one
does not reveal him- or herself to just anyone. Conversation also takes effort. To hear and articulate ultimate meaning carefully is to commit oneself
to engagement with the truth. Time is involved, and also disengagement
from life's many possible distractions.

Preaching, teaching, proclaiming the Scriptures, telling the stories of
God on a street corner or in a class of first graders, evangelizing, prophesy-
ing justice in situations of injustice, issuing a pastoral letter, writing theology: all are ministries of the Word that promote the divine–human conversation.

The goal of being human is to achieve communion and conversation
with God. Besides ministries that are specific in their promotion of that
goal, there are ministries that set up conditions that make the goal more
readily attainable. It is difficult, if not impossible, for people who are weak
from lack of food or nourishing food, or cold because of lack of ample
clothing or adequate shelter to be attentive to communion and conversation
with God. Often it is a matter of responsible Christian ministry to assist
with food, clothing, and shelter. When people are politically or religiously
oppressed they may be distracted and even prevented from the free pursuit

---

3. John 1:3, which is reminiscent of the word or speech of God in the creation story of the
first chapter of Genesis.

of communion and conversation with God. Other Christians not so restricted will consider it their ministerial duty to do what they can to create
a more just political order. To create a hospitable environment at worship,
to cheer up those who are sick or discouraged, to care for a weary couple's
small children so that the couple can refresh their relationship, to visit a
lonesome prisoner: these might possibly be diaconal actions, if they create
conditions conducive to the divine-human communion and conversation.

If we can arrive at some partial determination of what Christian ministry
is by coming to understand its goals, we are also assisted by coming to
understand its source. Activities are ministerial only when they originate in
the persons of God on mission to redeem and sanctify humanity. God acts
in the world as the triune community, and it is as the triune community that
God invites human persons to cooperate in the establishment of a redeemed and sanctified humanity. Inspired by the Holy Spirit, sent on
mission to human interiority, and guided by the risen Lord Jesus, sent on
mission into historical existence in his humanity as minister of the new
human-divine relationship, individual Christians accept responsibility to do
what they can to foster communion and conversation or to so arrange the
conditions of human existence that communion and conversation are advanced.

While the divine community can move any individual to act in favor of
communion and conversation, self-conscious ministers are those who have
been baptized into the Christian community. They come in faith and
understanding to recognize that the interpersonal relations created in baptism between themselves and God and the church entail service. As persons
become conscious that they live in a dynamic state of being gathered up
into intimacy with the divine community, they sense themselves to be compelled to relate to their fellow human beings on the basis of this loving
relationship with God. They want to reorganize their human relationships
on the basis of their life with God.

Self-giving service is a major direction that the reorganization takes.
Receiving God's love and returning it creates a dynamic toward service of
all the other human beings whom God loves. Besides, people who have
found new life with God in the community of the baptized know how much
they owe to others who have been instruments, that is, ministers, of the
triune God for them. In turn, they seek to be of service to others so that in
due time all can be gathered into self-conscious communion and conversation with the divine persons.

Loving service of this sort is a function of faith, the knowledge born of
love in which the baptized know the mystery of God's love for humanity,
know that they are part of this mystery, know that they have the privilege

of making some contribution to the insertion of human society into the mystery. Faith, then, as knowledge of one's role in the divine gift of redemption and sanctification is also a source of ministry. It may be understood as the subject's appropriation of the ministerial responsibility conferred in baptism. To sum up, the source of ministry is the triune God through the missions of the Spirit and the Son and mediated through baptism and faith. [4]

We are now in a better position to make an initial statement about which activities are ministerial. Actions can be classified as ministerial whose source is baptism and faith mediating to human individuals and ecclesial communities the divine invitation to service of humanity, both inside and outside the church, and whose goal is, ultimately, communion and conversation between humanity, individually and communally, and God. Given this approach to determining roles of service, an approach that is an interpretation of New Testament data, it becomes apparent that a wide variety of actual activities can be accepted as ministries. It is no surprise that St. Paul includes quite different activities in his lists of gifts conferred upon individuals to build up the Body of Christ. According to the variations of the sociocultural context and the character of the Christian community in that context, whether in Corinth or Rome or Ephesus, the triune God inspires service which takes shape in different ways, but always to promote communion and conversation.

I find no theological basis for designating as ministries the more public, official, or permanent roles of service, while classifying other less visible and more spontaneous actions by some other category, as, for example, when the former are named *ministries* but the latter *services*. On the contrary, as Paul himself teaches, giving alms, speaking in tongues, founding a church, and administering a church are all gifts given by God to individuals for the sake of the common good. Just as Paul seemed unconcerned to develop an exclusive list, so, over the centuries of Christian history, the list continues to expand.

At the same time, while the argument here does not allow for the distinction of ministries between formal and informal or between established functions and spontaneous activities, the criteria of goal and source do enable Christians to sort out what is and what is not ministry. Normally the services of a mayor, teacher, plumber, nurse, lawyer, chef, or auto mechanic are not Christian ministries. Those who exercise these roles are regularly of tremendous assistance to their fellow human beings in the execution of daily life in contemporary society. While both the agent and the recipient

---

4. In these paragraphs I have systematized what 1 Cor. 12:4-6 and Eph. 4:4-6 teach about the sources of the roles of service in the church.

of such goods and services may be committed Christians, seeking to offer honest service in return for just remuneration, ministry is not at issue here for the source and the goal is unrelated to life with the divine community.

There are situations, however, in which the exercise even of the activities mentioned above and others that are similar can be ministerial. If someone comes weekly to the home of a person who must use a wheelchair to clean the house and do the laundry, and performs this service primarily out of love of God and neighbor, respecting the dignity of the person and establishing a bond of love with a fellow human being that can lead to greater love of God on the part of both the agent and the recipient, whether this cleaning person is or is not paid for services rendered, it is an act of ministry. Contrarily, if the almsgiver or the TV evangelist or the interpreter of tongues is performing those more publicly Christian activities apart from the source and goal of ministry, then they are no more than the appearance of ministry. So I interpret 1 Cor. 13:1-3, which contends that speaking in tongues, when it is not motivated by divine love, is nothing but empty sound.

Who Can Minister?

As the end of the second millenium approaches, it is increasingly commonplace for Christians to assert that all the baptized are called to service for the sake of the gospel. The Second Vatican Council promoted this kind of talk among Catholics by teaching unequivocally that, before the members of the church are divided into clergy and laity, they are the one People of God. Moreover, the Council teaches, all the baptized share in the priesthood of Jesus, the one high priest of the new covenant with God.[5] Jesus exercised his high priesthood as a ministry of reconciliation of humanity with God, to initiate a new and final era of intimate interpersonal relationships between human persons and the divine persons. To have some share in this priesthood of Christ means that those human persons so blessed not only are beneficiaries of the new interpersonal relationships, but also are cooperators with Christ in extending those benefits to others.

The Council teaches further that because Jesus is the Christ, the anointed one of God, he not only exercises the ministry of God's anointed high priest, but also of God's anointed prophet and God's anointed king. The Council's attribution of the three anointed ministries to Jesus as the

---

5. On how the Council came to this teaching and how it is to be understood in the context of the Council, see my "Common and Ministerial Priesthood: *Lumen Gentium*, Article Ten," *Irish Theological Quarterly* 53 (1987): 81–99.

Christ is not a novelty. Sporadically since Eusebius of Caesarea in the early fourth century the threefold ministry of Christ has been acknowledged. In a related patristic theme, the three functions of Christ were applied to those anointed in baptism as Christ-ians. The Council chose to restore this attribution to a central place in contemporary Catholic Christology and ecclesiology, probably under the influence of the extensive development given the theme by Yves Congar in his 1953 study, *Lay People in the Church.*[6]

What is novel for the Catholic church with the Second Vatican Council is an explicit insistence that the ministry of all Christians is patterned in the same threefold manner after the ministry of Christ.[7] The church is made up of members who pattern their lives upon the life of Christ, including the activity of Christ. The activity of Christ on earth was a priestly, prophetic, and shepherding or pastoral activity.[8]

How useful is the threefold pattern for organizing ministry? After all, many more titles have been attributed to Jesus than the three of the pattern. And, while these three are governed by the practice in the Hebrew covenant of anointing, even there questions may be raised, for while priests and kings were surely anointed, it is not so clear that prophets were. The pattern, then, grounded as it is in the theme of anointing, is a conceptual device for relating Christians to Christ their leader, and sorting out the activities on behalf of humankind of the leader and his followers. Given its nonrigorous rationale we may wonder about the extensive use of the trilogy in Vatican II and contemporary theology.

Nevertheless, I favor retention of the pattern because of its ability to provide a conceptual umbrella for the diverse ministries exercised in the church according to the multiple charisms of the Holy Spirit. At the same time the pattern neatly distinguishes ministerial activities according to their contribution to the goals of ministry of communion, conversation, and creation of the conditions for both to happen and continue. It is not inconvenient to find a unifying category in the anointed one = Christ = Christian, with the anointing that issues forth in priestly, prophetic, and shepherding activities.

How, in fact, do the three functions take shape among the baptized? The

6. Translation of *Jalons pour une théologie du laïcat* (London: Chapman, 1959).

7. On the history and meaning of the Council's use of the threefold pattern of ministry, see my "The Priest, Prophet and King Trilogy: Elements of Its Meaning in *Lumen Gentium* and for Today," *Eglise et Théologie* 19 (1988): 179–206. John Calvin seems to have been the first theologian to apply the threefold pattern explicitly to all the baptized. See John Calvin, *Institutes of the Christian Religion* I, in Ford Lewis Battles, ed., The Library of Christian Classics (Philadelphia: Westminster, 1960), 494–503.

8. The kings of Israel were often referred to as the shepherds of Israel, just as Yahweh was referred to as the Shepherd of Israel.

priestly character of the whole people of God is perhaps given its earliest statement in Rom. 12:1-2. Paul exhorts the members of the local church at Rome "to present your bodies as a living sacrifice, holy and acceptable to God, which is your spiritual worship. Do not be conformed to this world but be transformed by the renewal of your mind, that you may prove what is the will of God, what is good and acceptable and perfect."

By their insertion into Christ through baptism the Christian people are enabled to create a new moment of goodness in the world in their own persons. It is not difficult to move from this personal, sacrificial transformation to an active priestly effort on behalf of the transformation of the world. Indeed, Paul says as much in what is now the last verse of the chapter: "Do not be overcome by evil, but overcome evil with good" (12:21).

What this priestly ministry serves, in all the ways in which it can be implemented, is communion. Communion is the first of the goals of ministry stated above, a goal sought in each of the types of ministry, but most especially in priestly ministry. What initiates communion with God on the part of a people alienated from God by sinfulness is reconciliation. Reconciliation is the first priestly ministry. Jesus is the definitive reconciler, through his self-sacrifice bringing about humanity's reconciliation with God so that an intimate communion is achieved. By the same action Jesus creates the possibility of communion within the human family. The priestly ministry of reconciliation, mediating communion with God, includes ministerial efforts of incorporation, nurture, and healing, and the establishment of bonds of friendship. Extending reconciliation to the whole of humanity engages Jesus' followers. We become "ambassadors for Christ, God as it were appealing through us."[9] This priestly ministry of reconciliation is not limited to a few of the baptized, but in some way falls to the whole People of God.[10]

Prophetic ministry is the second type. It serves the dialogue between the persons of God and human persons. God speaks the definitive word of love to humanity in the incarnation of the Logos, and that same Logos, the Word become flesh, in his utterly responsive humanity is the perfect human word addressed to God. God's purpose in the divine missions, however, is not simply the fundamental establishment of the dialogue, but the establishment of the further opportunity for each human person of every generation to enter personally and freely into the dialogue in partnership with

9. 2 Cor. 5:17-21. While Paul's terminology is of ministry of the word ("he has entrusted the message of reconciliation to us"), the reality of reconciliation is first communion. Conversation encourages and follows from reconciliation. See Eph. 2:12-22.

10. I suggest that this is what 1 Pet. 2:5, 9 has in mind when it addresses the Christian people as a priestly people in Christ.

the incarnate Logos. To this end baptism moves the whole People of God to prophetic ministry. Those who are already, by the grace of God, privileged to be partners in the conversation are impelled by gratitude for what they have received to serve others in such a way that they may respond to the Word of God as well. Thus, Paul, quoting Isaiah, celebrates the ministry of the word in Rom. 10: 15: "How beautiful are the feet of those who preach the good news."

Ministries of the Word abound, from the simple, wordless witness of a committed Christian life, so much extolled by Pope Paul VI in *On Evangelization in the Modern World*, to solemn declarations of belief proposed by the church, to lengthy and elaborate treatises penned by Christian theologians and philosophers to initiate dialogue among those educated in the sciences and the humanities. [11]

Pastoral care is the third type of Christian service. A continuation of the ministry of Christ in his role as Good Shepherd or Pastor, pastoring includes not only guiding a diocese on the part of a bishop or a parish on the part of the appointed pastor. It also includes counseling the grief-stricken, visiting the sick in hospitals or at home, providing food, clothing, and lodging for the indigent, teaching the illiterate to read. The baptized take up these ministries in the spirit of Matthew 25, where Jesus commends those who respond to him with compassionate care for those beleaguered by life's many physical, emotional, and mental problems. Efforts to effect change in the social causes of systemic hunger, homelessness, illiteracy, and so on, such as lobbying Congress for new legislation and educating against abortion or racism or sexism can also be pastoral ministries. In each of these instances the immediate goal is serving people in favor of a human physical or cultural good. But, when pursued out of inspiration by the triune God and with the long-term goal of communion and conversation between humanity and God, such activities are ministries, not so much of sacrament or word, but of pastoral care.

The bishops gathered in council at the Vatican from 1962 to 1965 went to a great deal of trouble to teach clearly that before there are any distinctions among members of the church there is unity and an equal privilege of the faith. They insisted that the text of the *Dogmatic Constitution on the Church* first treat of all the baptized as making up the one People of God, who share in common the priesthood of Jesus. They did not follow the original draft drawn up by a preparatory committee, in which the hierarchy was highlighted, as if those in the hierarchy were generators of the rest of the body of the faithful and superior to them, and in which the common priesthood

---

11. Pope Paul VI, *On Evangelization in the Modern World*, art. 21.

of the baptized was not introduced until after consideration of the hierarchy, and was discussed only in relation to the laity.[12] When the final document was completed and endorsed in 1964, the equality of all the baptized was firmly in place.[13]

Along with the equality of the entire People of God came a fresh appreciation of the need on the part of the church to abandon the sense that had long been in place that some members of the church were active on behalf of the others while the remainder of the church was passive, receiving the ministrations of the active members. Nonordained men and women had always been among the active members of the church, but chiefly the clergy were considered to be the active members. Now the Second Vatican Council has taught that this common perception is to be amended. The theological argument by which the restored Pauline teaching of universal service is promoted begins by proposing for the first time in conciliar teaching the traditional doctrine of the priesthood of the entire membership of the church, a Catholic appropriation of a doctrine earlier highlighted by Martin Luther in the sixteenth century. It then goes on to draw the entire membership of the church into the active implications of that priesthood by including every group of the faithful in the ongoing implementation of the threefold function (*munus*) of Christ, as John Calvin had done in the *Institutes on the Christian Religion*.[14] Thus, while the term *ministry* is not generally used by Vatican II in reference to all the Christian faithful, although there are exceptions, the reality is certainly recognized as pertinent to all, and Catholic church history subsequent to Vatican II is applying the term to the service of all the faithful as well.[15]

In the previous paragraphs of this section, I have avoided reference to ordained ministry to prevent the notion from cropping up at the start that the ministry of all the baptized is lay ministry, precisely the notion that Vatican II also deliberately avoids with its utilization of the image of the People of God. To view the ministry of all the baptized as lay ministry misses the point that all the Christian people, whether ordained or not, are

12. See my "Common and Ministerial Priesthood," 81–85.

13. Of course, *Lumen Gentium* does not reduce all ministries into one. It also proposes the particular significance of the ministry of the bishop (see chapter III, art. 20–27), the presbyter (III, 28), the deacon (III, 29), and lay people (IV).

14. Calvin, *Institutes of the Christian Religion* I, 494–503. See also my "The Priest, Prophet and King Trilogy," 184–86.

15. I have found at least two instances in the documents of Vatican II in which the term *ministry* is applied to the nonordained. See the *Decree on the Church's Missionary Activity*, art. 23, and the *Decree on the Apostolate of the Laity*, which notes: "*Est in Ecclesia diversitas ministerii, sed unitas missionis*" (art. 2). I quote the Latin text here because not all English versions are specific in their translation of the terms *ministry* and *mission*.

commissioned to implement the threefold role of Christ. The ordained have a particularized ministry to fulfill, but so do parents and catechists. Moreover, the latter ministries are as essential as the former.

All this is not meant in any way to undermine the value of ordained ministry, but to restore to their proper value the ministries of other members of the People of God. What purpose faithful to the Gospel of Jesus is accomplished by glorifying one or another ministry as if it were superior? Yet that is what happened to the ordained ministry under the influence of the historical conditions of the Constantinian Empire in the fourth century, the Gregorian reforms of the eleventh century, and the anti-Protestant Catholic Reformation of the sixteenth century. The result has been an unfortunate loss of balance on the part of the church (a loss of balance that the reformed churches of the sixteenth century and later have recognized but have not been successful in overcoming), to the detriment of the entire church. It is instructive to examine the history of the ministry of all the baptized, but before doing so a trinitarian theology of ministry is developed upon the foundations of Vatican II's opening toward a recovery of the balance between baptized and ordained ministry.

The Trinitarian Structure of Christian Ministry

As Cardinal Leon-Joseph Suenens has stated, order in the church is not characterized by democracy or aristocracy, but by collegiality.[16] Collegiality refers properly to the relationships among the bishops, but it, as well as Suenens's insight, is grounded in the ecclesial reality of communion, which is broader in its extension than bishops. It applies to all the church's members. The 1985 Extraordinary Synod of Bishops recalls that communion in the church has its source in and is patterned by the intimate communion of the divine persons with each other and by the missions into human history of the Word and of the Spirit.[17] The Synod is recalling the opening articles of the Second Vatican Council's *Dogmatic Constitution on the Church*, which grounds ecclesiology in trinitarian theology.[18] The church has its origin in the divine initiative, the principle of which is the first person of the Trinity;

16. Cardinal Leon-Joseph Suenens, in an interview with the U.S. National Catholic News Service, in *Origins* 15 (May 30, 1985): 18.
17. "The Final Report" of the 1985 Extraordinary Synod of Bishops, *Origins* 15 (Dec. 19, 1985), art. A2 (446); C1 (448–49).
18. See *Lumen Gentium*, art. 2, 3, 4; see also the *Decree on the Church's Missionary Activity*, art. 2, 3, 4.

the church is the community of the disciples of the incarnate Word; the church is animated by the divine Spirit.

Furthermore, the *Pastoral Constitution on the Church in the Modern World* teaches that the ultimate expectation for human society is that it be a community constituted in the image of the trinitarian community, an interpersonal communion of mutually exchanged truth and love.[19] Ideally, the church is the vanguard of society; it is to be now what society may be expected, by the grace of God and human cooperation, to become. The church, then, is to be a community constituting itself in the image of the trinitarian community. Once more we are back at the goals of ministry, namely, the promotion of communion and conversation between humanity and God and among human persons. In short, ministry's goal is to foster community in the image and likeness of the triune God in the church and in the wider society.

Which characteristics of the divine Trinity need to characterize the church?[20] The Creed of the Councils of Nicea (325 C.E.) and First Constantinople (381 C.E.) affirms the equality of each of the three divine persons with the others. Each person is equally, truly God. Yet each person is really distinct from the others. The Father is not the Son, nor the Son the Spirit, nor the Spirit the Father. The Father is the originating principle of persons in God. This characteristic of principle does not render the first person of the Trinity superior to the other two. It is only a statement of relationship, of an order among equals. The Son is distinguished as the Word that speaks divine truth within the Trinity. The Spirit is the movement of divine love. Each is personally distinct and yet no less sharing fully in the divine nature.

The relationship of the divine persons to each other is so total that each is said to dwell entirely in the other in a complete exchange of divine life. Greek theologians of the early Christian centuries gave this total, mutual self-giving on the part of the three divine persons the name of *perichoresis*, the going round about, that is, interpenetration, of the Three in One. The Latin terms for the same reality are also instructive. *Circumincessio* refers to

---

19. *Gaudium et Spes*, art. 24.

20. My considerations in the following paragraphs do not present, but only draw on, the church's long tradition of trinitarian theology. More complete theologies of the trinity are offered by Anthony Kelly, CSSR, *The Trinity of Love: A Theology of the Christian God* (Wilmington, Del.: Michael Glazier, 1989); William J. Hill, *The Three-Personed God: The Trinity as a Mystery of Salvation* (Washington: Catholic University of America Press, 1982); Walter Kasper, *The God of Jesus Christ* (New York: Crossroad, 1984); John J. O'Donnell, *The Mystery of the Triune God* (London: Sheed & Ward, 1988); Leonardo Boff, *Trinity and Society* (Maryknoll, N.Y.: Orbis, 1988); and a text which is not so much a theology itself as a summary of the data and theology of the trinitarian doctrine, Edmund J. Fortman, *The Triune God: A Historical Study of the Doctrine of the Trinity* (Grand Rapids: Baker Book House, 1972).

the entry of each divine person into the life of the others in total openness and freedom. The other Latin term, *circuminsessio*, refers to the residence of each person with the others, the welcoming and comfortable dwelling together of the three divine persons.

Not only does the triune God exist in itself, but it relates to the world it has created. The triune God has entered into this world in its human history. The Word entered into history by assuming a full human nature, and the Spirit entered into history as animator. Their missions in history are extensions of what the Word and the Spirit are within the divine community. Without any change in themselves or in the divine community, the Word and the Spirit bring changes to human reality, and the major change is the establishment of the church as a historical trinitarian community comprised of those people appropriating redemption and sanctification through baptism according to faith in the triune God. The church is the community of persons who self-consciously live out the new interpersonal relationships established by the divine missions in human history.

Three characteristics of the divine community have been distinguished. First, each person of the Trinity is equal to the others; there are no distinctions of superior and inferior. Second, each person within the Trinity has its own distinct personal identity, which is an identity only in relationship, but it distinguishes the person as real. In other words, each person of the Trinity is real in itself, but its reality consists in the distinctness of its relation to the others. Third, the persons of the Trinity act out their divinity in constant, mutual exchange of their life and truth and love. Finally, in the trinitarian missions both the life of the whole as well as the individual persons become intimately involved with the world. The missions do not add a fourth characteristic to the divine community. They are God's self-extension into the world.

The church is a community patterned after the divine community. How do the three characteristics of the divine community transfer to the community of the church? First, because the sacrament of baptism has the same effect within each member of the church, there is absolute equality of dignity among the church's membership. No person in the church is more reconciled to God than the next person. Christ has reconciled all equally through his absolutely effective saving life, death, and resurrection. Second, each member of the church has her or his distinct identity. Each is to be respected for the person she or he is, created equally with everyone else in the image of the intelligibility, truth, and love of God, and redeemed and sanctified as well by God's gracious gift as all the others who have been redeemed and sanctified, but always as an individual, a unique and free subject. Third, the church exists as a *koinonia*, a fellowship in which each member stands ready to offer the gifts (charisms) with which he or she has been blessed in service to the other and to receive from the other the gifts lacking in herself or himself. There is a constant, mutual exchange of all that promotes communion and conversation between humanity and God.

Just as the qualities of the life of the triune God have their analogous counterparts in the life of the church, so they have their counterparts in the church's ministry. For ministry is not distinct from the life of the church, but is a dimension of what the church is, the active dimension of rendering service. Communion, with its characteristics of equality, distinction, and mutuality, pertains as much to the ministerial as to every other dimension of church life, for the church is constituted to be communion in all its aspects.

At this point we return again to Karl Rahner's theology of symbol since it clarifies how the very expressions of God's activity in and by the membership of the church are God's presence gracing the church.[21] All the multiple ministries of the church are symbols of the active presence of the triune God. There is not some deep chasm across which God reaches to make the ministers and ministries of word, sacrament, and pastoral care effective. Rather God acts *in* the ministers and ministries; they are expressions of the divine community in the present situation insofar as their source is the triune God and their goal is communion and conversation with the divine community. One does not look outside the minister and the ministry to find how God might be at work here; one discovers the divine activity in minister and ministry. God's presence is embedded in the ministry. Moreover, the diverse array of ministries expresses the richness of the reality of God active in human history. Welcoming every baptized person to exercise the charisms with which she or he has been gifted manifests the beauty of the church, but also the beauty of the mysterious God who can be discovered in the activities of ministry.

Searching for the triune God inherently at work in human history, we discover the three qualities that characterize the divine Trinity and the church community patterned after the Trinity to be present as well in the church's ministry and ministers. Just as with the persons of God, there is a radical equality of each minister and of each ministry. Those that appear more humble and those that appear more grand are actually quite equal, for both contribute to the life of the church without which it would be so much the poorer. The diocesan bishop presiding over a eucharistic celebration of

---

21. In this section of his essay Rahner relates the theology of symbol only to the ministry of sacraments, but in light of the theology of ministry being developed in these pages Rahner's arguments apply to all the instances of ministry. See "Theology of the Symbol," 242.

the local church is surely performing a ministry that is a symbol of the saving action of God, but so is the woman or man afflicted with a spreading cancer, who suffers in union with the crucified Christ and who patiently and lovingly does so in service of humankind's appropriation of the redemption accomplished by Christ.

It may seem that ministries that are more publicly related to the functioning of the church are the more important. Pastoral leadership of the church by bishops and presbyters is one case in point. Administration of the sacraments is another. Public preaching and teaching of the word of God is a third. And indeed these are all ministries essential to the daily life of the church and to its extension from one generation to the next. We even name the group that is most responsible for these activities the hierarchy, those who perform the official ministries of leadership of the church as a matter of sacred trust. But what endows these ministries with their particular distinction is their way of extending the divine missions into the ongoing history of the church, and not their superiority, as if to imply that God is more active or more importantly active in the official ministers and ministries.

A second quality of the trinitarian community is the distinct identity of each of the divine persons constituted by the relationships each has to the others. The church is also constituted by this characteristic in its ministry, as the reality expressed by Paul's term *charism* manifests. It is a term, along with the reality, recovered by the Second Vatican Council.[22] Charisms are the ministerial gifts conferred upon the baptized in such a way that, by the grace of God, every member of the church has one or several gifts to offer in service of the goals of ministry. No one is entirely without charismatic gifts.

Whereas the equality of each minister and ministry in the church endows all with equal dignity, the dignity of being a person baptized into Christ who is also called to service, the charismatic gifts differentiate the People of God among themselves, so that they can relate to each other according to the rich diversity of the variety of gifts. We can think of three Christians, one caring for fellow human beings left to die on the streets of Calcutta, one teaching illiterate adults how to read so that they can enter more fully into the divine-human dialogue, one preaching to a congregation at Sunday worship. Each is exercising a different charism. Each minis-

22. See, among other references, *Lumen Gentium*, art. 4, 7, 11, 12. Article 4 distinguishes charismatic from hierarchical gifts, or charism from office, but I find no sound basis either in the New Testament or in the later tradition for making a qualitative distinction between them. Official recognition of some ministers is, of course, important in an ordered society. But office is not more divinely inspired than spontaneous charisms.

try is equally valuable, yet each is quite distinct. In the church the subjects of these charisms relate to each other, on the one hand as equals and on the other by means of their different ministries. Unless the three were equal the relationship would not be on the level of their common dignity; unless each of the three possessed a different gift there would be nothing to share in a relationship. Moreover, it is not just the three whose service is noted in the illustration who can relate to each other in their ministry, but the three recipients are also, when viewed differently or when active in a different context, at least potential subjects of ministry. So, the dying man of Calcutta, the illiterate adult, the worshiper in the pew possess their respective charismatic gifts for service of the common good.

Another element of ministry highlighted by this second quality is that everyone is not equally capable of all ministries. Ministries are not simply superficial functions anyone can pick up and accomplish at whim. Ministries express the graced being of the Christian people, which includes the diversity resulting from the distinctness of individuality in concert with God's diverse gifts. Ordination confirms the gifts of some to preside over the church. Spontaneous charisms endow some with the ability to preach effectively to small children, not a gift given to all. Still others have the charism to adapt readily to cultures other than their own for the sake of translating the gospel freshly in various cultural circumstances. It is a mistake to think of ministry as simply another role or task that all baptized persons can indiscriminately accomplish. The talents of individual persons and the skills in which they have been trained together with the endorsement of the church help the faithful discern which gifts have been granted to them by the triune God.

A third quality of the persons of the Trinity which is distinguished in the tradition of trinitarian theology underscores the constant, mutual, interpersonal activity of the three divine persons, who eternally and with total generosity share their life and truth and love. This quality transfers to the ministerial dimension of the ecclesial community specifically as the service which, ideally, the members of the church constantly offer to each other. It is the quality by which all are willing, as followers of the Master, to lay down their lives for the others.

In a recent book interpreting the philosophy of John Macmurray, Frank Kirkpatrick names this the mutual/personal model of community, considering it to be the highest form of social life attainable, the ultimate form of social life willed by God. [23] Based as it is upon the character of God's inter-

---

23. Frank G. Kirkpatrick, *Community: A Trinity of Models* (Washington: Georgetown University Press, 1986), 137ff.

personal life, this type of community consists of mutual relationships among persons who want simply to spend themselves for the others. Nor do they go to such lengths of service in order to get something out of it, although in such a mutual exchange not only do all serve but all are served as well. [24] Macmurray sums it up succinctly in the following sentence, which appears in his lectures on *Freedom in the Modern World*: "That capacity to live in terms of the other, and so of what is not ourselves, to live in others and through others and for others, is the unique property of human beings." [25]

The third trinitarian quality of ministry brings us to the heart of what ministry most characteristically is, what its very name signifies: it is all the members of the church giving *themselves* in service to each other according to the charisms with which they have been gifted. There is no sense in such service of gaining any advantage for oneself over against the others. [26] This third characteristic of ministry, analogous to the characteristic of mutuality within the divine community, gathers up and fulfills the characteristics of equality of dignity and differentiation of gifts of service.

The divine persons are not self-absorbed; they have come on mission into human history. Moreover, the church is a community of persons constituting human history. It is a way of living in the world and affecting the course of world events. [27] The church's life, including the ministerial dimension, participates, by reason of its self-constitutive quality, in the outgoing, missionary character of the Trinity.

At this point ordained ministry becomes intelligible. In the extension of God's trinitarian life in the divine missions throughout human history by means of the sacramental instrumentality of the church the distinction of the ordained ministry takes on its meaning.

Jesus, the incarnate Word of God, brings the triune God's redeeming activity into human history in a way that is most readily accessible to humanity, in the deeds and teachings of a historically existing human being. The First Letter of John (1:1) says it as well as it can be said: Jesus is "that which was from the beginning, which we have heard, which we have seen with our eyes, which we have looked upon and touched with our hands, concerning the word of life. . . ." After living a life as all human beings do, Jesus no longer walks the earth. However, a public ministry of the church

24. Ibid., 190–92.

25. John Macmurray, *Freedom in the Modern World* (London: Faber & Faber, 1932), 183–84. While Macmurray expresses this truth of human being in philosophical terms, he understands it to be at the heart of the teaching and life of Jesus.

26. Mark 10:42-45.

27. Karl Rahner and Bernard Lonergan both deal with the church's character of *Selbstvollzug*, self-constitution in history. See Lonergan, *Method in Theology* (New York: Herder & Herder, 1972), chap. 14. See also the works of Joseph Komonchak referred to in chap. 1, n. 12.

in the name of Jesus, the ordained ministry, continues throughout human history. Animated by the Spirit of God it is a ministry of leadership. It is Christ's leadership of the body of the church in a socially acknowledged and concretely recognizable way. Yves Congar notes that the continuance of the two divine missions provides a christological and a pneumatological balance within the church: "Such is the meaning of the hierarchy: it represents Christ in his quality of standing before the community which, nevertheless, he animates from within."[28]

In Congar's view the christological and the pneumatological are the two ways in which Christ works in the church. As the risen Lord he works through his Spirit to make all the members active in service. But Christ also continues a certain historical relationship vis-à-vis the ecclesial community in the hierarchy who act as representative of Christ to the community.

Congar's view has the merit of demonstrating that the church exists in a trinitarian way, as a community in which all the members are equal, differentiated by their charisms, and giving themselves in unhesitating, mutual service to each other, with a structure according to which authority is exercised, in positions of God-given leadership (hierarchy), but in all instances eschewing any crass exercise of power.[29] Thus, the distinction among ministers and ministries, including ordained ministry, has a trinitarian meaning as it derives from the second quality of the divine Trinity, the distinction of persons in the Trinity on the basis of relationships. Distinction in ministry also derives from the differentiated divine missions into human history; at this point ordained ministry is specified as leadership in the name of Christ the head of the church (in persona Christi capitis ecclesiae).

Insightful as Congar's interpretation of the hierarchical structure of the church is, caution must be exercised lest it be extended too far. For while ordained ministers serve the baptized and confirmed faithful as representatives of Christ, the baptized and confirmed faithful are likewise representative of Christ's saving presence to the wider world. For all the baptized share in the threefold ministry of Christ. Thus, there is a christological dimension to the ministry of all Christians.

Conversely, those who are ordained are animated in their ministry by the Holy Spirit, such that ordained ministry participates in the extension

---

28. Yves Congar, "Ministères et Structuration de L'Eglise," in *Ministères et Communion Ecclésiale* (Paris: Cerf, 1971), 41. Congar writes in a similar vein in the first essay of the volume, which has been translated as "My Path-findings in the Theology of the Laity and Ministries," *The Jurist* 32 (1972): 169–88.

29. Pertinent here is the distinction Lonergan draws between what he calls "naked power" and authority in "Dialectic of Authority," in *A Third Collection*, ed. Frederick E. Crowe (New York: Paulist, 1985), 5–12.

of the mission of the Holy Spirit into human history. Thus, there is a pneumatological dimension to the ministry of ordained bishops, priests, and deacons. The theological reason for the close connection between the christological and pneumatological dimensions of all ministry lies in the nature of Christ's resurrection. The risen Lord constantly bestows the gift of his life-giving Spirit upon all the faithful.

Another helpful distinction, again not to be exaggerated, was emphasized in the 1987 Synod on the Laity. There the baptized were understood chiefly to be entrusted with the church's mission to further the redemption and sanctification of the world, that is, the entire human environment, while the ordained were understood to minister within the church to the baptized so that they have the wherewithal to fulfill their world-oriented ministries. On this understanding both the baptized and the ordained serve the conversion of the world to communion and conversation with the divine community, but the former more directly and the latter indirectly.

Lumen Gentium makes prominent use of the images of the People of God and the Body of Christ to describe the nature of the church. The former is sometimes considered to be better suited to the trinitarian model of the church, while the latter can seem better to fit the organic model of the church as a body with some members more prominent than others. Edward Kilmartin has suggested that the trinitarian model clashes with the "christomonistic" model of Christ, the Head of his body, the church.[30] Kilmartin contends that the Second Vatican Council was unsuccessful in moving beyond a juridical model by which to understand the church because the Council fathers could not resolve the tensions that emerge when the attempt is made to place both trinitarian and christomonistic models of the church side by side.[31] While there may be some truth to Kilmartin's interpretation of the mentality of the Council fathers themselves, and while there may be some movement at the present to denigrate the image of People of God as less suited to the reality of the church than the image of the Body of Christ, there is no inherent reason to set one image of the church, or the models each suggests, over against the other. Both models illustrate a trinitarian theology of church that can be extended to ministry.

The image of the People of God expresses the unity of radically equal members who nevertheless contribute to the good order of the whole by their diversified roles. The image of the Body of Christ stresses the organic unity of the differentiated members of the body. Some members, and partic-

---

30. Edward J. Kilmartin, "Lay Participation in the Apostolate of the Hierarchy," *The Jurist* 41 (1981): 343–70.

31. Ibid., 353.

ularly the head, are more prominent than others. But Paul takes great care in 1 Corinthians 12 to interpret the meaning of the image in such a way that the less presentable members are in no way downgraded, in no way considered to be inferior. Nor are the other members passive, while the head is active. For without the contribution of each member exercising its particular role the body suffers severely or even breaks down. Thus, both the image of the People of God and the image of the Body of Christ communicate that the members of the Christian communion are equal, yet diverse, and intimately related to one another.

How the Ministry of All the Baptized Disappeared

What happened to the church community's perception of the active involvement of all the baptized in ministry from the moment of its unabashed acceptance in the Pauline Scriptures to the happy beginnings of its retrieval in the sixteenth century and its firm restoration in the twentieth? The history of the ministry of the baptized includes several moments that are important not just as a chronicle of what happened, but because they became catalysts for notions that entered into theology in the past, and still continue today, and that do disservice to the theology and reality of ministry. This particular history is most instructive about what went wrong and what, therefore, has needed to be changed.

First, the early years are examined, and for this examination I rely especially on the study by Alexandre Faivre of the gradual diminishment of the nonordained in the church during the first several centuries of Christianity.[32] Faivre begins by reminding the reader of the all-important fact that Jesus himself paid scant attention to the divisions of class and status among people, performing miracles for Jew and Gentile alike, welcoming among his followers women and men, relating not only to those who scrupulously adhered to the law, but also to public sinners. Jesus' basic acceptance of every human being, without any reference to the multiple stratifications of importance created repeatedly within society, has to be the reality to which the Christian community returns over and over as the pattern it follows in its own structure and decisions. None of these attitudes and moves on Jesus' part is a cultural particularity. Just the opposite—each demonstrates a countercultural intervention of Jesus into his society.

---

32. Alexandre Faivre, *Les laïcs aux origines de l'Église* (Paris: Centurion, 1984). For a related study see Jean-Paul Audet, "Priester und Laie in der christlichen Gemeinde: Der Weg in die gegenseitige Entfremdung" in *Der priesterliche Dienst I, Ursprung und Frühgeschichte* (Freiburg: Herder, 1970), 115–75.

The early Christians picked up on Jesus' practice (it hardly seems that they would have initiated such a custom) and addressed one another as *sister* and *brother*. This is the implication of texts such as Mark 3:35 and 10:30, although the appellations of Paul's letters refer only to "brothers." From the texts that remain extant, it seems that, even as specific titles and functions appear, and these before the end of the first century in the Pastoral Letters, the great concern of the Christian church, up to the end of the second century, is to define the bonds with Christ that are to be lived by all, rather than to set members of the church apart from each other. Faivre notes, for example, that the late-first-century *Letter of Clement of Rome to the Corinthians*, while calling its addressees to a sense of order, nevertheless looks upon all the members of the liturgical assembly as active: "Clement is not capable of subscribing to a theology which would make the offerings and liturgical functions the monopoly of certain ones to the detriment of the whole people of God."[33]

In addition, Clement's letter represents not so much the instruction of the church at Corinth by the leader of the church at Rome, but instead a reflection of the whole church at Rome, which is part of an ongoing exchange among the members of both churches.[34]

Throughout this period, several texts, such as *The Didache*, Ignatius of Antioch, Justin Martyr, Irenaeus, and Tertullian acknowledge distinct members of the Christian community as leaders, but they do not set them apart from the rest of the community as belonging to a special group.[35] Their concern, rather, is to set out the ideal of the community of disciples of Jesus, and in the process of doing that, to acknowledge the role that the leaders of the community play. There is neither diminishment nor exaggeration of any members of the Christian people.

At the beginning of the third century things begin to change. In both the Greek- and Latin-speaking spheres of the church, bishops come to be regarded as priests. Whereas in the New Testament all those who are baptized are named the people set apart, the *kleros*, the clergy, if you will, as distinct from the vast numbers of nonbaptized, toward the end of the second century this term becomes reserved for the ordained, as distinct from the baptized but nonordained members of the church.[36]

---

33. Faivre, *Les laïcs aux origines de l'Eglise*, 34. For the pertinent section of Clement, see the *Letter of Clement of Rome to the Corinthians*, 40, in Robert M. Grant and Holt H. Graham, eds., *The Apostolic Fathers* (New York: Thomas Nelson & Sons, 1965), 2:68–70.

34. Audet demonstrates this from the salutation of the letter in "Priester und Laie," 136.

35. See Hervé-Marie Legrand, "The Presidency of the Eucharist According to the Ancient Tradition," *Worship* 53 (1979): 413–38. See also Audet, "Priester und Laie," 137–39.

36. Acts 26:18; Col. 1:12.

In the same period the generality of Christians is slighted even further by being distinguished from the group formally named the laity. According to Origen, himself a nonordained Christian who respects the superior dignity of the clergy, there is an inner circle of the nonordained, the laity strictly so-called, from among whom the clergy can be chosen. These are men (women are not included) of requisite knowledge and virtue. Among the requisite virtues for men to belong to the laity is that they be celibate or married only once.[37]

Faivre interprets the shifts that are taking place in the third century as the onset of a certain inequality, which can be understood theologically on the analogy of the high priest, the notion increasingly employed to describe the meaning of episcopal ministry. The bishop/high priest alone possesses the sacred dignity to enter the Holy of Holies. As a result, the Christian people, who in the first century of Christianity all belonged to the priestly people, now becomes distinguished into the high priests, who are ordained, and the baptized people ministered to by the priests.[38] By the middle of the third century, the Syrian *Didascalia* treats the bishop as a monarch and the Christian people as infants whom the bishop needs to watch over carefully. Moreover, the bishop is accountable only to God.[39]

While the views expressed in the Syrian *Didascalia*, an Eastern text, cannot be assumed to be universal in the church of the mid-third century, they parallel those of another third-century author, a Latin Christian, Cyprian of Carthage (d. 258). The letters of Cyprian mention in passing the developing distinctions among Christians. Levels of responsibility are in place in the church, from the bishop who presides (*praepositus*), to the group set apart and just under the bishop, namely, the clergy (*clerus*), to the people (*plebs*).[40] The organization of the church is taking shape in the style of Roman society. Roles and tasks are being portioned out according to one's standing on the church's developing ladder of prominence (*cursus honorum*).

With the fourth-century endorsement of the church by the empire under Constantine, it is an easy move for the clergy to become officials of church and state. By the end of the fourth century, in a series of decretals of

---

37. Faivre, *Les laïcs aux origines de l'Eglise*, 82–83, 90. See Origen, *Homélies sur S. Luc*, 17.11 (Paris: Cerf, 1962), 262–63. See also Alexandre Faivre, "Une femme peut-elle devenir laïque?" *Revue des Sciences Religieuses* 58 (1984): 242–50. As Elaine Pagels argues in her recent study, *Adam, Eve, and the Serpent* (New York: Random House, 1988), for Origen's predecessor in the catechetical school of Alexandria, Clement, even to be married once is a less desirable way of being a Christian disciple than to remain unmarried for the sake of the kingdom (pp. 29–30), although at this early stage there is no direct link between ordination and celibacy.

38. Faivre, *Les laïcs aux origines de l'Eglise*, 94.

39. Ibid., 112–16. See F. X. Funk, ed., *Didascalia et Constitutiones Apostolorum*, vol. I, book II, 20, 1–2 (Paderborn: Schoeningh, 1905), 70–73.

40. Audet, "Priester und Laie," 150.

the bishops of Rome, the clergy and the laity become sharply distinguished as two disparate groups within the church, with almost all ecclesiastical functions becoming clerical. [41] During this same period, the number of the clergy grows rapidly, no doubt because of the increase of Christians generally, but also because, as the church and the state endorse each other, many privileges are accorded the clergy.

In response to this state of affairs the option of life away from normal society becomes increasingly inviting to those Christians who wish to live lives of evangelical commitment. Thus a third group gradually appears in the church, a group dedicated to holiness, eremitical or cenobitic monks, both men and women, eschewing marriage for the sake of the gospel. These are called the *continentes*, the continent, both sexually and otherwise. However, while increasingly numerous, they live on the margins of society.

Within civil society there remain two Christian groups, progressively separated from each other in dignity and way of life. One group is made up of the leaders of the church, called the *rectores*, who are the clergy, and who by the time of Pope Gregory the Great (pope from 590–604) wear the outer distinguishing mark of the tonsure. To maintain a separate and holier life-style for their clergy, many bishops, including Augustine, gather their clergy around them in the bishop's house or compound in a kind of monastery of the cenobitic life. Prayer is in common as is the possession of material goods; celibacy is required and together the assembled clergy study the Scriptures. [42] In the other group are those who are in the lowest Christian state, the *conjugati*, that is, the married. They receive the ministrations of the clergy. So low are the *conjugati* that the severe form of punishment for recalcitrant clergy is to reduce them to the lay state.

Just how far the division between clergy and laity could go is evidenced by the highly influential *Book of Pastoral Rule* of Gregory the Great. Written in the first year of his pontificate as a rule of life and ministry (especially the ministries of preaching and counseling) for bishops, the *rectores* in the church, the *Pastoral Rule* makes reference to 1 Pet. 2:9. In itself this text addresses the whole baptized people as a " holy nation, a royal priesthood." In Gregory's text, however, any notion of royal priesthood attaching to the baptized has given way to its application to bishops alone. They are the royal priesthood. [43] The laity are the subjects of the rulers within the church.

Although the division of the baptized People of God into two opposing,

41. Faivre, *Les laïcs aux origines de l'Eglise*, 185.
42. Peter Brown, *Augustine of Hippo* (Berkeley: University of California Press, 1967), 198.
43. See the *Book of Pastoral Rule* II, 3, 29. See also the commentary of Bruno Judic, "La Bible miroir des pasteurs dans la *Règle pastorale* de Grégoire le Grand," in *Le monde latin antique et la Bible*, ed. Jacques Fontaine and Charles Pietri (Paris: Beauchesne, 1985), 466.

rather than complementary, groups was firmly in place by the end of the fourth century and still continued in place without much change into our own century, it is worthwhile to continue to examine the ministry of the baptized in the centuries after the patristic period. Several instances of such ministry need to be highlighted in order to instruct us in our present efforts to construct a well-founded contemporary theology of ministry. What we discover in this history is that, despite the forces against their active role in the church, "ordinary" baptized Christians exercised their imaginations and initiative to find ways to assert their right and duty to join in the mission of the church.

For the so-called Middle Ages, here determined to be from 1100 to 1450, I rely chiefly upon a recent collection of essays by André Vauchez. [44] While the denigration of the nonordained Christian by the clergy, begun in earnest during the reign of Constantine, continues throughout the Middle Ages, complemented by a resentment of the clergy on the part of the laity, I choose to emphasize the instances in which the laity take their part in the ministry of the church, sometimes with and sometimes without the support of the clergy. [45] Such instances are important developments because of the changes they introduce into the history of ministry. Just such changes provide the key to understanding history, for change indicates shifts in meanings. [46]

The core of it all seems to be the twelfth century. It provided the ferment for the appearance of new groupings of the Christian faithful. The twelfth was a century of great social, intellectual, and technical change in which it was natural for movements to emerge. [47] One such movement, which had its beginnings in the eleventh century, but flowered in the twelfth, and continued in bloom into the fifteenth century, is that of the pious societies or confraternities for lay people and priests together, but especially lay people. The formation of these societies was an effort to retrieve the sense of community that, it was supposed, prevailed in the apostolic age. [48] While the communal life and the religious sophistication of these groups varied

44. André Vauchez, *Les laïcs au Moyen Age* (Paris: Cerf, 1987).

45. Vauchez quotes a 1296 decretal of Boniface VIII which is quite uncomplimentary of the laity: "History tells us that the laity has always been full of hostility toward clerics, a fact of which present experience provides an illustration" (ibid, 7). On the other hand, Innocent III, in the early years of the same century, was a great supporter of the new movements in the church, though he tended to want to clericalize them.

46. On change as the key to the meaning of history, see Lonergan, *Method in Theology,* 178–79, 187.

47. See the study of Marie-Dominique Chenu, *Nature, Man, and Society in the Twelfth Century* (Chicago: University of Chicago Press, 1968), esp. 219–30, 239–69.

48. See Acts 2:42-47; 4:32, and Luke 10:1-12 on the "apostolic life."

widely, they manifested that the nonordained were ready to take responsibility for their own Christian faith. Some, like the eleventh-century Patarines of Milan, even had as one of their goals the reform of the clergy. But primarily the confraternities sought the advancement in holiness of their members. Moreover, they were open to all the baptized, clergy and laity, women and men, young and old.

In almost all the pious societies, penitence became a valued way to achieve sanctity, and it was available without having to enter a monastery. The concern for penitence was not unrelated to Manichean tendencies, but whatever its motivations, the possibility of doing penance as a lay person included the assumption that it was not necessary to be a monk to become holy, but that a person could be married and continue to live in the world as a merchant or artisan. [49] Simplicity of life, various ascetical practices, and periods of sexual continence characterized the spiritual exercises of members of these pious societies. Monastic practices, such as flagellation, were also adopted by some societies, becoming especially popular during times of unusual stress such as the Black Death and the Great Schism. [50]

Vauchez has also noted the impact upon the emergence of an active laity of the call to the Crusades. From the point of view of the relationship of Western Christianity with Islam and with Eastern Christianity, the Crusades do not constitute a glorious moment in the history of Christianity. From another point of view, however, they stand as one more catalyst moving the otherwise largely passive masses of ordinary people, that is, those who were not clerics, monks, or nobles, to become active on behalf of the gospel. [51] In a sense, it is another opening to a new spirituality, for what most characterized this commitment to the Crusades was a move away from the need to escape the world by way of monastic contemplation, and a move toward spending one's life in the here and now of daily existence to conform oneself to Christ in his humanity. Making one's way eastward to recover the land of Jesus from the "infidel" and while there literally to walk in the footsteps of Jesus was one preeminent way in which this spirituality, perhaps crudely, expressed itself. [52] Beyond the Crusades, the spirituality of conformity to the humanity of Jesus was incorporated into the new confraternities generally, and reached its high point in the Middle Ages in the Dominican and Franciscan movements.

Both the desire to live the ascetical life and the desire to conform oneself

49. Vauchez, *Les laïcs au Moyen Age*, 99–100.
50. See André Vauchez, "La Bible dans les confréries et les mouvements de dévotion," in *Le Moyen Age et la Bible*, ed. Pierre Riché and Guy Lobrichon (Paris: Beauchsne, 1984), 587–89.
51. Vauchez, *Les laïcs au Moyen Age*, 57.
52. Ibid., 10, 27, 239.

to Christ in his humanity combined to give the members of the pious societies a socially oriented direction as well. Theirs was what we would today name a ministerial spirituality. For example, in the Low Countries, between 1170 and 1180, the movement of the Beguines was initiated. This was a community of women who devoted themselves to three occupations: manual labor, intense prayer, and care for the sick. Distribution of food to the indigent, the establishment of hospices for victims of plague, and of guest houses along the routes of the pilgrimages (especially to the three great centers of the Middle Ages, Saints Peter and Paul at Rome, Saint James at Santiago de Campostela, and Sainte Foy at Conques) were among the common types of outreach by the members of the confraternities. Vauchez notes that generosity and hospitality were the hallmarks of the religious life of devoted laity.[53] The inspiration for this remarkable dedication to works of mercy was again the spirituality of the humanity of Christ, in this case love for the crucified Savior as he is met in one's needy neighbors.

All this new activity on the part of those Christians who were to be counted neither among the clergy nor the monks became noticed by the hierarchy. Pope Innocent III (pope from 1198–1216) may be the most prominent among the bishops who supported the new movements. But Vauchez remarks that the hierarchy generally departed from their custom of celebrating the holiness only of monks and clerics dedicated to the monastic life, and began, during the thirteenth and fourteenth centuries, to praise members of the church, including the laity, involved in apostolic activities of various sorts.[54]

No movement can sustain itself over the long run without a literature. For Christian spiritualities the sustaining literature is mainly the Bible. The Bible is especially important for a spirituality that attempts to achieve conformity of life with the humanity of Jesus. Contact with the Bible on the part of most pious Christians of the Middle Ages, however, was rarely direct. Mothers taught their children the Our Father and the Hail Mary, and perhaps the Creed. Some pious Christians, who wanted to observe the monastic hours of prayer in their individual lives, would memorize the Psalter.

Preaching, too, was a way to communicate the life of Christ. It also came to be recognized as a chief way to live the apostolic life, extending the meaning of "apostolic" beyond the monastic life of self-contained commu-

---

53. Ibid., 128–30.
54. Ibid., 137. Throughout his study Vauchez has sprinkled biographical sketches of lay people who gained fame among their contemporaries for their distinguished holiness.

nity. Already in the eleventh century Peter Damian promoted itinerant preaching on the part of those who demonstrated evangelical fidelity by remaining aloof from material riches.[55] The Dominican and Franciscan movements of the new spirituality were dedicated to preaching the authentic gospel to the faithful; thus, the mendicants became itinerant preachers, doing much to provide an accurate evangelical base for the spiritual movements of the age.[56]

The Bible was also communicated to the people of the time through the stained glass windows of the great cathedrals and other churches constructed during the period, and through the frescoes and sculptures adorning churches both inside and out.[57] The artists and artisans, for the most part nonordained members of the church, who produced these works of art and of faith that abound in Europe, quite without self-consciousness, could be said to be engaged in ministry, for the purpose of their work was to instruct and edify the faithful. It was work undertaken for the love of God and of Mary, the mother of Jesus.

A religious language specific to the mentality of the new spirituality was also developed, especially from the thirteenth through the fifteenth centuries. Much of this literature can be characterized as prophetic/mystical and was authored by distinguished women of the time: Hildegarde of Bingen (d. 1172), Brigid of Sweden (d. 1373), Catherine of Siena, (d. 1380), and Julian of Norwich (d. 1413). Their writings emphasize individual religious experience and celebration of the sacraments as a means of one's individual union with Christ. The women authors had further handicaps to overcome: their gender and their lack of education.[58]

There is not much point to speculation about what might have happened to the spiritual movements of the Middle Ages if the clergy were not so much in control of the church and if education were extended to more than male nobles and clerics, but it seems clear that laypersons ready for more active participation in the life of the church and ready to be sustained by a biblically informed faith are at least partially responsible for the success of the Protestant efforts to reform the church during the sixteenth century. But nothing could have opened the doors more dramatically than Martin Lu-

55. Chenu, *Nature, Man, and Society,* 214–15.

56. Ibid., 130, 137. As early as the eighth century there was concern that the Bible be preached in the vernacular languages to those who could not read or understand Latin. See Michel Zink, "La prédication in langues vernaculaires," in *Le Moyen Age et la Bible,* ed. Riché and Lobrichon, 489–516.

57. See Francois Garnier, 'L'imagerie biblique médiévale' in *Le Moyen Age et la Bible,* ed. Riché and Lobrichon, 423.

58. Vauchez, *Les laïcs au Moyen Age,* 247–48, 266–69.

ther's assurance in *The Freedom of a Christian* (1520) that everyone who lives by faith in the word of God shares in the priesthood of all believers![59]

However, while the reformers are to be celebrated for their efforts to restore the whole Christian people to active participation in the life of the church and to provide opportunities for all to have access to an evangelical faith informed by the Bible, the Protestant Reformation reacted against the exaggerated emphasis of the ministerial priesthood and its sacramental meaning by rejecting them altogether.[60] On the other hand, the efforts of the Catholic Reformation simply to shut out the Protestant Reformation in its totality (despite earlier attempts at conciliation in the Augsburg Confession) prevented baptismal ministry from achieving the rightful place toward which it had been struggling through the spiritual movements of the Middle Ages.

Interestingly, both Protestants and Catholics in the centuries after the Reformation found ways of redressing their particular imbalances. Whatever their theology of ministerial priesthood and sacrament, the Protestant ecclesial communities have, for the most part, an ordained clergy who clearly preside over word, worship, and care. From the other side, whatever the denigration of the nonordained and the efforts to keep the laity as recipients rather than agents of ministry, the Catholic church found itself with increasing numbers of men and women choosing an apostolic life. During the late medieval period and into the modern centuries, scores of religious congregations were founded to do ministry: education, care for the sick, homeless, and orphans, and missionary activity. These new congregations were not monastic but sought to address the material and spiritual needs of society from within, although the power of monasticism was so strong that even such active congregations tried to adapt monasticism in some measure to themselves. Moreover, so powerful was the view that the clergy belong to a higher state that most of the male religious became ordained.[61]

---

59. Martin Luther, "The Freedom of a Christian," in *Luther's Works*, ed. Jaroslav Pelikan and Helmut T. Lehmann (Philadelphia: Fortress Press, 1957), 31:354–56. See also Luther's other two important works of 1520, *To the Christian Nobility of the German Nation*, 44:127, and *The Babylonian Captivity of the Church*, vol. 36, which includes Luther's claim that since all Christians are priests all have the same power (p. 116).

60. See E. Gordon Rupp, "The Age of the Reformation, 1500–1648," in *The Layman in Christian History*, ed. Stephen Charles Neill and Hans-Ruedi Weber (Philadelphia: Westminster, 1963), 147, and, in the same volume, Martin Schmidt, "The Continent of Europe, 1648–1800," 151. Both authors note how quickly the Reformation impetus to lay participation in the church's mission waned.

61. In fact, many of the new congregations began as communities whose intent was to be priests who would take up pastoral tasks otherwise neglected. See José Ignacio Telechea Idi-

In the nineteenth century, within the Catholic context, an attempt was quietly launched by a layman writing a compendium of canon law to retrieve the active place of all the baptized. Georg Phillips transposed the concept of the church's priestly, prophetic, and kingly functions from the Protestant context (first developed by John Calvin and taken up by the rationalist theologians of the eighteenth century) into the Catholic and proceeded to explain that every baptized Catholic shares in the threefold function of Christ.[62] The laity, in particular, exercise their priestly role in the church by offering their prayers to God; their teaching role when parents educate their children in the faith and when lay people serve as catechists; and their royal or kingly role by influencing the church's leadership. Admittedly, Phillips is making modest claims for the nonordained, but what is more to the point is that a door is finally being opened, three centuries after the Reformation, to a systematic understanding of active evangelical living on the part of baptized Catholics who are neither clergy nor religious without slighting the significance of the ordained ministry.

In the twentieth century the church generally began to awaken to the need for all Christian people to assume responsibility for the promotion and defense of the faith. Confronted with massive intellectual and political secularization, the hierarchy began to recognize that only the laity are immersed enough within normal social life, without any of the world-distancing practices of monasticism and celibacy, to be able to evangelize from within. Finally, with the twentieth-century opening to the apostolate of all the baptized, we are back again in the present.

Retrieving a Perception of the Ministry of All the Baptized

First, the formation of two rigidly defined groups in the church during the third and fourth centuries is an unfortunate legacy to the rest of the Christian centuries, continuing as it does even up to the present time. It is unfortunate, because theologically ill-founded, that the ordained became the clergy, the group set apart from the rest of the baptized as if their portion were the Lord, and even more unfortunate that the rest of the baptized became the laity, understood pejoratively to refer to those lesser Christians who have not achieved the dignity of orders or the holiness of monks.

---

goras, "La espiritualidad sacerdotal en la época moderna," in *Espiritualidad del Presbitero Diocesano Secular* (Madrid: Editorial de la Conferencia Episcopal Española, 1987), 413.

62. Georg Phillips, *Kirchenrecht* I (Graz: Akademische Druck- u. Verlaganstalt, 1959; a reprint of the 3d edition of 1855), #32, 33.

On the basis of a trinitarian theology of ministry, including the aspect of the divine missions in the world, there is no place, doctrinally, theologically, psychologically, or sociologically for any gap between the ordained and the rest of the baptized. Rather there ought to be a collaborative attitude characterizing the relationships of the ordained with the rest of the baptized people. For every baptized person is an equal member of the ecclesial community, with differing charisms for service, but all striving for the same goal of communion and conversation. A theology of ministry based on the trinitarian missions calls for collaboration.

A second evaluative position praises the beginnings in the Middle Ages of an apostolic spirituality for Christians of every sort. This endorsement of a move toward evangelical fermentation of society on the part of Christians living in its midst need be no slight of the value of monastic spirituality, which is, after all, also a way of living in society and bringing gospel values to bear upon it. But when monasticism is looked upon as the privileged way of Christian living, and life in the normal course, characterized by marriage, family, and secular work, is considered of lesser value, then the call to holiness of all the baptized is distorted. Unfortunately, as Vauchez notes, in the early Middle Ages, before the beginnings of the apostolic movements, holiness was considered almost impossible for anyone who was not a monk or a cleric, because persons not so designated were involved in war, sex, and money handling, the last being the worst. [63]

It is sad that the Christian people who were involved in the establishment of the new spirituality and the bishops and popes who supported them were not able to prevail. If they had prevailed the move toward equal participation of all the church's members in the church's mission might not have been delayed so long. Perhaps, although there were many other factors involved, the bad feelings among Christians of the sixteenth century and up to our own day might also have been avoided.

What we can draw from the history of the Middle Ages, in the area reviewed in the previous section, is the challenge to develop an integrating spirituality for all the baptized, a task that still remains because such a spirituality was not pushed beyond its infancy in the Middle Ages. As we have seen, the quest was abandoned in the centuries after the Reformation. Vatican II, on the other hand, teaches unequivocally that the call to holiness is universal. [64]

---

63. Vauchez, *Les laïcs au Moyen Age*, 79–80.
64. *Lumen gentium* devotes chap. 5 to this issue. "The Final Report" of the 1985 World Synod of Bishops renews the theme of "the vocation of all the faithful to holiness" (art. A4).

If a trinitarian spirituality were to pervade the thought and behavior of all the baptized, including the ordained, integrating all of every Christian's life, both the religious and the secular aspects, the Christian church would undoubtedly take on a more evangelical look and become more of a leaven in the mass of the broader society.

Chapter Three

THE MINISTRY OF THE ORDAINED AMONG THE CHRISTIAN PEOPLE

TAKING NOTICE OF A SHIFT OF PERSPECTIVE RELATIVE TO the meaning of the ordained priesthood, M. Edmund Hussey claims that "the post–Vatican II church no longer tends to see the bishop in terms of the priest, but tends rather to see the priest in terms of the bishop. In the Tridentine church the bishop was a 'priest plus.' In the post–Vatican II church, the priest is a 'bishop minus.' " [1]

More evaluative is the assessment of Christian Duquoc. He claims that the doctrine of the Second Vatican Council on the role of the priesthood fails. The Council instructs that the function of the ordained is to make Christian freedom accessible to the faithful who depend upon the pastoral activity of the priest acting as Christ's instrument. But the teaching fails because its undergirding theology retains the classical assumption that reserves sacred power to those who are ordained, ignoring the rights of all the baptized to active participation in the mission of the church. [2]

The dialectical interpretations of Hussey and Duquoc are instructive. They provide reminders that the Second Vatican Council does not merely pick up where Trent left off, and that the meaning of ordained ministry is still developing. The contemporary situation that the Second Vatican Council addresses requires a fresh interpretation of the meaning of the ordained priesthood. As they engaged in the process of responding to that situation the various Council Fathers found themselves, often enough, re-

---

1. M. Edmund Hussey, "Needed: A Theology of Priesthood," *Origins* 17 (Feb. 4, 1988): 581.

2. Christian Duquoc, "La riforma dei chierici," in G. Alberigo and J.-P. Jossua, eds., *Il Vaticano II e la Chiesa* (Brescia: Paideia, 1985), 412–13. Duquoc refers to the *Decree on the Ministry and Life of Priests.*

flecting quite different theologies, which do not always appear side by side in the conciliar documents in orderly, and even less in integrated, relationship.

Nevertheless I am going to take an organic approach to the development of the ordained priesthood in the Roman church. It seems to me that both history and theology allow of, and, in fact, support, an organic interpretative approach. This is not to say that there are not dialectical moments within the development of the priesthood, including the present moment. But I hope to demonstrate that the dialectic serves the organic development. I also submit the theology of ordained ministry that follows for consideration by Catholicism's partners in ecumenical dialogue.

The Role of Leader,
Teacher, and Priest

The lists of ministries that appear in 1 Cor. 12:8-10, 28; Roman 12:6-8; and Eph. 4:11 demonstrate that the gifts distributed by the Holy Spirit among the faithful vary from local church to local church. We may presume that the reason for the variations has to do with the different needs of the several communities. What would serve the common good (1 Cor. 12:7) or build up the Body of Christ (Eph. 4:12) in one community may not be necessary or desirable in another. Nevertheless, each of the three New Testament letters cited seems to be concerned about an order in the life of the church.[3]

Leader.   Each list includes ministries of leadership. First Corinthians even ranks three ministries: first, apostles; second, prophets; third, teachers. The Letter to the Romans includes a ministry of presidency.[4] The entire section of Ephesians in which the cited passage appears is likely an instruction on official ministries of leadership within the community. Specifically named are apostles, prophets, evangelists, pastors, and teachers.[5]

3. It would be excessive to list all the contemporary studies of the ministry of leadership in the New Testament. However, a few are: Jean Delorme, ed., *Le ministère et les ministères selon le Nouveau Testament* (Paris: Seuil, 1974); Bernard Cooke, *Ministry to Word and Sacraments: History and Theology* (Philadelphia: Fortress Press, 1976); Karl Kertelge, ed., *Das kirchliche Amt im Neuen Testament* (Darmstadt: Wissenschaftliche Buchgesellschaft, 1977); and Thomas Franklin O'Meara, *Theology of Ministry* (New York: Paulist, 1983), chap. 4.

4. This is a contemporary translation which I suggest for προΐστημι. That the word refers to a role of leadership, contrary to the first meaning given in the Revised Standard Version, is argued convincingly by Bo Reicke in Gerhard Friedrich, ed., *Theological Dictionary of the New Testament* (Grand Rapids: Wm. B. Eerdmans, 1968), 7:701–02.

5. Helmut Merklein, *Das kirchliche Amt nach dem Epheserbrief* (Munich: Kösel, 1973).

In several instances the Acts of the Apostles acknowledges groups of church members who exercise collegial responsibility for the guidance and direction of the community.[6] Besides recognizing some ministries that arise spontaneously, such as Paul's apostleship, the leadership groups appoint people to various ministries and invest them by imposing hands. They also resolve doctrinal and other community disputes.

With the pastoral letters comes a shift from making passing reference to leaders to an emphasis upon them. Concern for the day-to-day functioning and order of the church is the focus here. Instructions set forth which types of persons are to be office-holders such as overseers, deacons, elders, and, perhaps, widows. Reference is made to an ordination of the community's leader.[7] First Timothy seems to assume that leadership is exercised by the council of elders, with one of the elders chosen to preside in the role of overseer on a rotating basis. Titus implies that a single elder exercises leadership in the community.[8]

The Pastoral Letters give evidence of the New Testament origins of ordained bishops and elders and, perhaps, deacons serving as pastoral leaders within the local Christian communities. The letters, however, are not very helpful in their indications of what functions belonged to those who bore the titles. Whether the pastoral letters are to be dated in such a way as to indicate Pauline authorship or are to be dated toward the end of the first century, they compare rather than contrast with the other texts cited insofar as they add another perspective on the ministry of leadership within the early Christian community; mostly, a perspective on the qualities desirable in those who assume leadership of the community. If, in fact, the pastoral letters are writings authored around or after the year 80, they also indicate that the church of that day was becoming more engaged with structures and offices than it had been earlier.

Teacher.   Prominent among the ministries of leadership included in the lists cited above are those word-oriented ministries such as apostle, prophet, teacher, evangelist. Proclaiming the good news and teaching the way of God are the work of Jesus and continue after him to be the work of the church. While all are called to witness, some are called to take up the specific task of handing on what has been received, and to do so faithfully and accurately. Matthew's Gospel, in fact, places teaching at the center of

---

6. See Acts 1: 15-26; 6: 2-6; 8: 14-17; 11: 1-3, 18, 27-30; 13: 1-3; 14: 23; 15: 1-31; 20: 17-18, 28.
7. 1 Tim. 4: 14; 2 Tim. 1: 6.
8. See Hermann Von Lips, *Glaube-Gemeinde-Amt: Zum Verständnis der Ordination in den Pastoralbriefen* (Göttingen: Vandenhoeck & Ruprecht, 1979).

the church's task.[9] It is the chief ministry. As Jesus was the teacher, so in his discourse to the Twelve he sends them to teach in his name: "Go to the lost sheep of the house of Israel. And preach as you go. . . . A disciple is not above his teacher, nor a servant above his master; it is enough for the disciple to be like his teacher, and the servant like his master."[10]

At the same time Matthew warns those who exercise the role of teaching within the community not to consider themselves superior to their fellow Christians whom they teach. No one in the community is to be called rabbi or father or master.[11] All teaching is simply a ministry whose principal agent is Christ. It seems that "the fascination with developing structures and offices in the late first century had its dangers, and Matthew was alert to them."[12]

The Johannine community was even more concerned not to exaggerate the role of those officially designated to lead by teaching and pastoral care. The Spirit inspires broadly within the Christian community. The task is to discern the Spirit, not simply to look to the officially designated leaders.[13] However, even the Johannine community found it necessary to make room for designated leaders in order to counter false doctrines more effectively. "Thus, from 3 Jn and from Jn 21 (Peter as the shepherd) we may suspect that greater supervisory power of the presbyter-bishop type, although foreign to the theological genius of the Johannine community, was introduced over opposition into segments of the community in order to resist false teaching."[14]

This concern about sound doctrine became increasingly a matter to be dealt with by the leaders of the Christian communities. The Pastoral Letters come back to this theme again and again. Overseers, deacons and elders, as good ministers of Christ Jesus, are to preach and teach faithfully what they have received. They are to guard the truth diligently, always on the watch for those who deceive by teaching false doctrine.[15] Since we are dealing in these letters, as in the Johannine corpus, with the first hints of gnostic theories, it is not surprising that, as the church moves on through the second

9. See Wolfgang Trilling, "Amt und Amtsverständnis bei Matthäus," in *Mélanges bibliques en hommage au R. P. Béda Rigaux* (Gembloux: Duculot, 1970), 29–44.

10. Matt. 10:6-7, 24-25.

11. Matt. 23:8-12.

12. Raymond E. Brown, "Episkope and Episkopos: The New Testament Evidence," *Theological Studies* 41 (1980): 337.

13. Ibid., 337–38. See 1 John 4:1-6.

14. Ibid. See also Raymond E. Brown, *The Community of the Beloved Disciple* (New York: Paulist, 1979).

15. 1 Tim. 1:3-7, 4:1-16; 5:17; 6:2-3, 20; 2 Tim. 1:8-15, 2:1-2, 14-18; 4:1-5; Titus 1:9; 2:1, 7, 15.

century, when Gnosticism became a fully developed system of thought, concern about false doctrine and sound teaching increases so that by the latter part of the second century some way to ensure fidelity to the truth of the gospel has to be found, and is found through doctrinal and apostolic succession. [16]

Priest.   As the discussion moves from the ministry of community leader and official teacher to that of priesthood, it is necessary to distinguish between two Greek words, *presbuteros*, elder, and *hiereus*, priest in the sense of one whose role is to perform cultic activity. Both Greek words are translated in English as *priest. Presbuteros* is to be included in the cluster of words discussed in the preceding paragraphs that indicate ministries of direction, guidance, and care of the Christian community. *Hiereus* and its compound *arch-iereus* (high priest) do not appear in any of the lists. In the New Testament those words first appear as titles for officeholders within Jewish society. They are also used of Christ. The Letter to the Hebrews argues that with the coming of Christ there is now only one true priest, Jesus, the high priest who intercedes perfectly with God his Father for the whole human race. Because of the once-for-all nature of Jesus' priestly sacrifice the implication is that there is no need for additional priests who continue to offer sacrifice in the style of the Hebrew dispensation.

The New Testament also understands all those who have been baptized into a share in Christ's gifts and functions to exercise a priesthood. Sometimes this is understood individually, as when Christians at Rome are encouraged "to present your bodies as a living sacrifice, holy and acceptable to God, which is your spiritual worship" (Rom. 12:1). Sometimes the priesthood is understood as a Christian quality to be exercised both personally (1 Pet. 2:5) and corporately (1 Pet. 2:9, after Exod. 19:6). [17] The priesthood exercised by all the faithful, what Vatican II has named the common priesthood, is a participation in the one high-priesthood of Christ.

The New Testament names no Christian a priest in the sense of a person

16. See Walter J. Burghardt, "Apostolic Succession: Notes on the Early Patristic Era," in *Lutherans and Catholics in Dialogue*, vol. 4, *Eucharist and Ministry* (Minneapolis: Augsburg, 1979), 173–77. Tertullian and Irenaeus are the chief proponents of the position on succession. However, it is interesting to note that no such concern is prominent in earlier second-century works that are extant. James F. McCue claims that the reason lies in the purpose of the works. The earlier works are more concerned with Greek and Jewish questions, whereas the latter contend with the Gnostics. See McCue, "Apostles and Apostolic Succession in the Patristic Era," in *Eucharist and Ministry*, esp. 153.

17. On the Pauline use of priesthood, see Leopold Sabourin, *Priesthood: A Comparative Study* (Leiden: E. J. Brill, 1973), 229. On the interpretation of 1 Peter, see Daniel C. Arichea and Eugene A. Nida, *A Translator's Handbook on the First Letter of Peter* (New York: United Bible Societies, 1980).

deputed to perform or preside over specific cultic activity on behalf of the community. Christ is the priest who has definitively offered the sacrifice, which is himself, upon the altar of the cross. [18] Still, Paul clearly understands his ministry of the gospel to be priestly in character (Rom. 15:16). Moreover, the early Christian community eventually concludes that the final, eschatological meal of Jesus' earthly life, described in the Synoptics, in which the body and blood of Christ are to be eaten in his memory, requires a priestly presider because its character is sacrificial in the giving over of the body and the pouring out of the blood to establish the covenant. [19]

It is not necessary to maintain that the earliest disciples of Jesus understood the sacrificial, and therefore priestly, character of the eucharistic meal. It may be, as Raymond Brown suggests, that determination of the sacrificial character of the Eucharist and the priestly character of the presider at Eucharist entered into the Christian community only after the destruction of the temple in Jerusalem by the armies of Titus in 70 C.E. As long as the temple and its priesthood continued to function the Christian people may not have questioned their validity. Only when they ceased to exist did Christians have to ask more profound questions about the relation of Jesus' death on the cross to the temple sacrifice and priesthood. [20] In any case, at least in Rome, the sacrificial character of the Eucharist has clearly emerged by the time of Clement of Rome's letter to the Corinthians late in the first century. [21] It is not difficult to imagine how natural it would be for one of those chosen to exercise direction and guidance for the community in other matters to be the one to preside at the community's gathering for the eschatological meal as well. Indeed, this seems actually to have been the dynamic. [22]

What this brief survey of data from the first generations of Christianity

---

18. Nevertheless, Raymond E. Brown cautions against any tendencies to exaggerate the influence of the Letter to the Hebrews on Christian thinking in the New Testament period. See his *Priest and Bishop: Biblical Reflections* (Paramus, N.J.: Paulist, 1970), 14.

19. Evaluation of the development varies, of course, among Christians. For an evaluation different from mine, see, e.g., Dunn's comments in James D. G. Dunn and James P. Mackey, *New Testament Theology in Dialogue: Christology and Ministry* (Philadelphia: Westminster, 1987), 129–36.

20. Brown, *Priest and Bishop*, 17–18. Brown notes other historical factors coalescing around the year 70 which could open the way to attribution of a priestly character to the presider at Eucharist: numerical dominance in the Christian church of Gentiles who would not feel any responsibility to the Jewish institution of priesthood, movement of the church's center away from Jerusalem, and excommunication of Christians from the Jewish synagogue.

21. See the comments of Annie Jaubert on the eucharistic and sacrificial nature of "the gifts" (τὰ δῶρα) in *Clément de Rome, Epitre aux Corinthiens* (44), *Sources chrétiennes* (Paris: Cerf, 1971), 173 n. 4. Clement's letter sets up persons and institutions of the Hebrew dispensation as types of the new Christian community (see chaps. 2–4) and specifically ascribes continuity from the priestly ministry of the Hebrew dispensation to that of the Christian (chaps. 40–44).

22. See Hervé-Marie Legrand, "The Presidency of the Eucharist According to the Ancient Tradition," *Worship* 53 (1979): 413–38.

suggests is that the foundations are in place before the end of the first century, indeed within the New Testament itself, for the emergence of a specifically so-called ordained ministry. The church order we now have of bishop, priest, and deacon did not spring up overnight, but arose consistently out of the beginnings of Christianity, and, I will argue, in a way that expresses in symbol one dimension of God's continuing self-communication through the missions of Word and Spirit, namely, the dimension of leadership. By the end of the third century, ordained ministry understood as a priesthood is in place, primarily in the bishop of each local church who exercises a ministry of leadership of the community not only in pastoral governance, but also as chief liturgist and chief teacher. Presbyters gradually assume roles of eucharistic leadership as the bishop's surrogates in the rural areas of the local church too distant to be serviced from the urban centers. Deacons seem to function primarily as direct assistants of the bishop in some administrative and pastoral matters.

The ordained priesthood arrives at the end of the first stage of its development in the fourth century in the lyrical prose of Gregory Nazianzen's theology in his Second Oration (362 C.E.) and in John Chrysostom's elaboration of Gregory's work in his *Concerning the Priesthood* (after 373 C.E.). These theologies of the bishop (and by extension of the presbyter), especially Chrysostom's, are unfortunately much tainted by the clergy/laity division that is moving firmly into place at the same time as Nazianzen and Chrysostom are assuming office. Their treatises need to be read with a critical eye on that account, for their exalted view of the office is, to some degree, a function of the belittlement of the baptized. Both authors stand in awe of the priestly ordination they had hoped to avoid but now find themselves forced to accept. To their minds the office of priesthood is the outstanding way to live the Christian life, far superior to the monastic life for which they both longed, and on a different plane altogether from the search for Christian fidelity on the part of those who are neither ordained nor monks. Chrysostom asserts that no woman could possibly be worthy of the ordained ministry, nor most men either.[23]

This flaw having been noted, Nazianzen and Chrysostom both exhibit a genuine sense that ordination is a public trust, a ministry of leadership to be executed conscientiously on behalf of the Christian people. This ministry entails the *art of arts*, which is to understand and guide God's complex creatures, human beings, as if the bishop were a "physician of souls."[24] Such is the pastoral care that the bishop is called upon to exercise. Moreover, the

---

23. John Chrysostom, *Six Books on the Priesthood* (Crestwood, N.Y.: St. Vladimir's Seminary, 1984), II, 2 (p. 54).

24. Gregory Nazianzen, *Oration II*, in *Nicene and Post-Nicene Fathers of the Christian Church*, Second Series (Grand Rapids: Wm. B. Eerdmans), 7:16 (pp. 208–9).

bishop has to be available when and as people need his services, not according to his own choices of time.[25]

Guiding the Christian congregation through his preaching and teaching is also a major responsibility of the bishop. Chrysostom devotes the entire second chapter of his treatise to preaching. He notes the need for the bishop to preach the word of God and not himself; to issue a challenge when that is called for, but always to preach with charity.

Finally, both Chrysostom and Nazianzen are eloquent about their reverence for the bishop's role as president of the liturgical assembly. Nazianzen affirms that the priest has the awesome position of being "entrusted with . . . the office of mediator . . . between God and man."[26] For Chrysostom the office of priesthood is one of "excellence." It ranks among the "heavenly ordinances" for, because of the priest's invocation of the Holy Spirit in the epiklesis of the eucharistic prayer, those at worship are lifted to the heavenly realm.[27] Priests also perform the more-than-angelic functions of forgiving sins, healing the sick, and turning away the wrath of rulers and kings.

The Nature of the Priesthood according to Classical Theology

A second stage in the theology of ordained ministry introduces a more theoretical reflection upon the nature of priesthood. The intrinsic meaning of the ordained priesthood is to be found, I suggest, in the doctrine and theology of *character*. At the same time, the priesthood of the baptized, with which ordained priesthood is so closely linked in Vatican II's *Lumen gentium*, is also distinguished by its character. Thus, a study of the emergence of the theology of character enlightens us not only about the meaning of the priesthood of the ordained but also about the priesthood shared by all the baptized (and confirmed) and the close linkage of the two.

The theology of character develops in a genetic-dialectical process from its original formulation by St. Augustine through its metaphysical exposition in the thirteenth century to a contemporary theological understanding of its meaning. In the first moment the dialectic is between the catholic faith and the insistence of the Donatists and others that apostates who re-

---

25. Peter Brown describes the pressures of being a bishop in the Roman Empire of late antiquity. Augustine was called upon as bishop to sit as judge even over civil disputes, a reminder that public ministry carried with it civic as well as strictly religious responsibilities. See *Augustine of Hippo* (Berkeley: Univ. of California Press, 1967), 194ff.

26. Gregory Nazianzen, *Oration II*, 91 (p. 223).

27. John Chrysostom, *Six Books on the Priesthood*, III, 4 (pp. 70–71).

pented and heretics who came over to catholic faith be rebaptized or reordained. In a second moment, the period of the eleventh through the thirteenth centuries, the issue is first raised as the dialectic between the civil and the ecclesiastical authorities, and the question is of the relation between the realms of the sacred and the profane. Later in the same period Augustine's meaning of sacrament is conflated with his meaning of character to express the effect of baptism and ordination upon the recipient. In the sixteenth century, the Roman church's doctrine of ordained priesthood is perceived to be contrary to the reformers' doctrine of the priesthood of all believers. [28] In the contemporary situation the dialectic is between a secularism that would deny any validity to the religious dimension of human being and a critical insertion of human subjectivity into the realm of mystery.

Before beginning a review of the history of the classical theology of the nature of ministerial priesthood, it is important to state a caution. As with Nazianzen and Chrysostom, there is a major flaw in the theology that develops, even into the twentieth century; the flaw is present from the beginning and increases with the development of the classical theology of priesthood. That flaw is the diminishment of those who are not ordained. We have already uncovered the origins of this flaw and discussed how it distorts the gospel. Since the flaw was definitively in place before the start of the development of the theology of character, it is not surprising to discover its pervasive influence.

The previous chapter has structured the retrieval of the preeminence of baptism as the cause of the fundamental dignity and mission of every Christian. In the present section I set out to demonstrate that the theology of character as it pertains to the ordained priesthood can be, indeed ought to be, supported as long as it is separated from an exaggerated distinction between the ordained and the baptized. In addition to that separation, the theology of character needs to be transposed from its classical to a historically minded, intentional context. Once both moves have been made, appropriating sacramental character serves an understanding and evaluation of the priesthood common to all the baptized and the priesthood of the ordained, and the relationship between the two that is called for in *Lumen gentium*.[29] I trust that such appropriation also invites a reappraisal of ordained priesthood by Christians otherwise disposed to reject it.

---

28. Recent dialogues between Lutherans and Roman Catholics reveal that the two traditions are not, in fact, so far apart as it may formerly have seemed regarding the effect of ordination upon the recipient. See nos. 16–18 of "Eucharist and Ministry: A Lutheran–Roman Catholic Statement," in *Eucharist and Ministry*, 12–13. See also 215.

29. See *Lumen gentium*, art. 10.

Augustine's concern was in reaction to those of his fellow Christians who demanded rebaptism or reordination of those members of the church who repented and sought to return to communion after capitulating in the face of persecution or who had originally been baptized into heretical Christian communities. Augustine's effort was to solidify the tradition that held that the sacraments of baptism and order could be conferred only once because they were grounded in profession of a trinitarian faith. Surely penitence is required of the repentant Christian, for delinquency is evil, but a person's evil does not destroy the original insertion into the sphere of God's life, for God's action and its public celebration are irrevocable.

To express the effect of baptism and order upon those who receive them, the term *sphragis*, seal, was adopted from texts such as Eph. 1:13 and 2 Cor. 1:21-22: "But it is God who establishes us with you in Christ, and who has commissioned us; he has put his seal upon us and given us his Spirit in our hearts as a guarantee." While the Greek fathers thought of the Holy Spirit as the seal, the Western tradition develops in the line of an effect in the person to whom the Spirit is given.[30] *Sphragis* was translated into the Latin term *signaculum*, and this, in part, created the confusion about whether the sacraments could be conferred twice because when a repentant delinquent who had fallen away from communion with the church was restored, the ceremony of restoration included the gesture of imposition of hands and was named *signaculum*.

To distinguish the original conferral of the sacrament from the later rite of restoration to communion, Augustine sought a fresh word. He found his word in a term that had a similar meaning to *sphragis*, namely, *character*, character. The word refers to a distinctive mark, impression, or engraving. In Augustine's culture of late antiquity *character* denotes the permanent, that is, indelible, brand mark of a soldier. The soldier is marked until death by the title of the emperor under whom he serves; there is no escaping his allegiance.[31] Augustine found this word to be just what he was looking for to express the durable reality that resulted from the sacraments of baptism and order. By baptism the Christian is marked forever by the title of Christ so that she or he belongs to Christ from the moment of baptism onward. Infidelity does not destroy the fact that Christ has title to the person, although

---

30. Bernard Leeming, in a concise statement of the position of classical theology, mentions this difference between East and West in *Principles of Sacramental Theology* (Westminster, Md.: Newman, 1955), 227–28. But there is evidence that Eastern theologians also understood ordination to bring about a change in the ordinand. Gregory of Nyssa writes in his sermon *On the Baptism of Christ* that the priest is "transformed in respect of his invisible soul." See *Nicene and Post-Nicene Fathers*, Second Series (Grand Rapids: Wm. B. Eerdmans, 1954), 5:519.

31. J. Galot, *La Nature du Caractère Sacramentel: Étude de Théologie Médiévale* (Brussels: Desclée, 1956), 36–41.

it does destroy one's livelihood within the corps, because the person has chosen to alienate himself or herself from the unity of the church. To overcome the alienation reconciliation is necessary.

Augustine thus clarifies a distinction that had preceded him in the tradition but remained muddled until he used the word *character* to name the reality. Once the reality is clearly named, Augustine is able to add a further distinction and relate the character of the sacrament and the grace of the sacrament. Baptism and ordination confer something upon the person that is never thereafter lost: (*a*) a public character as a Christian or as an ordained minister, and (*b*) an interior consecration of the person to be a Christian or an ordained minister. The former is the character; the latter is the special grace of the two sacraments. [32]

After Augustine it is not until the lay investiture controversies of the eleventh century that a new element achieves full actuality in the theology of priesthood, particularly with the reforming efforts of Pope Gregory VII Hildebrand (pope from 1073–1085). In that century and throughout the twelfth century, the long-smoldering conflict between the spiritual power (*sacerdotium*) and the temporal power (*imperium*) reaches a theoretical and practical resolution. Gregory won his dispute with the emperor Henry IV when the latter, after having been excommunicated by Gregory because he would not yield on the matter of appointing bishops, offered his submission to the Pope at Canossa in 1077. By this act medieval society recognized spiritual power to be superior to temporal power. Practically speaking, however, it was from this time forward that each power was given its own domain. Instead of the two continuing intermingled, they became separated. This opened the door for ecclesiastical and civil society to embark upon a great burst of development, each within its own domain. [33]

Since the clergy and monks had already, since the fourth century, been distinguished as living the more perfect Christian life, they were the obvious candidates for the exercise of spiritual power. However, there was a differentiation established among those who had chosen the sacred as distinct from the profane life, so that the clergy were considered superior in *power* to the monks. This was at least partially due to the enthusiastic reception of the writings of Pseudo-Dionysius (fifth or sixth century), who taught that the highest ranks of Christians are the three orders of hierarch (bishop), presbyter, and other ministers. Below them rank the monks, and

---

32. Nicholas M. Haring demonstrates Augustine's use of the terms *character* and *sacrament* in this way. See his "St. Augustine's Use of the Word *Character*," *Mediaeval Studies* 14 (1952): 79–97.

33. Augustin Fliche, *La Réforme grégorienne*, vol. 2, *Grégoire VII* (Louvain: Spicilegium Sacrum Lovaniense, 1925), 317ff. See also Peter Brown, "Society and the Supernatural: A Medieval Change," *Daedalus* 104 (1975): 134.

below them the "sacred people," the baptized, and finally catechumens.[34] Whatever judgment is finally to be made about the extent of the influence of Pseudo-Dionysius, the fact is that during the twelfth century increasing numbers of monks were being ordained priests, and their principal work was the celebration of the Eucharist, that being the work in which the spiritual power was most effectively exercised.[35]

So it happened that during the very same period that the nonordained, nonmonastic Christian people were experiencing a growth of Christian self-consciousness, as was noted in the previous chapter, the clergy too, in a kind of paradoxical parallel development, were growing in numbers and in the differentiation of functions. Once one entered the clerical ranks by means of tonsure, there was a whole range of roles to be filled and titles to assume. Liturgies multiplied and also became more elaborate in the great cathedrals being constructed at the time. Ecclesiastical bureaus multiplied as well. Clerical rank and privilege was in full bloom.[36]

These enhancements of the clergy are an outgrowth of the distinctions introduced in the eleventh century between the spiritual and the temporal powers. The ordained ministers of the Christian people, who are deemed to be the carriers of spiritual power, are endowed with a quasi-divine prestige, for they represent God on earth. Vestments and ceremonies set the clergy and their sacred power apart from the rest of the world with its merely profane power. Processions are unusually important occasions because they allow medieval society to arrange everyone in proper rank. In the processions each is much concerned to be in the right place. "Each alleges a criterion of superiority to justify his pretension."[37]

The clear delineation of the realm of supernatural reality as distinct from the realm of nature included a perception that each realm is simply factual. Examination of one's personal disposition is obviously not necessary to determine acceptability for the natural realm; one is born into it. Similarly, in a Christendom in which the supernatural realm was also taken as an unquestioned fact, into which all but the ignorant or the recalcitrant entered through baptism, entrance into the clerical order of supernatural power also came to be a simple matter of fact. One's inner disposition was not a matter

34. Pseudo-Dionysius, *The Ecclesiastical Hierarchy*, in *Pseudo-Dionysius: The Complete Works* (New York: Paulist: 1987), V, 5–6 (pp. 236–38), VI, 1–3 (pp. 243–45).

35. Marie-Dominique Chenu, *Nature, Man, and Society in the Twelfth Century* (Chicago: University of Chicago Press, 1968), 210. See also Jean Leclercq, "Influence and Noninfluence of Dionysius in the Western Middle Ages," in *Pseudo-Dionysius: The Complete Works*, 27–29.

36. Gabriel Le Bras, *Institutions ecclésiastiques de la Chrétienté médiévale*, vol. 12 of *Histoire de L'Eglise*, ed. Augustin Fliche and Victor Martin (Paris: Bloud & Gay, 1959), 151ff.

37. Ibid., 266.

of much concern, only that a person make the moves that were most reasonable within that particular worldview.

However, as the clergy and clerical roles multiplied in the twelfth century an alarm was sounded here and there by some who perceived the abuses of spiritual power. Gregory's reform had already set in motion a massive effort to purge the clergy of their worldly ways, and parallel lay movements, such as those of the Patarines mentioned in the last chapter, also promoted a clergy more dedicated to holiness. Efforts like these continued and gathered greater momentum in the twelfth and thirteenth centuries. Peter Damian, decrying the wealth of the clergy, claimed that the only persons fit for the office of preaching are those who lack the support of earthly riches and live the common life, the "truly apostolic life."[38] Lay preaching was one result of this sort of mentality. Another was the move on the part of reform-minded clergy to join with the laity in forming the pious societies and confraternities that began in earnest in the latter half of the twelfth century. Dominic and Francis became the initiators of inspired movements which became new orders in the church.

This sort of development occurred in reaction to tenacious abuses which attached themselves to the relationship between holiness and spiritual power. This troublesome relationship was a legacy of the overdrawn separation between the permanent and indelible character of the sacrament of order and the factor in baptism and order of personal disposition. The most influential thinker to attempt to wend an interpretative way through the new distinction between nature and supernature and between the abuses of the clerical state and the lay and clerical reform movements was Thomas Aquinas. To do the job he enlisted the help of Aristotle, whose writings had been introduced slowly into the Latin West since Boethius (d. 524) and whose metaphysical works finally arrived in the thirteenth century, just in time for Thomas to make use of them. I quote Marie-Dominique Chenu on Aquinas's achievement:

> When St. Thomas Aquinas defined the transcendence of grace by invoking the Aristotelian idea of nature, he was not merely making a reasoned option in favor of the Philosopher. Rather he was giving supreme expression to that Christianity in which a return to the Gospel had secured for the believer a presence in the world, for the theologian a mature awareness of nature, and for the apostle an effective appreciation of man.[39]

38. Chenu, *Nature, Man, and Society*, 215.
39. Ibid., 238.

While Aquinas's use of Aristotle demonstrates that he was an innovator, he was also a traditionalist, accepting the acknowledged authorities of his day. He relies on the theology of the heavenly and the ecclesiastical hierarchies of Dionysius, whom he, along with his contemporaries, considered to be Dionysius the Areopagite of Acts 17:34 and first bishop of Paris.[40] According to Dionysius and Aquinas, the ecclesiastical hierarchy is patterned after the heavenly, a progressively ranked participation on earth of the order of heavenly glory. As the heavenly hierarchy is sacred, so the ecclesiastical. The further along one is in the sacred ranks, the more elevated vis-à-vis those of the lesser ranks. In the ecclesiastical hierarchy, bishops have the highest rank, followed by priests, deacons, and other ministers. In general the clergy belong to a higher state of life than do the laity.[41] The role of the clergy is to minister in a threefold way, just as Dionysius teaches, namely, by purifying of their unworthiness those initiated into the household of faith, illuminating them with sacred doctrine, and perfecting them in the divine life.

The Dionysian hierarchy worked well for Aquinas, whose cultural situation included a system of progressive movement through the ranks of the clergy from exorcist, lector, porter, and acolyte, to subdeacon and deacon, and finally to priest and bishop. Nevertheless, while it was an easy matter to accept these ranks as hierarchical in general according to a Dionysian understanding, it was not so easy to fit them exactly into the hierarchy of ministries of purification, illumination, and perfection.[42] So Aquinas takes from Dionysius the general idea of sacred order.

Within the sacred order of the church are the sacraments which are public acts that bring people into and sustain them in the sacred order. Ultimately the public order of the church is related to the hidden order of the life of God, which is greater than the human mind or heart. But the sacraments are acts accessible to human beings, and, for Aquinas, they relate people especially to the hidden God by way of worship.[43] All the ways in which worship of God can be initiated, sustained, restored, extended, and perfected may be expected to have a sacramental expression.

40. For the broader social meaning of ministry as conceived by Aquinas within his cultural context, see O'Meara, *Theology of Ministry*, 109–14.

41. *Summa theologiae* (hereafter, S.T.), Suppl., q. 40, a. 2, ad 3. While the Supplement to the *Summa* is not part of the *Summa* itself, but was added by Aquinas's disciples after his death, it is nevertheless composed of Aquinas's own words. They were gathered from his *Commentary* on the *Sentences* of Peter Lombard.

42. In S.T. III, q. 64, a. 1, ad 1, Aquinas discusses how both deacons and priests are involved in the ministry of purification, although for Dionysius priests exercise the ministry of illumination, while the lower ranks of ministry are active for purification.

43. S.T. III, q. 60, a. 1, Response.

Carrying forward the tradition Augustine inaugurated, and that the highly influential Peter Lombard had incorporated and systematized in his *Sentences* (1155), Aquinas teaches that three sacraments confer a permanent character upon their recipients: baptism, confirmation, and order. But Aquinas probes further to understand just what this reality might be. His conclusion is that a character is "a sort of sign with which the soul is impressed in order to be able to make one's own or hand on to others those things which are part of divine worship."[44] What is Aquinas getting at here? Three questions arise directly from the definition. What does it mean that something is impressed upon the soul? Why is the impression permanent? What is the reason that character's reference is to worship?

Let it be noted again that Aquinas arrives at his theological understanding by establishing a dialogue between the religious tradition and the metaphysics of Aristotle. He finds the latter to be helpful for understanding the basic structures of reality insofar as the human subject can investigate them by its natural, unenhanced abilities. The religious tradition, on the other hand, brings one into contact with the basic structures of reality by means of the human mind enlightened by divine truth communicated through the gift of revelation.[45] By reasoning about the relationship of the two, the theologian has the possibility both to gain "speculative" knowledge about the universe of uncreated and created reality and "practical" knowledge about how to recover from sin and achieve the beatific vision of God.

Reflecting upon the categories of Aristotle, Aquinas concludes that the sacramental character resides in the soul as a supernatural power (*potentia*), that is, as an ordering reality by which the soul is enabled to do what it could not do without that inherent power. What God does is confer the capacity to give proper worship to God. The whole purpose of the character, then, is to orient a person to action in the public, ecclesial setting, where worship is offered. Although humanity can never be fulfilled unless and until it relates to God in complete submission, the possibility to relate properly to God requires God's intervention. This intervention is most graciously offered by God in the conferral of the character. So character is a sacred, as distinct from a simply natural, capacity which by God's grace is impressed, that is, made to reside inherently in the rational, as distinct from the sensitive or physical, soul of a person.

---

44. S. T., III, q. 63, a. 4, Response: "character est quoddam signaculum quo anima insignitur ad suscipiendum vel aliis tradendum ea quae sunt divini cultus." See Peter Lombard on order and character in *Sententiae in IV Libris Distinctae* (Grottaferrata: Collegii S. Bonaventura Ad Claras Aquas, 1981), Lib. IV, Dist. XXIV, cap. 13, 1, 2.

45. See Marie-Dominique Chenu, *La théologie comme science au XIIIe siècle* (Paris: Vrin, 1957), chap. 5.

Aquinas is even more specific about how the human soul so gifted by God assumes a sacramental character. He discerns the reality of character in the faith of a person.[46] This is so because worship is a matter of mind. Surely, it is also a matter of the heart (of love) and of the senses (since it is a public human reality), but neither love nor the senses enter into worship unless they are directed to it by the mind that relates to God by imaging, affirming, and, to some extent, understanding. The power that is character is thus a cognitive power of the soul.

Aquinas's inquiry into the permanence of the sacramental character leads to two other elements of his theology, both intimately connected, namely, that character is a matter of participation in the priesthood of Christ and that it is a capacity that is not active for itself but only as an instrument of the priesthood of Christ. Its connection with priesthood is the reason that Aquinas defines character as a power that enables worship. Since the coming of Christ, perfect worship can be offered to God because Christ has complete and unhindered access to God, both because he is one of the divine persons himself and also because in his humanity he is completely united with God through grace and now in glory.[47] Whereas others before Christ exercised roles of leadership of their fellow human beings as they were given the particular graces of legislator, priest, and king, Christ relates to all humanity in the perfection of grace so that these functions come together in him as the source of all grace for all people.[48] These functions, and any others Christ might exercise, are all gathered into his role as the priest who is "mediator between God and the people."

The priesthood of Christ is a permanent priesthood. Christ remains forever the priest who once and for all accomplished the reconciliation of humanity with God. Because of the permanent effectiveness of Christ's priesthood, whatever he draws under the influence of his mediation remains consecrated for as long as it exists.[49] So, a first reason for the permanence of the sacramental character is on the side of the one impressing the character. It is on the side of Christ whose priesthood is permanently effective.

46. S.T., III, q. 63, a. 4, ad 3.

47. S.T., III, q. 22, a. 1, ad 1, 3.

48. While the function of legislator differs from that of prophet/teacher, the other two, namely, priest and king, are in keeping with the longer tradition of the three functions of Christ, and make an easy transition to the category of the three functions that has been restored to contemporary currency by the Second Vatican Council. At this point Aquinas is not thinking of Christ's functions in terms of his being the anointed one, although such a connection is not unknown to him. See *Ad Romanos*, lect. 1 in *Super Epistolas S. Pauli Lectura*, vol. 1, ed. Raphael Cai, O.P., 8th ed. (Rome: Marietti, 1953), n. 20.

49. S.T., III, q. 63, a. 5, Response.

When he takes someone or something into participation in his priestly mediation, he never needs to repeat that act. It is done once for all.

There is also permanence on the side of the recipient of Christ's consecrating action. In this case it depends on the quality of the recipient to continue in existence. For, obviously, the effect can last only as long as the recipient. If an altar or a church is consecrated, it remains consecrated until it is destroyed. If a person is consecrated, the consecration is forever indestructible, for the human rational soul in its intellective power is consecrated. And the rational soul with its intellective capacity does not die.

In Aquinas's view, the sacramental character is chiefly a divine reality, conferred by God's choice upon a person. Its purpose is to be an instrument by which Christ's priesthood becomes effective throughout humanity and its world in order that the priestly worship of Christ may be offered to God through the participation of more and more people. Primarily the worship is the act of Christ. Persons cannot share in Christ's priesthood unless God communicates it to them. Those who serve this worship by being impressed with the character of baptism, confirmation, or order are instruments of Christ's priestly worship.[50] The new power of worship now granted to their intellect derives entirely from Christ's priesthood. It is not their own power. Christ is the "principal mover" and each subject of the spiritual power of character is named by Aquinas a minister.[51]

The particular instrumental quality of the sacramental character of order gives to ordained ministry, according to Aquinas, its nature as activity that represents Christ. But the baptized and confirmed also have their character, by which they are configured to Christ the priest. So it is not as if they "delegate the priests to pray in the place of the ecclesial community."[52] Rather Christ deputes the whole community to participate in his priestly worship. At worship, the ordained minister represents both Christ (*in persona Christi*) and the church (*in persona ecclesiae*), but he does not usurp the role of either.

The sacramental character of baptism is mainly an enabling one. The baptized person is equipped by this participation in Christ's priesthood to receive the other sacraments. Aquinas does not, however, think of this en-

50. S.T., III, q. 63, a. 5, ad 1 and 2.

51. In light of the contemporary Roman Catholic retrieval of the meaning of ministry, this is a momentous statement by Aquinas so I quote it here: "Habere enim sacramenti characterem competit ministris Dei: minister autem habet se per modum instrumenti . . ." (S.T., III, q. 63, a. 2, Response).

52. B.-D. Marliangeas, *Clés pour une théologie du ministère: In persona Christi, In persona Ecclesiae* (Paris: Beauchesnes, 1978), 138.

tirely as a passive instrumental power. For betaking oneself to receive the other sacraments is itself an active profession of faith.[53] In this sense one becomes an instrument of Christ's priestly power because through baptism a person is enabled to spend the rest of life offering fitting worship to God.[54]

But the sacramental character of confirmation specifically confers the capacity actively to assume responsibility for the evangelizing mission "as a sort of office" or duty.[55] Aquinas describes the mission conferred by the character of confirmation as an apostolic power to profess one's faith in public, and particularly to defend the faith against its enemies.[56]

Order is the third sacrament that confers a character. Here the character deputes the ordained person to hand on the sacraments to others.[57] For Aquinas this means that ordination relates especially to liturgy (*divina officia*), primarily Eucharist. But he also notes that the offices of bishop, presbyter, and deacon include pastoral care, especially on the part of bishops, and proclamation of the word, which ranges from reading the Gospel in church on the part of deacons to official teaching on the part of bishops.[58]

Nearly three centuries after Aquinas's detailed study of the nature of the character Augustine had named, the bitter controversy of the Reformation led to the Council of Trent's dogmatic affirmation that the sacraments of baptism, confirmation, and order confer a character within their recipients.[59] Trent thus implies an endorsement of the priestly character of all the baptized, although it was hardly interested in dealing with the implications of that sacramental character at the time. There is reason to conclude that the lack of a sufficiently developed theology of Christian ministry in the sixteenth century, in addition to concern about the "new faith" (*die neue Glaube*) of the reformers, kept the Council of Trent from answering the crit-

---

53. S.T., III, q. 63, a. 6, Response and III, q. 72, a. 5, ad 2.

54. This interpretation parallels the priestly statement of Rom. 1:1-2.

55. S.T. III, q. 72, a. 5.

56. From his discussion here any mistaken notion can be cleared away that Aquinas thinks of worship only in terms of liturgical activity or specifically of the seven sacraments. For the importance of the Christian departure from narrower meanings of worship to the Christian meaning of worship as broad activity exercised in conscious freedom in the Spirit of God, see O'Meara, *Theology of Ministry*, chap. 3.

57. S.T., III, q. 63, a. 6, Response.

58. S.T., III, q. 65, a. 3, Response; III, q. 67, a. 2, Response; II–II, q. 184, a. 5, 6, Response; III, q. 67, a. 1, ad 1; III, q. 82, a. 1, ad. 4. In this view, however, the sacramentality of order did not seem to pertain to the roles of teaching and pastoral leadership so directly as it did to Eucharist. See Kenan Osborne, *Priesthood: A History of the Ordained Ministry in the Roman Catholic Church* (New York: Paulist, 1988), 209–14.

59. Henricus Denzinger and Adolfus Schönmetzer, *Enchiridion Symbolorum* (Freiburg-im-Breisgau: Herder, 1963), nos. 1609, 1767, 1774. For a brief history of the formation of Trent's doctrine of order, see André Duval, "Les Données Dogmatiques sur le Sacerdoce," in *Des Sacrements au Concile de Trente* (Paris: Cerf, 1985; the essay was originally published in 1962), 327–61.

icism leveled against the Catholic tradition even as it might have accepted those aspects of the Protestant interpretation of Christian doctrine that have since been adopted by the Roman church. [60]

Recognition of the meaning of the sacramental characters as empowerments of the whole Christian people to assume responsibility for the mission of the church had to await developments that began to come to fruition in the Second Vatican Council. It was the judgment of the Council that the three sacraments of baptism, confirmation, and order are the basis of the Christian people's participation in the priesthood of Christ. As the meaning of baptism, confirmation, and order becomes more clearly focused in the present age of the church's long history, earlier aberrations of identity begin to be recognized for what they are and the agonizing process of reshaping the church's ministry is undertaken. Some turmoil in ministerial practice results. The same is true of ministerial theology. One approach to resolving the turmoil on both levels is to make the doctrine of character serviceable in the present late twentieth-century ecumenical context of the church by transposing the classical, metaphysically grounded theology of Aquinas into a theology that is historically minded.

A Contemporary Conception of Character

Aquinas's considerable effort to achieve a synthetic understanding of Christian faith within the intellectual context of a metaphysical worldview makes a valuable contribution to the history of the meaning of sacramental character. It was a great advance to relate the unrepeatability of baptism and order to the divine conferral of a spiritual capacity permanently resident in the soul by which the baptized, confirmed, and/or ordained person is deputed to offer fitting worship because of being inserted into the priesthood of Christ as an instrument of that priesthood.

However, the metaphysical worldview began to crumble within years of Aquinas's death. Bernard Lonergan believes that the reason for the decadence of scholasticism resides in its search for the necessary and immutable expression of necessary and immutable truths and its inability to recognize

---

60. This is the well-argued thesis of Severino Dianich, "La teologia del presbiterato al Concilio di Trento," *Scuola cattolica* 99 (1971): 331–58. The author's thesis is succinctly stated on pp. 339–40. See also José Ignacio Tellechea Idigoras, "La espiritualidad en la época moderna," in *Espiritualidad del Presbítero Diocesano Secular* (Madrid: Editorial de la Conferencia Episcopal Española, 1987), who argues that there was also a lack of moral energy to move away from the benefice system and the abuses it fostered (pp. 417–19).

that human understanding and affirmation are historical.[61] Because human reflection draws its life from developing understanding that continually refers to data, scholasticism was left behind in an unassimilated way by those movements more committed either to the uncovering of new data or to developing understanding: the Renaissance, the Reformation, the modern formation of the natural sciences and the humanities.

Thus, if the advance of Aquinas's theology is to be made serviceable it must be transposed into a context that combines the rigor of Thomistic metaphysics and its drive to get to the very core of the matter with the contribution of the intervening movements that have demonstrated the importance of starting from concrete human experience and never abandoning the historicity of human subjectivity. In particular, a post-Kantian theology of sacramental character is well served by attending to the data of human interiority. More specifically, the data that have accumulated from the Scriptures and the history of the Christian tradition, and which I have summarized in the previous pages of this chapter, exhibit their normativity for contemporary ordained ministry as they relate to the experience of themselves on the part of baptized and ordained Christians.

So how does the tradition combine with the interiority of the baptized and confirmed, as well as the ordained, to lead us to a contemporary understanding of sacramental character that both clarifies its meaning within the Catholic church and also contributes to the promotion of ecumenical dialogue regarding ministry?

Fundamentally, character means that conferral of the sacraments of baptism, confirmation, and order grounds a new orientation of the consciousness of their recipients. Orientation of consciousness is to values or to disvalues. A subject is aware of being attracted to some person or way of life in a manner that involves the whole self. In the case of the sacraments of baptism, confirmation, and order, the subject senses being drawn into a self-conscious dynamic where more is demanded than simply taking care of one's own needs and desires; the subject is drawn into a more expansive, self-giving stance. This may happen before reception of the sacrament itself, in which case directions that have been developing in a variety of vague ways become specified in catechumenate and seminary programs. If subjects become conscious of the dynamic at some time after receiving the sacrament, they feel impelled to service of God and of their fellow human beings with a sense of urgency unknown before, perhaps vaguely felt but

61. See Bernard Lonergan, "Philosophy and Theology," in *A Second Collection*, ed. William F. J. Ryan and Bernard J. Tyrrell (Philadelphia: Westminster, 1974), 193–97; and "The Subject," *idem*, 71–73, where Lonergan criticizes those theologians who "seem to have thought of truth as so objective as to get along without minds."

never acted upon. In either case, we find the root of the dynamism in the ineffable call of God to lose ourselves in an unlimited love.

The orientation that is character, however, while it is grounded in the mutual love of the persons of God and the human person, is more specific. Developing Christian doctrine and theology inform us that sacramental character constitutes the recipient's specific participation in the priesthood of Christ. Henceforth, the baptized or ordained Christian is an instrument on his or her own behalf and, even more, on behalf of the world, of the divine worship that has been effected once for all by Jesus in his paschal mystery. As a person responds to the character he or she becomes conscious of a longing or drive to be of service as Jesus was of service. Thus, a person seeks to be formed according to the mind and heart of Jesus. Increasingly, the orientations a person has to other values (or disvalues) become subservient to the predominant orientation to service—priestly service that seeks to reconcile the world to God through communion and conversation.

I repeat the argument a bit differently. Every orientation of the free and conscious human subject is a matter of heading toward particular values. The orientation begins with an apprehension of the value and is confirmed by the determined choice of the individual. In the case of sacramental character, the church hopes that, at least gradually, both the apprehension and the choice become acts of the human subject. The initiation of the new orientation, however, is wholly a creation of God. We are led to this conclusion because we know that no human being is capable of offering fitting worship of God with the adequacy of the priesthood of Christ unless God confers that capacity. At the same time, once God confers the capacity it is never thereafter lost, for the God who confers remains faithful. Should a baptized or ordained person choose not to follow through on the orientation at any time after its conferral, she or he nevertheless retains the possibility of a later return simply by reawakening consciousness of the orientation, which continues as a kind of undertow, and then proceeding on to repentance and renewal.

When we speak of sacramental character our attention is first drawn, as Augustine's was also, to the public nature of the new orientation conferred by the sacrament. The sacraments are celebrated by the ecclesial community; the recipients are publicly established in their sacramental role; ever after they can be identified as having been baptized or confirmed or ordained. The public celebration of the sacraments provides a clear point of reference for the recipient of the sacrament and for the other members of the church to identify who has and who has not been gifted with a sacramental character.

But the public celebration is an expression and a confirmation of the interior reality God bestows upon the baptized and ordained. Ecclesial celebration and endorsement is confirmation of a new, inner, existential orientation of the subject. To lose sight of the less visible, but ultimately more profound, orientation of the subject to priestly service in the spirit and name of Jesus, the one high priest, is to lose sight of the fuller meaning of character.

The differentiation between baptism and order lies in the direction of the priestly service. All the baptized are oriented to the service of reconciling all humanity to God in all the world's myriad details. The ordained are oriented to serve the Christian life and ministry of the baptized through their particular ministry of word, sacrament, and care within the community. This is not to say that the baptized have no orientation to service within the church and that the ordained have no orientation to service of the world, but leadership within the church is the main area of service of the ordained, while attentiveness to the world's conversion is the main area of service of the baptized.

In the case both of the baptized and of the ordained, ministry is in service of worship in the broadest meaning of that term. Whereas Aquinas tended to view the meaning of worship chiefly in terms of the Eucharist, contemporary theology has expanded the meaning of participation in the priesthood of Christ to include the three functions of Christ. The baptized, confirmed, and ordained all engage in the ministry of worship, but worship includes word, sacrament, and care. This expanded view brings with it a more varied and far-reaching meaning of Christian living. For one thing, the totality of the human person, material, cultural, and religious, becomes the object of ministry. For another, we are not so limited to liturgical functions and intrachurch matters as we were formerly; worship is a matter of all the dimensions of life. All this lends itself to a broader view of the functioning of the sacramental characters.

Thus, the subject who receives the sacrament of baptism is thenceforward interiorly ordered to stand with the Christian community as a full member. Her or his subjectivity has been lifted to the capacity of participation in the priestly worship of Christ. She or he is now empowered to share in Christ's priestly, prophetic, and pastoral role in company with the entire baptized community. While this capacity is most fully employed at Eucharist, the baptismal character empowers one to worship in all the aspects of one's life, and to draw others into the sphere of Christ's worthy worship of God as well. However, confirmation is recognized as the sacrament whose character confers the duty (the *officium*, as Aquinas names it) to give public witness to the faith.

Baptism and confirmation confer characters that order their recipients to live out their faith, to give public witness to their faith, to be instruments of the invitation of God to others to become people of faith as well. All this is deputation for ministry, as the Second Vatican Council's *Decree on the Apostolate of the Laity* teaches:

> In the church there is a diversity of ministry, but unity of mission. It was upon the apostles and their successors that Christ conferred the function of teaching, sanctifying and governing in his name and by his power. But the laity, as participants in the priestly, prophetic and governing function of Christ, fulfill their own part in the mission of the whole People of God in the church and in the world. [62]
>
> Inserted into the mystical Body of Christ through baptism and strengthened by the power of the Holy Spirit through confirmation, [the laity] are deputed to the apostolate by the Lord himself. [63]

By the sacrament of order subjects are consciously ordained to spend themselves in service of the worship of their sisters and brothers who are baptized and confirmed, so that the latter may be informed, strengthened, and guided to and in their respective ministries in service of church and world. Order deputes its recipients to priestly, prophetic, and pastoral roles in the person of Christ and in favor of the activity of the Spirit-filled faithful. Order is, thus, not for the recipient's enhancement but for the service of others.

Obviously, such an expanded notion of ministry, moving into so many areas besides Eucharist and sacraments, leaves much more room for human qualification of ministry. Earlier understandings of character that paid little heed to the receptivity of the subject of the character are in the process of being replaced by greater concern that Christian subjects be fully alert to the meaning for their daily living of the sacramental characters that have been conferred upon them.

The baptized, confirmed, and ordained are instruments of Christ and of his Spirit. The effectiveness of God can never be thwarted by human beings. At the same time, human instruments are free and intelligent centers of consciousness whose degree of self-conscious actuation of the sacramental characters is a significant component of effective ministry. [64] With so

62. *Decree on the Apostolate of the Laity,* art. 2.

63. Ibid., art. 3.

64. The lay reform movements of the Middle Ages, discussed in chap. 2, and the Council of Trent's first canon on the reformation of those who have the care of souls demonstrate that concern for behavior consistent with baptism and ordination was not lacking in the church, but it was not integrated into the theology of sacramental character in the way that the contemporary appreciation of human subjectivity allows.

many more areas qualifying for ministry because of the endorsement of the threefold function that pertains to each sacramental character, we are able to recognize far more room than formerly for human error and mistakes. There is also far more possibility for a richer mutual ministry within the church and for a new perspective on Christian influence in society, since the myriad charisms of the Christian people prove to be a wealth of riches.

Bernard Lonergan's historically minded philosophy of the human subject is helpful in this dimension of the meaning of sacramental character, calling as he does for the authentic human subject, and the authentic human community, to make a commitment to a self-correcting process of learning. This advice is as appropriate in the implementation of the sacramental characters as in any other area of life, perhaps more so since the recipients of the characters are responsive sincerely, generously, intelligently, reasonably, and responsibly to the ongoing missions of the Word and of the Spirit of God through them.

The Trinitarian Meaning of
Sacramental Character

In the previous chapter the meaning of Christian ministry was shown to be illumined by analogy with the meaning of the divine Trinity. Equality, diversity, and mutuality as constitutive of community are characteristics of the Trinity and the church and its ministry. Moreover, within the Christian community ministry is an extension of the missions of the Word and of the Spirit in the world.

Now we are in a position to extend the analogy further by means of sacramental character. Character clarifies how the divine Trinity and human ministers are related, and how the relationship is sustained by the Trinity. The triune God chooses to establish an analogous extension of its own divine missions in the instrumental activity of the baptized and confirmed Christians upon whom is conferred a character enabling them to bring Christ to the world through the power of the Holy Spirit. The baptized and confirmed act as instruments of Christ to mediate his saving reconciliation in the world.

Because of the ministerial responsibility conferred upon them, baptized and confirmed Christians are in need of ministry for themselves. They need Christ to be active on their behalf in the power of his Spirit. And because Christ continues to act incarnately through sacramentally empowered human instruments, there is the third sacrament to confer a character, order, which enables its recipients to minister within the church to the baptized and confirmed members of the faithful. No bishop, priest, or deacon could assume on his own, or even simply by the action of the church, the role of acting on behalf of the members of the Christian church as Christ's agent. The role must be conferred by the triune God. Moreover, the role that is conferred is not a passing function, but a spiritual capacity that endures because it does not depend for its existence upon the person upon whom it is conferred, but upon the triune God who confers it. The character of order confers a capacity for leadership of the Christian people so that the whole people, in turn, may exercise their ministry to the world.

Through the activities of those upon whom the sacramental characters are conferred the missions of the Word and Spirit continue in humanly accessible ways for the salvation and sanctification of humanity and its world. Those who are marked by the characters of baptism, confirmation, and order become symbols of God at work in the world in Christ Jesus and the Holy Spirit, in the Rahnerian sense discussed in the first two chapters. How do ordained bishops, priests, and deacons, and baptized and confirmed Christians relate to each other within the church according to their distinct sacramental characters? This is a question that can be approached by applying the triad of ministerial functions.[65]

Priestly Ministry.   The sacramental characters of baptism and confirmation confer upon their recipients a particular priestly capacity to touch the lives of the people with whom they associate to draw them into reception of the reconciliation with God that Christ has won for them. By the quality of their presence as persons caught up in love of God, the baptized and confirmed invite their spouses, children, and co-workers, as well as anyone else whose spirit they might touch, into a moment or even a way of life that glorifies, reverences, and praises God. In addition to the quality of their presence to the people around them, baptized and confirmed Christians may explicitly gather others into priestly self-sacrifice as they form and lead, or simply participate, in groups that gather to pray (see Matt. 18:20).

The direction in which the priestly ministry of each baptized and confirmed Christian leads is always toward the worshiping community of the people of God. At the liturgy the role of the ordained priest receives its particular expression in presidency over sacramental action. The ordained priest's specific priestly ministry is within the church, to gather it together and build it up through the liturgical assemblies of the faithful. There in the person and name of Jesus the Lord, and as the servant of the baptized and confirmed faithful, the priest incorporates new members into the worshiping body of the faithful through the sacraments of initiation. The priest

---

65. The following paragraphs repeat the argument as I express it in my "The Priest, Prophet and King Trilogy, Elements of Its Meaning in *Lumen Gentium and for Today,*" *Eglise et Théologie* 19 (1988): 201–6.

nourishes for daily living through the Eucharist, heals the wounds of sin through the liturgy of reconciliation and the weakness of spirit caused by human ailment through the anointing of the sick, and (along with deacons) offers the church's blessing upon women and men who administer marriage vows to each other.

Because priests are usually associated with a parish in which the sacraments are usually celebrated, they gather people into the concrete worshiping community when they preside, and because priests are ordained by a bishop who is in communion with the worldwide college of bishops, their presidency over the particular community for worship at the same time links the particular act of worship with the worship of the church catholic. Because the priest presides in the name and in the person of the Lord, each particular act of worship on the local scale is also a participation in the eternal and heavenly worship of the whole creation.

The bishop presides over the worship of the local church of each diocese as chief liturgist. The church is never more itself than when it is gathered around its local bishop at liturgy, especially eucharistic liturgy. When at worship with the bishop as he exercises his liturgical ministry the priestly ministry of each baptized member should be recognized as achieving its most public expression. This is so because liturgy is the public act of worship of the whole People of God. At Eucharist, in particular, the priestly sacrifice of Christ himself is brought to bear upon the presently worshiping congregation, especially through the eucharistic prayer, and their lives and activities are brought into explicit participation in the priestly sacrifice of Christ, especially through the rite of communion.

Prophetic Ministry.   The meaning of the prophetic ministry of all the members of the church centers upon being absorbed by the word of God. The truth of God's activity in favor of the human world so engages the minds and hearts of believers that they feel themselves compelled to live that truth, form communities with like-minded believers, and proclaim the truth to the world according to their particular capacity and graces. By the capacity conferred in the character of order priests have the responsibility of proclaiming Christ's gospel by preaching to and teaching their congregations. By reason of the sacramental characters of baptism and confirmation and of their particular charisms, individual Christians may be called upon to exercise the prophetic ministry of catechist, theologian, and missionary. By virtue of the charisms that come with the sacrament of marriage, parents are "the first teachers of their children in the ways of faith."[66]

As supervisor of the local church the bishop exercises the prophetic

---

66. Rite of Baptism for Children, art. 39, 105.

ministry of chief teacher in his diocese, and as a member of the worldwide college of bishops he joins with the other members of the college corporately to exercise the ministry of teacher of the universal church. So important for the well-being of the church is the bishop's exercise of the ministry of preaching and teaching that the Second Vatican Council claims: "Among the principal duties of bishops, the preaching of the gospel occupies an eminent place."[67]

More than the words they speak, the way the baptized live makes a statement of the good news of Christ. The countercultural quality of the lives of some Christians may become an ultimate witness to the gospel through martyrdom. The degree to which gospel meaning, truth, and value become the common expression of the Christian people corporately in base communities, religious congregations, parishes, dioceses, and the universal church determines the effectiveness of the witness of the entire community of believers. The Second Vatican Council's *Decree on the Missionary Activity of the Church* teaches that individual and communal living complement actual preaching and teaching as occurrences of prophetic ministry.[68]

Royal/Pastoral/Political Ministry.   Extending the kingdom of God into the world and offering pastoral leadership and care within the church may be looked upon as two aspects of the third function of Christian ministry. According to the circumstances of their lives and the charisms with which they have been blessed, all the members of the church have a ministry to perform in cooperating with the risen Lord to bring about God's kingdom.

Baptized and confirmed Christians have the particular responsibility to gather the data on their talents and on the environment in which they find themselves in order to determine the ways in which they can be of service to engender in the people around them lives expressive of the fruits of the Spirit. Ministerial activities promoting the kingdom of God on earth admit of great diversity.

By reason of the sacrament of order bishops and priests have the shepherd's role to provide leadership of the Christian church so that all the church's members are equipped by sacraments, education, and opportunities to exercise their royal ministry. This is a major reason for order in the church, and for the governance that keeps church life orderly. All the needs that call out for response by God's people are to be met, and some people must oversee the activity of the church's members to assure that all the needs are being met. Spontaneously, the church's individual members may

---

67. *Lumen gentium*, art. 25.
68. *Decree on the Missionary Activity of the Church*, art. 11, 12, 15.

not recognize or choose to fill all the ministerial roles that have to be filled if needs are to be met. Oversight is the ministry that asks some people to respond to unmet needs, some people to leave one ministry to others while taking up another instead, to find a ministry more suited to their gifts and talents, to have the courage to do what might intimidate them. Pastoral leadership is not a usurpation of the multiple ministries of baptized/confirmed Christians, but an enablement of them in an orderly way that promotes the common good.

It has not been easy to include the deaconate among the differentiated ministries discussed in the preceding paragraphs because it is not easy to specify the roles of deacons. Diaconal ministry is not clearly expressed either in the New Testament or in documentation of the first five centuries or so when it was a more prominent ministry in the church. Still, I suggest that the first role of deacons is to serve as administrative assistants to diocesan bishops. That is one role deacons apparently exercised in the early centuries of Christianity. Deacons can bring the pastoral care of the bishop to groups that are not parishes, and therefore have no ordained pastor. Such might be extended-care facilities, homes for the aged, prisons, hospitals, and schools, although there is no inherent reason why any of these institutions could not be incorporated appropriately into the life of a local parish. Perhaps more to the point is the assistance deacons can afford bishops as directors of diocesan departments (roles that hardly seem presbyteral although they are often filled by presbyters): offices of education, social services, ecumenical affairs, marriage tribunals, and other supervisory ministries.

Belgian Cardinal Leon-Joseph Suenens offered another suggestion for the deaconate in a speech he delivered in 1979.[69] Since the large size of so many urban and suburban parishes as well as the isolation of rural parishes prevent personal attention to church members by the pastor in an age when personal attention is precisely what people seem to desire, ministry needs to find new ways to develop "its capacity to assume a truly human dimension," if the faithful's sense of ecclesial belonging is to be sustained. The deaconate may be admirably suited to meet this need. The wider parish can remain the eucharistic community, but leadership in prayer, study, action, and simple social exchange could be provided in smaller groups under the leadership of carefully trained deacons.

---

69. I have been able to locate Cardinal Suenen's remarks only in a *Newsletter* of January 1980 published by the Catholic Diocese of Buffalo's Office of Permanent Dioconate. For a current reflection of persons in the field of diaconal ministry, see Rev. Patrick McCaslin and Michael G. Lawler, *Sacrament of Service: A Vision of the Permanent Diaconate Today* (New York: Paulist, 1986).

Two Types of Presbyter:
Regular and Diocesan?

For centuries the church has promoted three types of ordained presbyter: priests to serve the local church as associates of the bishop, monks ordained as priests primarily to celebrate the eucharistic liturgy, and priests belonging to religious institutes whose particularity is determined by their religious vows and specific ministries or ministerial approaches. Since, at least in the contemporary church, monks are ordained primarily to meet the needs of their own monastery for liturgical service, they are simply acknowledged in passing. Of greater concern for the present theology of ministry are the other two types of priest. In a recent article, John J. O'Malley, has raised the question whether the two types of priest actually represent two types of priesthood within the Roman church.[70] O'Malley encourages the recognition of two types of priesthood for the sake of maintaining a tradition of ministerial enrichment. His thesis raises an important issue for the meaning of ordained ministry.

O'Malley recognizes that by the end of the second century the pattern of "a bishop surrounded by his presbyters emerged."[71] However, he highlights the conclusions of New Testament scholars that "the New Testament does not yield an altogether clear or consistent picture about church order, about the relationship between authority and community." In any case, O'Malley does not want to equate the earliest with the normative, especially since such an approach has not practically guided the church's life consistently. Instead, he goes on to show that a different sort of priesthood from the supposedly typical pattern emerged first in the thirteenth century with the Dominicans and Franciscans, and then in the sixteenth century with the Jesuits.

The pattern of the priest serving the local church under the supervision of the bishop became characterized by "order, status, office, and stable functions" and focused on "ritual and sacramental" activity, a church-type priesthood.[72] The pattern of the regular priests, that is, those living according to a *regula* or rule, became characterized as a voluntary community whose ministry arose in response to a specific need of the time, especially with the Dominicans, or in response to an inner inspiration, especially with Francis of Assisi. O'Malley names this sort a sect-type priesthood. Here is O'Malley's summary statement about the Dominican and Franciscan friars:

---

70. John J. O'Malley, "Priesthood, Ministry, and Religious Life: Some Historical and Historiographical Considerations," *Theological Studies* 49 (1988): 223–57.
71. Ibid., 229.
72. Ibid., 233.

If we should at this point construct a profile of the friar, therefore, we would note that his ministry originated in charism and need, that the minister transcended local lines and moved about "like the apostles," that his ministry consisted to a large degree in preaching and thus required an education, that it related to personal life-style and to the style of governance within the order, which in effect removed him from the governance operative in the church-type. If this profile is inserted into the history of religious life as we now have it, strong continuities emerge because of the ascetical tradition involved. If this profile is inserted into the history of ministry and of church order, however, we perceive a sharp break not only with the preceding monastic and feudal era but to some extent even with the presumably more normative paradigms of, say, the fourth and fifth centuries.[73]

The sixteenth century brought another upsurge of creative ministries within Roman Catholicism, not only in response to the Protestant Reform, but also consistent with the age of discovery and then, in the seventeenth century, the scientific revolution. The chief carrier of the new creativity was the Society of Jesus. Ministry of the word dominated: not only liturgical preaching, but novenas, Forty Hours, the Three Hours, missions, street preaching, spiritual direction and retreats, lectures on the Bible and theological subjects, and the establishment of schools. Social ministries burgeoned too. And the Jesuits took a special vow, the antithesis of stable, localized ministry, to go anywhere and to anyone as the needs were greatest.[74] The Council of Trent, on the other hand, when it dealt with the practical determination of ministry, issued reform decrees bent on promoting the authority of bishops and pastors and the prominence of parish-based ministry. Trent paid no attention to the ministerial creativity alive within Roman Catholicism at the time.

Vatican Council II made great strides forward in developing the broader meaning of priestly ministry by moving beyond its ritual, sacramental role to give prominence to the priest's ministry of the word and to the ministry of pastoral care and leadership. But, O'Malley contends, the basic documents spelling out the roles of priests make three fundamental assumptions that militate against the regular clergy as they have traditionally existed: (1) normally the priest will serve a stable community; (2) the stable community is composed of the faithful; (3) at all times the priest collaborates closely with the bishop.[75] On the other hand, the Council's statements about the

73. Ibid., 235.
74. Ibid., 237–43.
75. Ibid., 250–51. O'Malley refers especially to the *Decree on the Ministry and Life of Priests*, the *Decree on Priestly Formation*, and the *Decree on the Bishops' Pastoral Office in the Church*.

regular clergy emphasize the vows and give scant attention to their ministries.[76] There seems to be no room in the Vatican II model of priesthood for
the more prophetic, less sacramental ministries of the regular clergy, which
are wide-ranging in their missions both to serve those Christians who do
not belong to stable communities or who need to receive priestly ministry
in other situations, as well as to seek out and evangelize those who are not
Christians.

In the conclusion of his study O'Malley pleads for greater receptivity to
"the tradition of ministry and priesthood in the religious orders."[77] By making more room both theoretically and practically for other ways to be priest
than the local-church model, the church is able to reach more people with
the message of the gospel. O'Malley sees a special urgency for this diversity
in the present time for "even among the faithful, many persons seem to be
falling through the cracks of 'normative' ministry, at least in Western Europe
and North America."[78]

Who could dispute O'Malley's claim that the church's ministry has been
immeasurably enriched by both the greater and the smaller religious institutes which were founded not only to promote the personal holiness of the
members but also to meet the ministerial needs of various times and places?
The facts of history are indisputable in this regard. Moreover, I would support O'Malley's call to continue to respect long-existing as well as new
movements of ordained priests that complement the parochial structure of
the local church.

However, it seems to me that essential to the sacramental character of
all ordained priesthood is liturgical and pastoral leadership, so that the regular clergy cannot ignore this dimension of their priesthood. Moreover,
prophetic leadership, that is, ministry of the word, is also essential to the
character of all ordained priesthood, and thus a constitutive element of the
ministerial priesthood of the diocesan clergy.[79] Only the rare priest can be
equally adept at all three functions, but all, regular and diocesan, must be
able to manage some integration of the three so that they can guide the
Christian community in the person of Christ as their ordination deputes
them to do. Beyond a basic implementation of the three roles, there may be

76. O'Malley, "Priesthood, Ministry, and Religious Life," 249. The conciliar document is the
Decree on the Appropriate Renewal of the Religious Life. The post-conciliar document *Essentials of Religious Life* is also mentioned.

77. O'Malley, "Priesthood, Ministry, and Religious Life," 253.

78. Ibid., 256.

79. There is nothing stronger in the *Decree on the Ministry and Life of Priests* than that the
"primary duty" of priests, in cooperation with the bishops, is the "proclamation of the gospel
of God to all" (art. 4).

a variety of charisms, enjoyed both by the regular and the diocesan clergy, which enhance one or the other function.

Given the contribution that the religious orders have made and continue to make to the church's ministry, and without any desire to forbid, halt, or hinder those who presently seek to follow the Lord and serve the church as members of a religious institute, accurate assessment of whether there are two types of priesthood requires a further consideration. Why did two types of priest arise in the first place? Recall that it was in the fourth and fifth centuries that several bishops arranged to have their local presbyterate live the common life as far as was feasible. Augustine is the most famous of these bishops, and in his efforts one of the first semimonastic, semiministerial movements finds its origin. [80] At the same time, as we have seen, ordained Christians were endowed with higher status at the expense of baptized Christians. From that time forward it behooved anyone seeking to live "the perfect life" to consider seriously whether he ought not choose the monastic or the clerical state, and both if possible.

With the enormous social changes of the twelfth century, monasticism began to lose its appeal as an active, apostolic life became a vehicle of the quest for Christian perfection. Poverty, celibacy, and the common life continued, however, to stand before medieval and later Christians as highly desirable evangelical ideals, although it was conceded that one could achieve holiness as a married person with a secular occupation. The ordained ministry, too, was still looked upon as the religiously superior way to live. In such a situation does it not make sense that the great movements founded by the laymen Francis of Assisi and Ignatius of Loyola (Dominic de Guzman was a diocesan priest when he first attracted followers) should soon become clerical orders?[81]

But if, as the theology developed in these pages promotes, the baptized were to recover their status, would it any longer be necessary for missionary efforts, colleges and universities, care for the marginalized, and involvement in political efforts to be sponsored and staffed by groups of ordained priests? Do not these ministries belong to all the baptized? Is it not perhaps a usurpation of the role of all the baptized even to create the impression that

---

80. See F. Van der Meer, *Augustine the Bishop*, trans. B. Battershaw and G. R. Lamb (New York: Sheed & Ward, 1961), 199; Brown, *Augustine of Hippo*, 198; and James A. Mohler, *The Heresy of Monasticism* (Staten Island, N. Y.: Alba House, 1971), 119.

81. Francis would have preferred that he and his followers remain lay people, but church authorities demanded that those friars engaged in preaching be ordained. See the historical study of Edward Schillebeeckx, "The Right of Every Christian to Speak in the Light of Evangelical Experience 'In the Midst of Brothers and Sisters,'" in Nadine Foley, ed., *Preaching and the Non-Ordained* (Collegeville, Minn.: Liturgical Press, 1983), 32.

somehow these ministries are better implemented by those who are ordained? Should not the number of ordained in any community be limited to those who are needed to preside over each community in word, sacrament, and governance? This is the reason for the ordained ministry. Beyond that, all the baptized may implement needed ministries.

Chapter Four

WOMEN IN
MINISTRY

THE LAST THREE POPES (APART FROM JOHN PAUL I) HAVE specifically brought the discussion on the role of women into the Catholic context. In his final encyclical, published shortly before his death in June 1963, John XXIII commented briefly, but significantly, that the impetus toward greater participation of women in the life of society was one of the major currents in contemporary society.[1] Thirteen years later, during the pontificate of Paul VI, the Congregation for the Doctrine of the Faith made a pronouncement setting the Roman church against the admission of women to ordained priesthood. At the same time, and for the first time, the pronouncement continues at length to assert the equal dignity of women and the call of women along with men to the ministry of the baptized. Surprisingly, a Vatican commentary even acknowledges that some fathers of the church suffered from misogynism and that Thomas Aquinas proposed arguments against the ordination of women that are indefensible.[2]

Most recently Pope John Paul II has issued his own reflections on the matter in an apostolic letter *On the Dignity and Vocation of Women*, a document that provides the theological foundations for suggestions in the postsynodal apostolic exhortation, *On the Christian Laity*.[3] In the latter pronounce-

---

1. *Pacem in Terris*, art. 41.
2. *Declaration on the Question of the Admission of Women to the Ministerial Priesthood*, Origins 6 (Feb. 3, 1977): 517, 519–24. "A Commentary on the Declaration" follows in the same issue of *Origins*, 524–31. For the point on misogynism, see p. 526.
3. John Paul II, *On the Dignity and Vocation of Women* (Mulieris Dignitatem), Origins 18 (Oct. 6, 1988): 261, 263–83; *On the Christian Laity* (Christifideles Laici), Origins 18 (Feb. 9, 1989), 561–95.

ment, the pope invites persons who are interested in these matters to use *On the Dignity and Vocation of Women* as a dialogue partner. This I propose to do in the present chapter. Accordingly, it is appropriate to quote the pope's invitation:

> May the reading of the apostolic letter *Mulieris Dignitatem*, in particular, as a biblical-theological meditation, be an incentive for everyone, both women and men, and especially for those who devote their lives to the human sciences and theological disciplines, to pursue on the basis of the personal dignity of man and woman and their mutual relationship a critical study to better and more deeply understand the values and specific gifts of feminity and masculinity not only in the surroundings of social living, but also and above all in living as Christians and as members of the church. [4]

The question of women in ministry is complicated by interdisciplinary issues of the meaning of the feminine and the masculine. The theological reality exists side by side with the anthropological, sociological, psychological, and biological aspects of the meaning of the feminine and the masculine in the human. No single person can be an expert in all these areas. In the present instance, then, as I propose a theological perspective on women in ministry, I recognize but am not competent to judge the findings of experts in other relevant fields. For this reason interdisciplinary dialogue is necessary.

There is also the matter of the New Testament witness to women in the church and ministry. Interpretation of these texts is as much a complicating as a clarifying factor at the present stage of biblical scholarship on women; still, New Testament interpretation must also be brought to bear upon the topic at hand. Suggestions on how to do that are relevant.

Positions That Will Not Be Considered

There are two views of men and women that are incompatible with Christian faith. The first has had a lengthy history. It is the position that holds that there is some inherent superiority of men over women. An outpouring of contemporary literature excoriates the long and oppressive history of patriarchy. But because the notion of the superiority of men has held sway for so long, there are still tenacious remnants of its tenure in those viewpoints that hold that some roles of leadership and work in society belong

---

4. *On the Christian Laity*, art. 50.

only to men, or only to women. Notions that men manage the office and
women belong to the support system, that only men do heavy labor and
only women light work, that men make decisions while women exercise
their influence in the background do not disappear easily from the common
perception of how things should be. While recognizing that a society characterized by the collaboration of equals is still far from achievement, I take
the view that the theoretical war against patriarchy has been waged and
won. In any case, it is not a tenable Christian position.

Equally untenable is the view that women are superior to men. This position has a shorter and more current history, and is advocated by some
feminists as an authentic Christian theology. Basically, the extreme feminist
theological position turns the tables on the patriarchal position. Instead of
men being created by God to be inherently superior to women, it is women
who have been created to be inherently superior to men. Instead of sin
coming into the world through the deception of Eve, it takes its entry
through the infidelity of Adam. Instead of salvation achieving its cure and
enhancing humanity's relationship with God first of all in and through the
male members of the species, it is women who are salvation's first recipients
and its transmitters to men, or, in the theories of some feminists, it is only
women who are the recipients of salvation.[5] None of these feminist positions is any more acceptable than the masculinist position of patriarchy as
an interpretation of the Christian meaning of being female and male in the
human world. Both are to be left aside.

I divide my dialogue with John Paul II in his *Mulieris Dignitatem* into three
segments on the basis of three areas of theological reflection that I take to
be operative in a theology of women in ministry: creation, incarnation,
Trinity. I do not propose any of what follows as definitive, but rather as one
more contribution to the "critical study" called for by the pope, to be submitted to thoughtful criticism from every side of the current discussion.

Female and Male in the Image
and Likeness of God

The first theological principle to govern a theology of women in ministry
may be simply stated: by God's gracious creative act every human being is
of equal worth and dignity. Gender, potential talents and skills, eventual
social or economic standing are irrelevant to fundamental human worth.

5. For a survey of several feminist positions on Christian doctrine see Patricia Wilson-
Kastner, "Contemporary Feminism and Christian Doctrine of the Human," in *Word and World* 2
(1985): 234–42.

This theological principle is grounded in biblical faith. *Mulieris Dignitatem* does a tremendous service in promoting this principle by its extensive discussion of the biblical foundations of the equality of women and men. Both by the cogency of his reasoning and by the authority of his office, the pope goes a long way to advance the interpretation of biblical faith in this regard beyond long-held interpretations within the tradition and beyond the contemporary arguments of some biblical fundamentalists. [6]

John Paul enters into his biblical reflections in a way that we have come to recognize as characteristic in his writings. He sets out on a kind of phenomenological meditation. Taking up the stories of creation in the first two chapters of Genesis he argues that both chapters teach the intrinsic equality of women and men, with the first chapter's proposition that human beings are created in the image and likeness of God constituting "the immutable basis of all Christian anthropology: . . . the human race, which takes its origin from the calling into existence of man and woman, crowns the whole work of creation; both man and woman are human beings to an equal degree, both are created in God's image." [7]

Moving to the second chapter of Genesis, *Mulieris Dignitatem* finds a development of the theme of the equality of men and women complementing that in the first chapter. In the second chapter the differences between men and women are noted in the narrative of building Eve from Adam's rib, but the pope does not discern any note of inequality in the difference:

> In the description found in Genesis 2:18-25, the woman is created by God "from the rib" of the man and is placed at his side as another "I," as the companion of the man, who is alone in the surrounding world of living creatures and who finds in none of them a "helper" suitable for himself. Called into existence in this way, the woman is immediately recognized by the man as "flesh of his flesh and bone of his bones" (cf. Gen. 2:23), and for this very reason she is called *woman*. In biblical language this name indicates her essential identity with regard to the man—*'is-'issah*—something which unfortunately modern languages in general are unable to express: "She shall be called woman ['*issah*] because she was taken out of man" ['*is*] (Gen. 2:23).

Subsequently, when the entrance of sin into the world is narrated in Genesis 3, and a distinction of the roles of man and woman is described at some length, this is not, in the mind of John Paul II, to be interpreted as an attribution of distinct or more guilt to one or the other. The sin is the sin of

---

6. The conclusions of John Paul II and Wilson-Kastner on the witness of the biblical data to equality between the genders coincide. See ibid., 239ff.

7. *Mulieris Dignitatem*, art. 6.

human beings, both male and female. Neither can be blamed more or less than the other for introducing the dire fact of alienation from God into human existence.[8] Thus, when God's salvific action enters into human history to rescue humanity from the destructive consequences of its alienating behavior, a unified humanity, both female and male, is saved. Both are equally saved. In fact, one consequence of salvation is to restore the equality of relationships between women and men, a consequence that requires constant attention and effort as do all the other salutary consequences of God's redemptive and sanctifying activity on behalf of humanity. Thus, while a result of the entry of sin into human history was the domination of women by men ("he shall rule over you," Gen. 3:16), a consequence of salvation is to restore male-female relationships as a collaboration of equals.[9]

The restoration of equality in the Christian dispensation is not contradicted by Eph. 5:22-23, which speaks of the husband as head of the wife and, because of that headship, of the duty of wives to be submissive to their husbands. Here, as Margaret Hebblethwaite has noted, the pope differs markedly from a favorite theme of some biblical fundamentalists.[10] He recognizes no authority for male domination in the text of Ephesians, but rather mutual deference, to the statement of which he adds a call for conversion:

> The "innovation" of Christ is a fact: It constitutes the unambiguous intent of the evangelical message and is the result of the redemption. However, the awareness that in marriage there is mutual "subjection of the spouses out of reverence for Christ" and not just that of the wife to the husband must gradually establish itself in hearts, consciences, behaviors, and customs. This is a call which from that time onward does not cease to challenge succeeding generations; it is a call which people have to accept ever anew.[11]

From every side the pope finds the biblical data supporting an interpretation of the complete equality of men and women in a basic appreciation

---

8. What a far cry the pope's statement is from very influential writings of early Christian authors such as Tertullian, who wrote of Eve as the villain who seduced Adam to sin, and of every other woman as Eve redivivus: "Do you not realize that you are each an Eve? The curse of God on this sex of yours lives on even in our time. . . . You are the devil's gateway; you desecrated the fatal tree; you softened up with your cajoling words the one against whom the devil could not prevail by force. All too easily you destroyed the image of God, Adam." Quoted in Elizabeth A. Johnson, "The Marian Tradition and the Reality of Women," *Horizons* 12 (1985): 122.

9. *Mulieris Dignitatem*, art. 9, 10.

10. Margaret Hebblethwaite, "Pope Seems More Conservative Than Misogynist," *National Catholic Reporter*, Nov. 11, 1988, p. 15.

11. *Mulieris Dignitatem*, art. 24.

that persons of both genders are human beings created in the image and likeness of God and redeemed from a devastating sinfulness by the gracious redemptive activity of the same God. Further, the Bible calls for this basic appreciation to be worked out in equal and collaborative social relationships among men and women. The paradigm for this equality is God who is neither male nor female and who creates human beings of both genders in the divine image and likeness. In my view this paradigm is the heart of the theology relevant to the interpretation of the role of gender in ministry. The papal argument on this matter is cogent.

If we ask how women and men are created in the image and likeness of God, our first response is a negative one: not by reason of their gender. The God affirmed by the Hebrew and Christian Testaments is not male or female, but spirit, which is not differentiated by any qualities of matter. Gender belongs to the material dimension of being. To the extent, then, that human beings are differentiated into female and male none of this participates in the qualities that render them creatures in the image and likeness of God. For, apart from the incarnation of the Word as a male at a particular moment of history, the triune God is entirely spirit.

To reflect upon God at length and to address God in language that is appropriate for creed and worship requires the use of metaphor. So it is not surprising to find that the Scriptures are full of anthropomorphic language about God. Most often the metaphors are masculine, reflecting the patriarchal society in which the language functions. God is often referred to as a father. The Word is named the father's son. God is the king and the shepherd of Israel. Often this language has been taken literally so that the masculine image of God has been interpreted to mean a masculine God. Certainly the trinitarian doctrine formulated in the first four centuries of Christianity went a long way to promote this equivalence of metaphor with essence, although that was surely not the intention of those who formulated the doctrine nor of the theologians involved in the debate about God, all of whom were fully cognizant of the spiritual character of God by virtue of their philosophical roots in Middle Platonism. But through Jesus' own address of God as Father and through the trinitarian doctrine of Nicea the generative language of Father and Son became a permanent fixture of Christian tradition, and without advertence to the metaphorical character of this language. After all, the Nicene Creed would have been just as faithful to the truth of God if it had named the generator and the generated by the more inclusive metaphors of Parent and Child.

Specifically feminine language, as much as masculine, is just as easily capable of expressing generativity, as well as protection, comfort, nurture, all of which are descriptive of God's character. Nor are feminine descriptions of God in this vein absent from the Bible. But until recently it would seem shocking to suggest that the biblical data also includes texts that attribute feminine qualities to God. [12] Now it is more commonplace, and with Pope John Paul explicit attention to the biblical descriptions of God's feminine qualities has found its way into papal documentation. Already in his encyclical on the first Person of the divine Trinity, *Dives in Misericordia*, John Paul separated himself from exclusively masculine references to the qualities of God. There he discusses in a lengthy footnote how the Hebrew word, *rahamim*, used to attribute to God the characteristic of gracious mercy, expresses the more feminine side of God as distinct from the more masculine connotations of *hesed*, fidelity. [13]

Determining which qualities of the human personality are feminine and which masculine, however, carries its own dangers. It is certainly possible to argue, and I would surely do so, that it is an old trap to fall into if we determine that there are essentially masculine and essentially feminine *spiritual* qualities, since spiritual qualities have no gender characteristics. It seems that John Paul II is also moving away from that stereotypical mentality, for in *Mulieris Dignitatem*, even as he lists side by side the biblical references to God in the masculine and the feminine metaphor, he insists that both are just that, metaphors, for God "possesses no property typical of the body." [14]

What all this comes to is that, first, we find in the Bible the attribution of both masculine and feminine qualities to God, although the majority of references are masculine. Cultural factors probably are the reason for the imbalance. Nevertheless, the presence of both types of reference is ample evidence that the Bible cannot be brought forth as a witness to God's masculinity. A second interpretation is more significant, namely, that both feminine and masculine qualities can be attributed to God only as metaphors for something essential about God that is neither masculine nor feminine, that is beyond both, because God is spirit. Spirit cannot be imagined accurately. It can be affirmed and, since it is personal, it can be loved. Those willing to make the effort to move beyond imagination can also achieve some halting, inadequate understanding of God's spiritual nature, as mystics and theologians have done through the centuries.

Still, the normal way in which we experience persons is as women and men, embodied spirits. It seems to me that we do not need to fear imagining God as man and woman, as long as the whole Christian people, and not

---

12. Sallie McFague has suggested several biblically based, nonmasculine images of God in *Metaphorical Theology: Models of God in Religious Language* (Philadelphia: Fortress Press, 1982).

13. *Dives in Misericordia* (Rich in Mercy), n. 52.

14. *Mulieris Dignitatem*, art. 8.

just theologians, is made aware of the limitations of imagination when it comes to relating to God.

If God is not feminine or masculine, but spirit, and if the glory of humanity is that each human person is created in the image and likeness of God, then clearly, despite all the expenditure of time, money, and imagination on gender and sex, and despite the grandeur of both, gender and sexuality being gifts of a beneficent creator, we do not arrive at the heart of our humanity until we recognize the distinct and equal dignity of each human being in the spirit which informs each of us. Human differences and distinctions, which are also evident and noteworthy, are not of the same importance as what all human beings share, a spirit like the divine spirit.

Human spirituality denotes the essential meaning of the human subject, which is to be an intelligent and free center of consciousness. Human spirituality is the image and likeness of God in the human being. For God is spirit, and spirit is the subject who understands and knows and freely chooses and loves. These are all spiritual activities. In human beings the activities of spirit are much affected by the bodily presence of humans in space and time. But the spiritual activities themselves are distinct from materiality, and link human persons most intimately to the divine persons.

This view of how persons exist in the image and likeness of God is very much within the pale of contemporary Catholic theology and philosophy. The Second Vatican Council's *Pastoral Constitution on the Church in the Modern World* proposed the same view of the divine–human similarity.[15] The Constitution declares:

> Humanity is not deceived when it acknowledges that it is superior to material things, and does not consider itself to be simply one more piece of nature or an anonymous element of human society. For by their interiority human beings surpass the entire universe of things; human persons arrive at this profound interiority when they become converted to the heart, where God, who scrutinizes human hearts, is waiting, and where, under the eyes of God, each human subject discerns its destiny. And so, recognizing in themselves a spiritual and immortal soul, human persons are not deceived by some illusion arising from physical and social conditions, but, on the contrary, they attain the profound truth of the matter.[16]

Along the same lines, Karol Wojtyla published a lengthy study of the human person in 1969, *The Acting Person*, in which he treats the cognitive and determinative structure of the person by bringing together Thomistic

---

15. *Pastoral Constitution on the Church in the Modern World*, art. 12–17.
16. Ibid., art. 14.

metaphysics and Max Scheler's phenomenological studies of value into an existential personalism whose emphasis is upon love as the most character- istic human quality.[17] For Wojtyla the core of the human subject is the self- determining conscience which, when actuated at its full potential, is in love. The most responsible persons live generously interpersonal lives, in love with God and with their fellow human beings. This love takes shape in two ways: it always values the other as a person, never treating the other as a thing; and it always looks out for the genuine good. In both instances, Wojtyla argues, employing Max Scheler's phenomenology of ethics, the subject begins by relating to the good through values that are discerned through feelings. Through feelings one "experiences" the truth of values, and through feelings one is oriented to esteem some values as higher than others.

One might ask what criterion exists within feelings that enables the dis- cernment of distinct values and of the priority among values. For Wojtyla the basis is human spirituality. It is the ontological ground for the objectiv- ity of the subject's discernment between the fundamental feelings of love and hate, the former actualizing human freedom that is realistic and the latter leading to illusory freedom that is enslavement.[18] When the feelings of the individual human subject, which emerge out of spirituality, are being actuated ever more fully, then the process of self-completion is under way, a process made up both of self-possession, by which a person appropriates herself or himself and self-dominion, by which a person is the responsible guide of her or his actuation. Ultimately, the capacity for self-completion in love is the most distinctive characteristic of the human subject, and the point at which humanity most exists as the image of God.

Bernard Lonergan's long years spent working out a critical method of philosophy and theology led him, too, to a fresh articulation of how human spirituality is what specifically constitutes the human creature as the image and likeness of God. Lonergan speaks of the intelligent subject as the intel- ligible in act. In human beings this takes shape as "an unrestricted desire to know" which, however, "is mated to a limited capacity to attain knowl- edge."[19] God, however, is the primary intelligible who is intelligence in act, "the unrestricted act of understanding."[20]

17. Karol Wojtyla, *The Acting Person* (Dordrecht: Reidel, 1979, orig. publ. 1969). See also Andrew N. Woznicki, *Karol Wojtyla's Existential Personalism* (New Britain, Conn.: Mariel, 1980). My summary of Wojtyla's existential personalism comes from a reading of Woznicki.

18. Wojtyla's argumentation seems to be quite close to the philosophy of John Macmurray discussed above in chap. 2.

19. Bernard Lonergan, *Insight: A Study of Human Understanding* (London: Longmans, Green, 1957), 639.

20. Ibid., 648.

Intelligence as the intelligible in act is what God and God's human creatures share in common, although the intelligence of God is vastly different
by virtue of its perfection from the limited intelligence of human subjects.
God, the unresricted act of understanding, understands both the divine self
as the subject of the unrestricted act and then every other possible intelligibility as potentially a divine creation. Joined necessarily to the unrestricted act of understanding is a commensurate freedom by which possible
intelligibilities may be actualized. In God freedom is always exercised on
behalf of the good.[21] In other words, God is a God of love.[22]

In a way that is similar, but far more dissimilar because of the distance
between unrestricted act and unrestricted desire but limited act, human subjects are intelligibilities in act. They too have the potential to come to
understand and know themselves and their world, although the order is
reversed because it is only after human subjects have come to some knowledge of the universe of which they are a part that they can begin to appreciate their own place as subjects within the world and how they are so
constituted as subjects. Joined with their intelligence, as a component of
their subjectivity, is the capacity of human subjects to evaluate possible
choices of the good, to make decisions, and thus to determine the course
of their own lives as well as the course of nature and society.[23] Freedom is a
function of this determinative capacity. It is a freedom limited by historicity.
It confers upon human subjects the potential to constitute both themselves
and their world. Still, limited as they are, human subjects, women and men,
not only equally but without distinction, are constituted in the image and
likeness of God by their spirituality.

Would It Have Been Possible
for God to Have Become
Incarnate as a Woman?

My second thesis follows from the first. It seems to me that there is no
theological significance to be attached to the incarnation of God as a male,
but that the second person of the Trinity might have come as a woman
without in any theologically significant way changing the process of human
redemption. This conclusion results, in the first place, from the essential
equality of every human being as created in the image and likeness of God.

---

21. Ibid., 664–68.
22. Ibid., 725–26.
23. Relying on Dietrich von Hildebrand and Max Scheler, in a way similar to Wojtyla,
Lonergan locates feelings as intentional responses to value in *Method in Theology* (New York:
Herder & Herder, 1972), 30–34.

Second, it results from the interpretation of metaphorical language about God. Connected with the argument of the first two points to be made is the issue of the level of significance of the differences between male and female in the human species. Finally, questions of biblical hermeneutics need to be addressed.

On the level of spirituality, that is, on the basis of the essential equality of women and men as human creatures of the loving God, there is no theological significance attendant upon the divine incarnation as a male or a female. For both women and men are equally intelligent and free conscious subjects. Theologians of the Trinity concur that it makes sense that the second person of the Trinity should be the one to become human, for the second person is the Word, the *expression*, the first person's generated image. The Word is understood to be the truth of God. It is an appropriate extension of the eternally begotten expression of God to enter into human history as God's expression as well. The first person, on the other hand, who is the eternal principle of relations in the divinity and the begetter of the Word, more appropriately remains hidden and inaccessible to human knowledge as the source and also the goal of human striving, mediated to humanity through the Word. The Spirit, too, as love, more appropriately enters into human history not as incarnate in a single individual, visible and accessible as a historical figure, but as the spirit-animator of human spirits desiring to enter into communion with the triune God.

It is the Word that became flesh. *Word* is an analogy for the divine individual, distinct from the other two individuals, who is the eternal expression of the divinity, the divine affirmation of divine truth. Word denotes the expression of truth generated by a source that generates. Human beings normally relate to words that are spoken or written. But before there is either speaking or writing, there is the spiritual formation of word in the mind of the speaker or author. Thus, the word is first spiritual before it takes on a material form. But, as spiritual, it is an expression of the mind that understands, and even more an expression when it is a product of the mind that affirms the truth. Then it becomes not just the word of insight, which needs further reflection to determine the accuracy of the insight, but the word of truth, which takes a stand because the insight has been verified.

When we name the divine Word the Son, and its generator the Father, we have moved from analogy to metaphor. For whereas we know that the generation of the word is first and always spiritual, we also know that paternity (and maternity) and filiation are first and always material. Because of their essential materiality, paternity and filiation can never be more than a metaphor for the distinction of individuals within the divine Trinity. Still, the metaphor of father and son rather than the analogy of act of understanding and word has embedded itself into the Christian mind over the centuries. Our prayers begin and end in the name of the divine Trinity, Father, Son, and Holy Spirit. I do not doubt that, at least until recently, preachers rarely troubled themselves about any other names for the divine three than Father, Son, and Spirit. However, the analogy rather than the metaphor needs to govern our theological reasoning. The analogy leads to the conclusion that there is nothing inherent in the divine generativity, as explicitly professed by the Christian church since the fourth century, which leads to the assertion that it was necessary or even convenient or desirable that the Word become flesh as a male.

Moving from the spiritual to the material, we ask if there is anything of religious significance in the order in which human beings are in fact women and men that renders it necessary, convenient, or desirable that the incarnation should have been masculine rather than feminine, or if either might have been equally significant. Here we need to attend both to biblical data and to the present views of the human and natural sciences.

The biblical image of Christ and the church as bridegroom and bride is prominent in the reflection of the 1976 Vatican declaration *Inter Insigniores* and in *Mulieris Dignitatem*.[24] Both documents argue that this image indicates the reason that the incarnation had to take place in a male rather than a female person. The 1976 declaration expresses it this way:

> It is through this scriptural language, all interwoven with symbols, and which expresses and affects man and woman in their profound identity, that there is revealed to us the mystery of God and Christ, a mystery which of itself is unfathomable.

> That is why we can never ignore the fact that Christ is a man. And therefore, unless one is to disregard the importance of this symbolism for the economy of revelation, it must be admitted that, in actions which demand the character of ordination and in which Christ himself, the author of the covenant, the bridegroom and head of the church, is represented, exercising his ministry of salvation—which is in the highest degree the case of the eucharist—his role (this is the original sense of the word *persona*) must be taken by a man. This does not stem from any personal superiority of the latter in the order of values, but only from a difference of fact on the level of functions and service.[25]

At this point the discussion is not of the analogy of human relationships with the immanent Trinity, nor is the issue the reality of redemption in its

24. *Inter Insigniores*, 522, "A Commentary on the Declaration," 530; and *Mulieris Dignitatem*, art. 25–27.

25. *Inter Insigniores*, 522.

effectiveness to forgive humanity's sinfulness. Neither of these issues enters into the declaration's argument. Rather the question regards redemption in its effectiveness to draw humanity into intimate communion with God. The triune God's effectiveness in both aspects of redemption takes place in the created order by the missions of the Word and the Spirit. The aspect of divine-human intimacy is expressed in the Bible, both Old and New Testaments, by the image of the wedding feast. The bridegroom lovingly welcomes the bride into his home and, as she lovingly responds, the two of them achieve a state of intimate communion. In the new dispensation Christ is the bridegroom and the church is the bride. Through Christ the church achieves communion with the triune God. Communion will be definitively achieved in the life of resurrection; now it is symbolically, most perfectly achieved in the church's celebration of the Eucharist.

The ordained priest has a particular role in the extension of Christ's visible mission into the present time of the church's life, acting in the threefold function of leader of word, sacrament, and pastoral care. In all this the priest acts as a ministerial instrument of Christ the one high priest. In the priest the church community, of which the priest is also a member, must be able to recognize Christ. Thus, the symbolic character of the priest is of theological significance. The priest represents Christ in his redemptive role in such a way that the utterly incomprehensible divine mystery becomes in some human way visible and accessible to the faithful.

But how theologically significant is the incarnate Word's maleness or the maleness of the priest who represents Christ when what is being administered is a redemption from a sinfulness that is equally attributable to men and women, and when the redemption is rooted in the totally submissive, loving self-sacrifice of the incarnate Word? Moreover, when it comes to the establishment of the new interpersonal relationship of grace between God and humanity, the relationship is between a totally spiritual triune God and human persons on the level of their spirituality, which does not differ between women and men. How could the masculine mediate this intimate communion any more than the feminine?

It is important to take care with the interpretation of the nuptial imagery. Since, in fact, the divine Word became incarnate in the male, Jesus of Nazareth, it is not surprising that in the employment of nuptial imagery Christ be imaged as the bridegroom. However, in attributing the lead in the nuptial union to the groom, we may be once more locked in a stereotype of patriarchal society. I cannot speak for all cultures, even contemporary, but recently in Western society the role of wooing is not essentially that of the man but can be just as much the woman's. Nor is this any aberration. It is just as intelligent and reasonable that a woman initiate a relationship with a man and that in marriage the bride lead the groom into the intimate communion of their marital relationship. Indeed, whether it be the man or the woman, the groom or the bride who takes the leadership in the relationship is quite accidental, ultimately irrelevant to a healthy marriage. More important, and of theological significance on the basis of sound trinitarian theology, is that, to quote John Paul II, "in the relationship between husband and wife the 'subjection' is not one-sided but mutual."[26] Both spouses give and both receive. Mutuality is the essential theological dimension of the female-male relationship, and marriage is the sacrament most symbolic of this relational quality. Male leadership and female following or female leadership and male following are elements in the relationship to be left behind as the relationship grows.[27]

Of course, as the pope also reminds his readers, in the relationship between Christ and the church, Christ always remains the leader and the church is always subject to him.[28] From what has been argued above, however, the reason for this is not because Christ is male but because Christ is the incarnate Word. The reality governs the nuptial imagery, not the other way around. Thus, if the Word had been incarnated as a woman, then she would be the leader and the church would be subject to her. The nuptial imagery could still be appropriate as a metaphor of the relationship between the incarnate Word and the church, but the bride would take the lead rather than the bridegroom. Admittedly, it is not likely that nuptial imagery would have lent itself to such interpretation in the cultures of the Bible in which it was introduced, but that does not prevent people of later cultures from recognizing that the image is just that, an image, which does not transfer without remainder to the reality, and indeed, as the reality becomes better known itself, the image can serve in a new way to make it intelligible.

If I have been successful in my demonstration that there are insufficient theoretical bases upon which to build a theologically significant differentiation for salvation or ministry on the part of women and men, it remains that the incarnate Word did enter human history as a male. Thus, while I have argued that it would not have contradicted the immanent reality of the triune God nor would it have made any significant difference to the divine saving activity if the Word had become incarnate as a woman, how does this sort of argumentation line up against the New Testament texts that indicate that even as Jesus chose women and men to join him in salvation and ministry, he chose only men to be in the inner circle of the Twelve? And

---

26. *Mulieris Dignitatem*, art. 24.

27. Here, once again, the danger of inflating metaphor into analogy becomes apparent. However, for some biblical metaphors can be normative, as Manfred Hauke argues regarding biblical nuptial imagery in *Women in the Priesthood?* (San Francisco: Ignatius, 1988), 249ff.

28. *Mulieris Dignatatem*, art. 24.

what about those New Testament texts that attest to the conferral in at least some early Christian communities of the ministry of leadership upon men while women are relegated to the background? Each of these issues calls for separate consideration.

A wide range of contemporary students of the New Testament are persuaded that Jesus was remarkable in his openness to women as compared with other men of his time and culture.[29] There is no doubt that Jesus treated women with unusual respect, listened to and addressed them as equal to men, proclaimed the kingdom of God to women on an equal footing with men, and welcomed them into the group of his disciples. Particularly remarkable is that women are the first witnesses to the Lord's resurrection. Also remarkable is that in John's Gospel it is not Peter, the first among the group of the Twelve, who makes the great profession of faith, "You are the Christ," but a woman, Martha (John 11:27).

Despite these unusual departures from the sociocultural conditioning of his time, the New Testament testifies that Jesus chose twelve men to belong to the inner group of his followers. Moreover, it is argued, it was to these twelve that Jesus entrusted the future leadership of his church in word, sacrament, and pastoral care. By choosing only men Jesus was making his will known that only men were to serve the church of the centuries to follow in the ministerial priesthood of episcopate and presbyterate. What confirms this intentionality of Jesus is that since he felt free to contravene established religious and cultural custom in the rest of his interactions with women, there is no reason to suppose that in this one instance of the choice of the Twelve he would act differently unless he specifically intended to do so for a very good reason.[30]

This is in response to those who argue that Jesus was a man of his time, who could not break with custom entirely, even if he had so wanted. Those who argue out of sociocultural considerations contend that Jesus would have felt that he could advance the acceptance of women in the kingdom of God, but that he could not go all the way at that time.

Is there more, however, to be discerned in the New Testament data? Since the question of the distinction in ministry between the baptized and ordained and of women in ministry, either baptized or ordained, is of contemporary origin, must we not take care lest we impose our questions upon

29. Among other studies see Jean Galot, "La femme dans l'Eglise," *Gregorianum* 68 (1987): 187–213; Olivette Genest, "Femmes et ministères dans le Nouveau Testament," *Studies in Religion* 16 (1987): 7–20; Pontifical Biblical Commission, "Can Women Be Priests?" *Origins* 6 (July 1, 1976): 92–96; Elisabeth Schuessler-Fiorenza, *In Memory of Her: A Feminist Theological Reconstruction of Christian Origins* (New York: Crossroad, 1984), chap. 4; Elisabeth Tetlow, *Women and Ministry in the New Testament* (New York: Paulist, 1980); the 1976 Declaration *Inter Insigniores*; and Pope John Paul II's apostolic letter of 1988, *Mulieris Dignitatem*.

30. *Mulieris Dignitatem*, art. 26.

the church of the New Testament? Exercising historical imagination, it seems that we can create a scenario that is perhaps approximately faithful to the times. In taking this approach to the texts of the New Testament I am keeping in mind a statement of the Pontifical Biblical Commission: "In general the role of women does not constitute the principal subject of biblical texts."[31] This reminds contemporary students of the Bible that our concern about women was probably not a concern of the authors of the New Testament, or at least not in the same way as it is a concern for us.

Minding these cautions, can we not imagine that, although in every instance in which he had occasion to interact with them, Jesus certainly treated women with uncommon respect, acting as he did from within his grace-filled humanity, talking with them and treating them as equals, inviting them to be his followers and join in his mission of proclaiming the kingdom of God, still he was not self-conscious or calculating about his actions? Could they not be the actions of an enlightened man of his time, who was nevertheless not entirely out of step with his culture, in much the same way as Paul can suggest the full equality of Greeks, women, and slaves, and still not feel constrained to argue for a change in the cultural or even the religious situation of any of the three in as thoroughgoing a way as we might expect him to do if he were acting today?[32] Thus, when it came to choosing his inner circle of disciples, would it be out of order to expect that Jesus would act like any other man of his time (and of most times since), not by determinedly leaving women out, but simply by not determinedly bringing them in? It may not have occurred to Jesus to go to such lengths as to include women among the Twelve. Nor would it have occurred to anyone else, including women, that women might be chosen. In that case, the determination of Jesus' intentionality should not weigh so heavily upon the texts narrating Jesus' choice of twelve men to make up his closest circle of disciples.

In a parallel example, it seems that for all the openness to women in church and ministry on the part of Jesus and Paul, and Acts and John, men mainly occupied the positions of leadership in the communities mentioned in the New Testament.[33] Moreover, as often as the congregation is addressed in New Testament sermons and letters, the appellation used is

31. Pontifical Biblical Commission, "Can Women Be Priests?" p. 92.

32. This is the argument of Karl Rahner, "Women and the Priesthood," in *Concern for the Church*, vol. 20 of Rahner's *Theological Investigations*, trans. Edward Quinn (New York: Crossroad, 1981), 42.

33. However, there is not unanimity on this point. Schuessler-Fiorenza argues in *In Memory of Her* that women did hold positions of leadership in early Christian communities (pp. 175–84). Dunn argues similarly in James D. G. Dunn and James P. Mackey, *New Testament Theology in Dialogue: Christology and Ministry* (Philadelphia: Westminster, 1987), 135.

"brothers."[34] Interpreting this exclusivity on the basis of the reading of the New Testament that I have suggested above, the conclusion is that although women were more freely accepted as active participants in the early Christian communities than in Judaism, there was no clear and consistent break with the general bias that favored men over women for prominent positions in social life. While we can laud the discoveries of recent years that cast a new and more inclusive light on the place of women in the Christian community of the first generations, the truth remains that they were not entirely on a par with men, however Jesus may or may not have treated them.

Another hermeneutical question arises with regard to the interpretation of the epistular texts on the place of women in the liturgical assembly of the faithful. To demonstrate the complexity of the present state of biblical scholarship on women it is useful to single out one text for attention. First Corinthians 14:33-36 is illustrative.

There are basically two approaches to the text. One set of exegetes considers vv. 34–35 to be an interpolation. This contention is based either on textual or theological considerations. C. K. Barrett notes the textual oddity that the phrase "in all the churches" should appear in v. 33b and "in the churches" immediately follow in v. 34a.[35] Jerome Murphy-O'Connor contends that without vv. 34–35 the text "gains in clarity."[36] Murphy-O'Connor also claims that the text is non-Pauline because of its theology. For one thing, Paul was not against women speaking in the assembly; this is clear from 1 Cor. 11:5, which no one finds to be a questionable text. It is also clear from the many instances in which Paul speaks of women as his collaborators in ministry. In addition, the text's use of the law to resolve a problem is not an authority to which Paul would appeal. It is much more likely, according to Murphy-O'Connor, that the author of 1 Timothy inserted these verses into 1 Corinthians 14 to bolster his prohibition in 1 Tim. 2:11-12 of women's interventions at liturgy. Barrett also suggests that the language of vv. 34–35 is so similar to that of 1 Tim. 2:11-12, which seems to be a later work much concerned about church order, that it could have been inserted into the earlier work by the author of the later.[37]

Another group of exegetes argues that the text is authentically Pauline, but a number of various interpretations are offered to determine its mean-

34. I have discovered no instance of the use of "brothers and sisters," and only one instance where a woman is addressed. (Philem. 1:2).

35. C. K. Barrett, A Commentary on the First Epistle to the Corinthians (New York: Harper & Row, 1968), 330.

36. Jerome Murphy-O'Connor, 1 Corinthians (Wilmington, Del.: Michael Glazier, 1982), 133.

37. Barrett, Commentary on the First Epistle to the Corinthians, 332.

ing. Barrett again argues the position of authenticity as equally possible. In this case Paul would be concerned lest the female prophets (or the male prophets in a similar situation) disrupt the assemblies by their excessive interventions. What if husbands and wives should get into public debates! Best that the women be silent. Although Paul issues this injunction it is not that he is opposed in principle to the prophecies of women at liturgy, as 11:5 makes clear. So his command is simply a call for good order. Barrett quotes Calvin similarly: "The discerning reader should come to the decision, that the things which Paul is dealing with here, are indifferent, neither good or bad; and that they are forbidden only because they work against seemliness and edification."[38]

Other exegetes maintain that Paul's injunction is normative not only for the Corinthian community but for all Christian communities at all times. This is the argument of the 1976 Vatican declaration. According to this understanding 1 Cor. 11:5 refers to the situation of women speaking inspired utterances in the Christian assembly; Paul accepts the right of women to do this. On the other hand, 1 Cor. 14:34-35 along with 1 Tim. 2:12 refers to a different situation, namely, official teaching in the assembly; this women are not allowed to do, and not for any cultural reason but as the divine will for all times and congregations.[39]

Elisabeth Schüssler Fiorenza argues that the injunction is restricted to married women.[40] Paul's opinion about married women speaking in the assembly "probably" comes from the Jewish-Hellenistic missionary tradition and the Roman tradition which frowned upon married women speaking in public. It was unseemly. As such it was simply a convention to which Paul was adhering. But why? Because Corinth was notorious for its many cults, some of which involved prophetesses who would work themselves into a frenzy. Paul wanted none of this sort of behavior to mar the dignity of the Christian assembly, so he adopted the strict convention of silence on the part of women in the assembly.

Schüssler Fiorenza admits that we cannot say whether Paul's injunction extends to unmarried women. Perhaps it did not, for Paul had a high regard for the woman who dedicated herself as a virgin for Christ, as we know from 1 Corinthians 7. The women allowed to speak in 11:5 may have been those holier in body and spirit, the unmarried women. In any case, Paul's words do not command women to "subordinate themselves either to the

---

38. Ibid., 333.
39. *Inter Insigniores*, p. 521.
40. Schüssler Fiorenza, *In Memory of Her*, 230–33.

community leadership or to their husbands. It asks simply that they keep quiet and remain subdued in the assembly of the community."

Finally, I mention the exegesis of David W. O'Dell-Scott who also argues for the authenticity of the text and who claims that it "is one of the most emphatic statements *for* female participation in the worship of the church to be found in the New Testament."[41] O'Dell-Scott contends that the accurate interpretation of the text hinges on the particle ἤ *What!* in v. 36. He compares the present text to 1 Cor. 11:22, where, as O'Dell-Scott reads it, Paul uses a similar construction to reject the behavior listed in the sentences just preceding: You do not eat the Lord's Supper; you eat and get drunk while others go hungry.[42] So in 1 Cor. 14:36 Paul uses the particle to reject the behavior listed in the sentences just preceding: You do not allow the women to speak in church; you use old arguments from the law to support your decision; you insist that women wait to ask their husbands at home; you consider it shameful for women to speak in church. Paul will not tolerate this behavior, for its perpetrators think that they have control of God's word or that they are its only recipients.[43]

Theologians and other Christians alike face this confusing plethora of interpretations of many important biblical texts, of which this text about the important question of women's place in the liturgical assembly serves as an example. All the interpretations cannot be correct. Yet how is one to know which to choose? Each has something to commend it. More important, can we make decisions on the basis of our preference for one interpretation or another? That does not seem reasonable, for the situation remains too fluid at the present time to make definitive choices. My own view is that we should appropriate as foundational Jesus' groundbreaking attitude with regard to women and move from there to affirmation of the insignificance for salvation and ministry of the differentiation of humanity into male and female. (This in no way denies that in marriage and parenting the male-female differentiation is of great import.) From that basis we can continue

41. David W. O'Dell-Scott, "Let the Women Speak in Church: An Egalitarian Interpretation of 1 Cor 14:33b-36," *Biblical Theology Bulletin* 13 (1983): 90–93 and 17 (1987), 100–103.

42. The term emphasizes a statement. The New American Bible (1986) does not include any translation of the particle. The Revised Standard Version uses the exclamation "What!" both in 1 Cor. 11:22 and 14:36.

43. Jerome Murphy-O'Connor argues against the interpretations of O'Dell-Scott (agreeing that the particle is a negative disjunctive, but claiming that the rejection is of the practices cited in vv. 26-33) and of Schüssler Fiorenza (claiming that in patriarchal society unmarried women stand in less regard than married) in "Interpolations in 1 Corinthians," *Catholic Biblical Quarterly* 48 (1986): 90–92. O'Dell-Scott replies to Murphy-O'Connor in his 1987 article cited above, n. 41.

to work to be the community of disciples of Jesus, even as we read and live by the thrust of the New Testament, while awaiting more consensus about interpretations of some of the particularly controverted texts.

Arguments against the Ordination of Women

I have pointed out some weaknesses I discern in arguments that claim a theological significance to the incarnation of the second person of the Trinity as male, and the consequent differentiation of roles in the church such that only men are suitable candidates for ordained ministry. Now I turn to the strengths of the argumentation that promotes the differentiation of women and men in ministry.

Once again, there is the biblical data. Jesus chose only men to be included among the Twelve. Women evidently did not fill many positions of leadership in the New Testament communities of which we have some knowledge. Women are not even addressed in the appellations of New Testament letters and sermons.

The 1976 declaration of the Vatican on the ordination of women claims that this data, at least the data on Jesus' choice of the Twelve, has theological significance. While I have suggested that the action of Jesus may be given more theological weight than it deserves, it needs to be said that on the basis of the data itself, given the widely held determination of scholars that Jesus very deliberately supported the equality of women in several instances, and given the context of the generally male leadership of early Christian communities, the argument in favor of Jesus' specific choice of men to be numbered among the Twelve cannot be discounted.

Once one interprets the New Testament texts on the supposition that Jesus purposely chose only men to constitute the Twelve because he had a theological reason in mind, the argumentation follows coherently that the incarnation of the divine Word was male so that he could be the groom in a marriage with his bride, the church, and that the church's insistence on the ordination of men only serves the sound christological function in ministry of providing a fitting symbol of Christ's presence to his bride, the church.

From within this perspective Pope John Paul II defines God's as a "spousal love."[44] Making this love effective for the redemption of the world the Word must and does assume human nature as a man. The sacramental reality that most completely celebrates the redemption Christ effects is the Eucharist.

44. *Mulieris Dignitatem*, art. 26.

Thus, the pope states, "It is the eucharist above all that expresses the re-demptive act of Christ, the bridegroom, toward the church, the bride."

At the present time the argumentation in favor of ordination exclusively for men and that in favor of extending orders to women is, to say the least, unsettled. To offer but one example, *The Tablet* of Feb. 18, 1989 includes two articles on the issue. Adopting argumentation similar to that which I have just recounted in this section, Sara Butler cautions that, on theological grounds, ordination of women may be a most inappropriate Christian deci-sion. Taking up opposite argumentation, Charles Davis contends that there is no theological reason to deny ordination to women, although there may be cultural reasons for doing so.

In the volatile state in which we find ourselves, the wise option is to let the reflection and dialogue that the pope calls for in *Mulieris Dignitatem* go forward as objectively as possible. Let all listen carefully to those who argue positions different from their preference. Let those who speak do so re-spectful of interpreters who honestly differ.

Collaborative Ministry among Women and Men

While recognizing that the issue of women's ordination continues to vex the Christian churches, and after offering my own modest reflections on the issue, I hope that the church will not be paralyzed by the strong feelings that bring sincere and good Christians on both sides of the issue into heated conflict. What I mean by paralysis is that those who oppose the ordination of women do not perpetuate the discrimination against women that continues to exist in church and society, and that those who find the reasons for the ordination of women cogent do not lapse into cynicism with regard to all the possibilities for women to serve in ministerial roles, includ-ing official and decision-making roles especially in church institutions.

Of great importance in continuing to move toward practical equality in church life and ministry is the promotion of collaboration among women and men in the church. It is only when men and women are able to value each other as persons and as Christians, and to appreciate the contributions to communion and conversation that each makes, not so much as woman or man, but as a human being, that the church will be another step closer to being that witness to the world of the new community filled with the Spirit of God's kingdom. What will it take to value each other as persons and to be able to work side by side as the children of God freed from false inhibitions?

For one thing, it is beneficial to subject the tradition that informs present thinking and behavior to a twofold hermeneutic, as Paul Ricoeur invites, one of recovery, which seeks a restoration of meaning, and one of suspicion, which seeks to reduce illusions.[45] Ricoeur writes, "Hermeneutics seems to me to be animated by this double motivation: willingness to suspect, willingness to listen; vow of rigor, vow of obedience."

Each of the previous two chapters has included both moments of a hermeneutics of the tradition. In the present instance we begin by taking note of the hindrances to closer and freer collaboration between women and men in the church. I speak especially of the Roman Catholic church, with which I am familiar. Some hindrances are not hindrances properly so-called; they refer rather to the respectful care that Christian men and women will always want to take when associating with each other so that the natural male-female (and for those to whom it pertains, the male-male and female-female) attraction does not intrude upon Christian commitments to marriage and celibacy (keeping in mind that every unmarried person committed to an evangelical life-style is called to practice celibacy). Obviously, because of the way in which such attraction naturally happens quite spontaneously, it will always be necessary to maintain a good deal of sensitivity and delicacy in the social, including ministerial, relationships of women and men.

Apart from this quite understandable caution, however, there is endemic to Christianity, because of its long historical maintenance not only in the church but generally in society, a division between women and men that often hinders collaboration. The division is rooted in the gratuitous exclusion of women for so long from roles of influence because of the assumption of male supremacy. Because it has so systemically pervaded social thought and action, patriarchalism can forcefully influence utterly good-willed women and men without any awareness thereof on their part. John Paul's challenge with regard to marriage can with good reason be applied to ministerial relationships among men and women: "However, the awareness that in marriage there is mutual 'subjection of the spouses out of reverence for Christ' and not just that of the wife to the husband must gradually establish itself in hearts, consciences, behaviors and customs."[46] Also of great importance is the pope's cogent argument that the domination of women by men is one of the dreadful consequences of humanity's sinfulness, a consequence overcome in principle by the redemptive work of Christ, and exemplified in the dignity of Mary which excels that of every other human being.[47]

45. Paul Ricoeur, *Freud and Philosophy: An Essay on Interpretation* (New Haven: Yale University Press, 1970), 27ff.

46. *Mulieris Dignitatem*, art. 24.

47. Ibid., art. 10–11.

However, even as the arguments of the pope and the feminists coincide to set us on the path out of patriarchalism to mutual deference and collaboration, there are dangers. Feminism can get caught in resentment and the papal argument can retain the vestiges of patriarchalism. A recent book by Anne Carr led me to a collection of essays by French feminists.[48] It is dismaying to come upon the bitter and angry sentiments so deeply lodged in these women. It leads the reader to realize how overwhelming is the hurt that has been sustained by women through centuries of patriarchal social life, including ecclesial life. But if the hurt engenders even more profound divisions just at a time when there is effort in so many quarters to move beyond patriarchy to mutuality, then there is no possibility for anything but paralysis in the social situation.

On the other hand, there is a lingering patriarchalism in the social institutions that are making the effort to change. For example, in *Mulieris Dignitatem* the pope reflects upon Mary, the woman, as the first member of humanity in the new dispensation of grace.[49] Thus she becomes a model of the saved human person, not only female but male as well; however, in particular, she is held up as a model of the feminine.

The pope's purpose in so presenting Mary is to show that sound Christian theology exalts rather than diminishes women, and thus should lead the Christian church out of patriarchalism. Curiously, however, two qualities of Mary's excellence that are promoted militate against the practical dislodgement of patriarchalism. First, Mary's close collaboration with God is so superior to any other human involvement with God that it is hardly applicable in any practical way to the faltering attempts of sinful women and men to live the life of grace; thus, we all, men and women alike, look up to Mary and ask her intercession. We also strive to emulate her, but she remains so far our superior.

Second, in addition to her superiority, Mary's excellence is a matter of profound interiority. Again, this is a quality every sincere Christian tries to emulate, seeking intimate union with the will of God, but it is easily set apart from the actual structures of ecclesiastical life and decisions. The issue of ministry, however, is to involve women and men in the practical service of building up the body of Christ on the basis of conversion. This sort of use of Mary as a paradigm for the relationships of women and men in the church can actually reinforce patriarchalism by promoting a mystification of the feminine that leaves no room for a fully public role for women.

48. Anne E. Carr, *Transforming Grace: Christian Tradition and Women's Experience* (San Francisco: Harper & Row, 1988), n. 30, p. 223, referring the reader to Elaine Marks and Isabelle de Courtivron, eds., *New French Feminisms* (New York: Schocken, 1981).
    49. *Mulieris Dignitatem*, art. 11.

But now I reverse myself and move from a hermeneutic of suspicion to a hermeneutic of recovery. To make the move I continue with the papal reflection on Mary. In a footnote toward the end of his apostolic letter the pope quotes an earlier talk of his which includes a reference to the theology of Hans Urs Von Balthasar on the role of Mary:

> This Marian profile is also—even perhaps more so—fundamental and characteristic for the church as is the apostolic and Petrine profile to which it is profoundly united. . . . The Marian dimension of the church is antecedent to that of the Petrine, without being in any way divided from it or being less complementary. Mary Immaculate precedes all others, including obviously Peter himself and the apostles. This is so, not only because Peter and the apostles, being born of the human race under the burden of sin, form part of the church which is "holy from out of sinners," but also because their triple function has no other purpose except to form the church in line with the ideal of sanctity already programmed and prefigured in Mary. A contemporary theologian has rightly stated that Mary is "queen of the apostles without any pretensions to apostolic powers: She has other and greater powers."[50]

In view of the fact that Mary, with her "other and greater powers," is the model for every sort of Christian living, perhaps Christians of every ministerial category and exercising every ministerial role would do well to downplay the differentiations, prerogatives, and authority attaching to particular ministries. Instead, we might embark upon a more wholesome effort—to encourage the search for holiness as disciples of Christ to blossom in a far richer variety and mutuality of ministries than we have thus far witnessed because we have been too preoccupied with difference, status, and power. Mary's utterly unpretentious openness simply to be of service to the divine will can lead the entire ecclesial community back to its trinitarian grounding. As I read it, this is the pope's actual intention in his letter. What sort of collaboration might ensue?

A collaboration that comes out of communion and conversation with the divine Trinity is a collaboration grounded in an utterly respectful love by each member of each other member of the People of God for their truth as persons. This is the way in which we can glimpse how the three divine persons relate to each other. It is the way in which human beings can best relate as persons created in God's image and likeness. There is never any effort to push oneself forward, nor an effort to belittle the other (usually in order to gain some sort of false superiority). Instead, each is quite content to be herself or himself, and to allow the other to do the same. There is also

50. Ibid., n. 55.

an uncommon effort, for it takes that sort of effort in this age still tainted by original sin, to recognize the truth and value of the other person, especially in her or his contribution to the common good. Moreover, when criticism is called for, as it so often is, there is the unfailing recognition that those who criticize are just as much in need of criticism as those whom they criticize.

At a second level, just as with the Trinity, the members of the church acknowledge diversity in their equality. The three persons of God are distinct individuals whose distinction is in their relationship to each other. So in the church there is distinction of roles, all of them relative to, in the sense of being of service to, the others. Thus, there will be an order in the church, as there is order in God, the divine economy. The first person in God is the principle of the other two. But the other two are not less significant on that account. Their contribution to the divine Trinity is equal to that of the first person. So in the church there are lines of authority, but the authorities also respect those in whose service they have been placed in authority. Nor are those without roles of authority hesitant to obey those in authority. What keeps the authority from being domination and the obedience from being subservience is that, as in the Trinity, there is mutual giving and mutual reception of life, truth, and love. All enjoy communion with each other. There is both give and take, talking and listening, in the extension of the divine-human conversation to the human-human conversation of the members of the church.

Is there any distinction of male and female to be attended to in the collaborative model of Christian ministry? Perhaps. But if so it must be an actuation of a principle formulated by Karl Lehmann: "equal rank and equal dignity for women and men in the recognition of a human existence stamped by diversity."[51] But what would that distinction be? I have argued in this chapter that there are no convincing arguments that advance a theologically significant distinction of male and female in the areas of salvation and ministry in Christ. Theologically grounded diversity in the church community is found rather in the differentiation of roles by reason of charisms, including office. Some of these roles may be taken up more by men and others more by women, but the reason for that lies more in the socio-cultural situation, which is not simply to be discounted, than in any more profound dimension of human reality.

What is of great significance if the church, and finally, we may hope, humanity, is to grow continually more to exist as the image and likeness of

---

51. Karl Lehmann, "The Place of Women as a Problem in Theological Anthropology," *Communio* 10 (1983): 231.

God, is *perichoresis*. Perichoresis, as has been discussed in chapter 2, names the harmonious exchange of life joyfully and continually shared by the three persons of God, such that each person lives totally in and for the others. This transfers to the church as completely generous service of each for all the others without any concern about one's own or the other's greater or lesser significance because, of course, no one is more or less significant than the other. Greater or lesser skill, greater or lesser publicity are irrelevant in the church, or ought to be if a trinitarian theology is the guide for ecclesial life and action. Instead each member of the church delights in the other; each is sorrowful with the other. The more mature are not put off by the less. Those who espouse one perspective on issues (ideology?) do not despise those who espouse another even when emotions run high as exchanges grow heated. For, in the last analysis, all the baptized share a common communion and conversation with the Trinity and therefore a communion and conversation with each other that exists on a deeper level than differing viewpoints. Such a trinitarian theology of collaborative ministry may sound utopian, but it is actually the heart of Christian realism.

What gets in the way of collaborative ministry among men and women, even apart from the issue of ordaining women, are long-ingrained attitudes that keep the domain of men separate from the domain of women. These attitudes are sometimes held unreflectively, in which case men are patronizing, and women allow themselves to be patronized. Sometimes the attitudes are rooted in suspicion and fear, and then they lead to mutual distrust. Gender stereotypes and taboos often underlie these attitudes. In this case people of one gender or the other are perceived to be bent on wielding power over the other, thus putting people of the other gender on the defensive. Gender stereotypes are like racial, ethnic, and class stereotypes, sociocultural realities that can be very stubborn. They are not likely to be replaced under the influence of a theology, but more likely by the persuasion of a trusted authority, or even more likely by the slow, gradual self-correcting process of learning in a practical setting where, in situations small and great, women and men learn to collaborate on the job.

Chapter Five

MUTUAL RECOGNITION OF ORDAINED MINISTRIES

WHILE WINGING HIS WAY NORTH AT THE BEGINNING OF June 1989 to visit the Scandinavian nations, Pope John Paul II was asked by a reporter accompanying him on the plane what concrete steps might best generate a unified Christianity in Scandinavia. "The best solution for ecumenism and for the rapprochement of the churches would be if the pope, the king of Sweden or the king of Norway could go skiing together," John Paul answered.[1] The pope's surprising response alerts us to the importance of friendly personal relations, even having fun together, to the furtherance of serious efforts at reconciliation. When people are comfortable with each other, when they enjoy each other's company, they can talk more openly and honestly about what divides them, and probably with a greater readiness for new insights into possibilities that would otherwise elude them. Acknowledging the value of simple human companionship and exchange, the present chapter nevertheless takes up some of the theological questions involved in mutual recognition of ministries. As with problems discussed previously, the trinitarian qualities of equality, diversity, and mutuality provide a basis for resolution of the impasse regarding mutual recognition.

Is there anything that all Christians hold in common? Increasingly in this century Christians of different denominations have come to acknowledge that they share this one objective: to know and to follow the Lord Jesus, and to live and act so that Jesus' gospel has an influence in the world. Nevertheless, there remain Christians who find it difficult to accept even

---

1. *The National Catholic Reporter,* June 16, 1989, p. 9.

the premise that, however else they may differ, all who choose the name Christian at least want to know and follow Jesus. And there are Christians who, having acknowledged that much common ground, accede little else. So there is no easy or generalized way to deal with the issue of promoting a unified worldwide Christianity.

For that reason the approach of the present chapter is not to attempt to carry on a dialogue with Christians of other persuasions. There are so many groups of Christians who differ more or less from each other that the pages of one volume, let alone one chapter, could not suffice to deal with the varying issues. The attempt of the present chapter is rather to interpret, from a Roman Catholic perspective, a few positions to carry into the dialogue with each other group of Christians. From what I have been able to determine these are the core positions of Roman Catholicism on Christian ministry.[2] Partially, they repeat presentations of previous chapters. However, since a systematic theology for Roman Catholics can assume some things that are accepted within the Roman communion, the present chapter adds positions that need to be made explicit in ecumenical conversations. These positions are statements of what Catholics bring to the dialogue with the hope that other Christians find them truthful and valuable. My concern also is to state the positions in such a way that they further the movement toward mutual recognition of ordained ministries.[3]

A caution is in order. Faith in Jesus Christ held in common does not imply that uniformity among the many Christian churches and ecclesial communities is necessary or even desirable. Although it may not always have seemed so ready to espouse this principle, the Catholic church certainly affirms it in the decree on ecumenism of the Second Vatican Council.[4] Rites, customs, doctrinal and theological formulations are mentioned as areas where diversity can be legitimately countenanced. We could perhaps add structures and doctrines themselves.[5] Conviction about who Jesus is,

2. A source worthy of special mention here is the reception document of the 1982 Faith and Order Paper, *Baptism, Eucharist and Ministry,* by the Roman Catholic church through the Secretariat for Promoting Christian Unity, "Baptism, Eucharist and Ministry: An Appraisal," *Origins* 17 (Nov. 19, 1987); and in vol. 6 of *Churches Respond to BEM,* 1–40.

3. Of course, these issues have been widely discussed in ecumenical conversations among the churches, and often the results of the discussions have been published. The present chapter draws on the fruits of some of these discussions. But the purpose here is to address the issues of mutual recognition of ministry within the context of a trinitarian theology of ministry. It seems to me that the context offers new possibilities for the churches in their pursuit of Christian unity.

4. Art. 16 and 17 of the *Decree on Ecumenism* refer to the Eastern churches, but the principle applies generally.

5. This is one way in which to interpret "hierarchy of truths" in the *Decree on Ecumenism,* art. 11.

what he came to accomplish and what he has accomplished, and what his coming means for the world encompasses the areas mentioned. On some significant issues of church formation and development Jesus is not recorded as having taken a stand, or at least Christians differ about whether he took a stand. Moreover, the churches of the New Testament themselves were not unanimous or uniform in belief and practice.[6]

Baptism, the Sacrament of Unity, the Ground of Ministry

It would be too much to claim unanimity on the part of Christians that baptism is the initiating sacrament that unites all who put their faith in Jesus. Some Christian communities accept only their own baptisms. There are communities that do not put much emphasis upon baptism by water and the invocation of the Trinity; these instead emphasize "Spirit baptism." But it is not an exaggeration to attribute to the majority of Christians the understanding that baptism unites in a common faith Christians of even widely differing denominations. Mutual recognition of each other's baptisms is common among the ecclesial communities.

The sacramental character of baptism emphasizes the human, visible dimension of the People of God. Neither a secret society nor a society divorced from the rest of human affairs, the church is animated interiorly, invisibly by the Holy Spirit, but also has a clearly demarcated existence within public human life. Thus, all those who are baptized by water and the invocation of the Trinity have entered into communion with one another.[7] Whatever the differences dividing them from one another, the baptized have something to say and do together in the world in the name of Jesus the Lord.

One way of expressing the communion of all the baptized is in the vocabulary of ministry. For the same baptism which publicly identifies Christians of diverse stripes as nevertheless belonging to a single Christian communion also is the reason for a responsibility all Christians share, namely, to be servants with Jesus the servant of humanity. Jesus gave his life so that human beings could be freed from the shackles that bind their spirits. Christians of every denomination, by virtue of the faith into which they have been baptized, need to participate in the mission of the church. Since their Christian being is to be in communion, so their ministry is best enacted in communion as cooperation.

6. On this point see Yves Congar, *Diversity and Communion* (Mystic, Conn.: Twenty-Third, 1985), 9–11.
7. See the *Decree on Ecumenism*, art. 3.

Happily, the Christian community effected by baptism is already being lived out by innumerable Christians both in mutual communion and in co-operation, especially in ways that often seem small and are unsung. How many individual Christians of different denominations join with one another in their neighborhoods, in their nations, and internationally in service of the promotion of gospel values within their society! Taizé, Mother Teresa's ministry in Calcutta, and Chautauqua in New York state come to mind as major instances of ecumenical Christian community and ministry. The spirit of ministry in this sense has been significantly furthered by the ecumenical movement.

Perhaps when we reflect upon Christian unity this dimension of flourishing cooperation, which never died out completely even in the times of worst division among Christians, is often overlooked as if it were not actually a most important witness to the love of Christ active among us. The quiet service that a small group of people initiates spontaneously can appear to be so insignificant when one thinks of the global dimension of the problem of divided Christianity. And yet such cooperation witnesses to reconciliation which has taken place on the level where people live their lives with one another, no matter how long and tortuous the process may be for healing to take place on the institutional level.

Indeed, such cooperation is sometimes a witness that no reconciliation needed to take place since no division had occurred on that level. For often enough the division is institutional. But all life is not lived institutionally, and many Christians are united in their efforts in service of the gospel on the level of interpersonal and small-group relations.

It is important in this connection to keep in mind that the parish is a remarkable segment of the institutional church. For at the same time as it is clearly an institutional reality, the parish is also, in so many instances, the scene of thriving ecumenical activity which can go on almost oblivious to the trying divisions on the institutional level.

Episcopal Leadership as the Guarantor of Apostolic Tradition and Succession

Whatever its ability to go forward in a certain unified manner despite the divisions that plague the institutional church, Christian life, whether communal or individual, cannot simply divorce itself from questions of order and jurisdiction. These are theological realities, too. So much is this the case that the sacrament of Baptism itself is normally celebrated, according to the conviction of the Catholic church, by a minister so deputed by proper church authority. Even when an extraordinary minister of baptism is the administrator of the sacrament the action takes place with a connection to the local church and under the bishop who is the steward of the mysteries of God.[8]

The issue, then, of the reality and role of episcopal oversight to which are intimately connected priestly ordination and Petrine ministry is the most vexing when it comes to Catholic involvement in ecumenical discussions that seek to advance the possibility of mutual recognition of ministries among the churches. To these three issues we now turn our attention, and first to that of episcopal leadership as the guarantor of apostolic tradition and succession. For upon this issue not only the other two depend, but also the legitimation of the ministries of word, sacrament, and care.[9]

As has been discussed in chapter 3 of the present work, a ministry of leadership arose at the start of the community of disciples of Jesus and has continued since. The New Testament gives witness to the emergence of at least two models of leadership during the apostolic age, that of the single individual who bears a certain responsibility of oversight, and that of a council of elders who perform that function. How long and in how many local churches each type of leadership, and perhaps others, continued cannot be determined on the basis of data in extant documents of the period. But before long Clement of Rome's *Letter to the Corinthians* and Ignatius of Antioch's letters to the churches of Asia Minor testify to leadership by a single bishop with a presbyteral council and offer reasons for this form of government.

In both writings the bishop's leadership of the church functions as the vehicle by which Christ and his gospel continue to be verifiably effective in the Christian community as its historical life proceeds beyond the life spans of the disciples who actually sat at Jesus' feet. The Lima Paper of the Faith and Order Commission (No. 111) of the World Council of Churches summarizes the position of these works thus:

> In the early Church the bond between the episcopate and the apostolic community was understood in two ways. Clement of Rome linked the mission of the bishop with the sending of Christ by the Father and the sending of the apostles by Christ (Cor. 42:44). This made the bishop a successor of the apostles, ensuring the permanence of the apostolic mission in the Church.

---

8. See *Lumen gentium*, art. 21.

9. Since oversight (*episcopé*) is already in some way a part of the structure of all ecclesial groups, it obviously becomes a starting position to relate to issues of episcopal leadership and to seek points of contact with the way that oversight is implemented on the part of the ecclesial dialogue partners.

Clement is primarily interested in the means whereby the *historical* continuity of Christ's presence is ensured in the Church thanks to the apostolic succession. For Ignatius of Antioch (Magn. 6: 1, 3: 1–2; Trall. 3: 1), it is Christ surrounded by the Twelve who is permanently in the Church in the person of the bishop surrounded by the presbyters. Ignatius regards the Christian community assembled around the bishop in the midst of presbyters and deacons as the *actual* manifestation in the Spirit of the apostolic community. The sign of apostolic succession thus not only points to historical continuity; it also manifests an actual spiritual reality.[10]

By the end of the second century church apologists claim to have evidence of the succession of bishops from the Twelve themselves.[11] To a great extent the gnostic movement was the occasion for the effort to authenticate authority in the church. Whose teaching was to be trusted: the gnostics or their opponents? Lists of the successors of the apostles, one following the other, in several local churches, was one way to authenticate the authority of the opponents of gnostic interpretations of the Christian way. While it cannot be argued that each name on the list was that of a person specifically called a bishop, bishops were looked upon as the successors of these apostolic successors whose names appeared in the lists.

Succession, then, was not significant for its own sake. Its importance was to function as an assurance of fidelity on the part of a local church to the teaching the apostles received from the Lord and handed on to their successors in the office of oversight. No one expresses this more clearly than Irenaeus:

> It is clear to all who wish to see the truth that the tradition of the apostles is manifest throughout the whole world in every Church, and we can list those who have been established as bishops in the church by the apostles, including their successors up to ourselves, and who neither taught nor even knew of any such thing as is being madly ranted about by these people. For if the apostles had known recondite mysteries, which they separately taught to the perfect while keeping it from the rest, they would most especially have handed them on to those to whom they were committing the Churches themselves. For they wanted those whom they left behind as their successors to be utterly perfect and blameless in all things, handing on to them their own role of teachers of these things. If these successors outstandingly fulfilled

---

10. *Baptism, Eucharist and Ministry* (Geneva: World Council of Churches, 1982), 29 n. 36.

11. See Walter J. Burghardt, "Apostolic Succession: Notes on the Early Patristic Era," in Paul C. Empie and T. Austin Murphy, eds., *Eucharist and Ministry*, vol. 4 of *Lutherans and Catholics in Dialogue* (Minneapolis: Augsburg, 1979), 174. See also, in the same volume, James F. McCue, "Apostles and Apostolic Succession in the Patristic Era," 156–58.

their role it would be something of great use; but if they were to fall away it would be a great disaster. [12]

It is not possible to line up exactly how Christians of the first and second centuries determined just what constituted the tradition and what were aberrations. Certainly living memory was an important criterion for some time. This was transmitted orally. But tradition was also connected with the Scriptures, which originally meant the Old Testament. [13] What was transmitted was the event of Jesus Christ, the good news of his life, death, and resurrection. The tradition handed on this event not only by repeating what had happened but also by interpreting and reinterpreting its meaning within the new circumstances of each particular moment of the church's existence.

As contemporary Christians come to recognize more adequately how doctrines and church life developed, it is possible to trace the emergence of new things along with the preservation of old as the tradition moves along from one moment to the next. For example, study of the development of the trinitarian and christological doctrines uncovers the process by which new dimensions of the event of Jesus Christ were brought forth on the way to Nicea and Chalcedon. Routes are taken that might not have been taken; routes that might have been taken are not chosen. At a later time there is opportunity to correct and expand.

Since tradition, then, does not mean handing on exactly, without any change, what Jesus said and did or exactly what the apostolic church chose to do, how is the church to determine which new things are developments and which aberrations? This is the problem the church faced as the power of the gnostic movement increased. The answer that became universally adopted was to interconnect tradition and succession. Implicit in the witness of these first- and second-century authors is the mutual reenforcement of succession and tradition in the church. And the "ecclesial subject" upon whom rests the responsibility of maintaining both is the persons responsible for leadership of the churches, namely, the bishops.

Catholics maintain that the interdependence of episcopal succession and catholic tradition is rooted in God's will for the church. It is not simply a matter of ancient custom; that would not be sufficient cause to commit the church so steadfastly to continuance of that structure. Rather, whereas historians have determined the fact that the early development of the mu-

---

12. Irenaeus of Lyons, *Adversus Haereses*, Book III, 3.1.

13. See Yves M.-J. Congar, *Tradition and Traditions: An Historical and a Theological Essay* (London: Burns & Oates, 1966; originally published 1960), 30–31; and Christian Duquoc, *Dieu différent: Essai sur la symbolique trinitaire* (Paris: Cerf, 1978), 61.

tual reenforcement of tradition and succession was occasioned by early problems, notably the threat of gnostic interpretations of the event of Jesus Christ, the Catholic position maintains that the truth is more than the fact. The theological truth is that the tradition-succession pattern emerged as the divinely instituted order of church life. Expressed otherwise, the joint existence of succession guaranteeing the tradition and the tradition being maintained through succession is essential to authentic reception and implementation of the gospel.

The theological meaning of the apostolic succession going forward jointly with the apostolic tradition is the preservation of ecclesial communion. The church is the participation of the baptized faithful in the communion of the divine Trinity. All the members are active in the ecclesial communion. All are the subjects of faith in the Christ-event; all celebrate and are nourished in this faith through the sacramental liturgies of the church. All are called to serve the church's mission of conversation and communion.

To repeat, communion is the way in which the Christian ethos receives and expresses the order of God brought into human history by the divine missions of Word and Spirit and extended beyond that historical moment of incarnation through the church. According to the trinitarian order communicated to the church every member is equal to every other in the faith. All are blessed in the absolute love of God. But there is diversity of service within the one life and mission of the church.

Diversity in church order includes the ministry of the bishop who functions within the local church as the sacramental representative of Christ, the church's absolute head. The bishop is the hierarch, the sacred source, sacramentally, of the divine life of the church. Of course, the bishop does not replace Christ, always rather standing under Christ as the Word of God. Nor is the bishop any less a disciple of Christ than every other baptized member of the church. Still, in the human order of communion the bishop functions as head.

The bishop is the guarantor of communion on the local level.[14] He is the chief teacher, the chief liturgist, and the governor of the local church. While the bishop shares the ministry of word, sacrament, pastoring, and care with the presbyters and baptized members of the church over which he presides, and while the other members are free to initiate ministry in

---

14. Severino Dianich claims that the churches of the Reformation also understand ordination to establish its recipients in a ministry of oversight for the sake of unity among the faithful. See his "Sacramento e Carisma," in Giustino Farnedi and Philippe Rouillard, eds., *Il Ministero Ordinato nel Dialogo Ecumenico* (Roma: S. Anselmo, 1985), 60.

various areas, it is the bishop's role to legitimate all the ministry that goes on within the local church.

Moreover, communion exists not just within the local church but among the many local churches throughout the world. The guarantor of communion among the many local churches is the college of bishops. Collegiality is expressed through ordination, letters and consultations, and synods. Bishops may be nominated in several ways (by the pope, the head of state, the faithful whom they will lead, vote of the clergy), but only another bishop ordains a newly nominated bishop who is then welcomed into episcopal ministry by the bishops of the surrounding churches. Bishops consult with one another on matters of importance to their pastoring, often, at the present time, through regional and national conferences. Synods of bishops and ecumenical councils are more solemn ways of expressing episcopal collegiality.

If examined simply from a logical viewpoint, it stands as something of a circular argument to claim that the Christian tradition is authentic by showing that it is taught by bishops enjoying apostolic succession and to claim that succession is apostolic because it remains faithful to the rule of faith (*regula fidei*) of the tradition as it is maintained by the episcopal college. Nevertheless, neither side of the equation is superior to the other; the balance is what is important. For this reason, despite the fact that a divinely constituted church order is being implemented, agreement by the college of bishops about a point of tradition, including the resolution of disagreements, becomes most credible when the usual procedures of right thinking (the transcendental method discussed in chapter 1, which is a particular meaning of orthodoxy) remain in force throughout the process of study, consultation, discussion, and formulation that lead to the agreement.

Indeed, I would say that since the same God who wills the tradition-succession balance also creates the human mode of arriving at meaning, truth, and value, the members of the episcopal college ought to be especially devoted to rigorous pursuit of the dynamic process of understanding, reflection, and evaluation, including consultation of the entire people of God whose religious experience and intelligent, reasonable, and responsible fidelity to the gospel of Christ count for a great deal within the communion that is the church. This is not to say that the faithful are constitutive of the teaching authority, that is, authorship, within the church. But it is to say that teachers who do not consult, on a wide basis, sincere and genuine, thoughtful and reasonable Christian faithful who seek to love God with their whole heart, soul, mind, and strength would be failing in some measure to fulfill their responsibilities.

Having sketched the Catholic position on the bishop's ministry of oversight in the church, the question naturally emerges about what can be done to bring about unity among the churches in this important aspect of communion. A first approach to dealing with this question seeks to clarify again the problem that led to the loss of the succession-tradition balance at the time of the sixteenth-century Reformation. Lutheran participants in the Lutheran-Catholic dialogues held in the United States hint at the problem in the joint statement on Eucharist and ministry: "It is to be noted . . . that the Lutheran confessions indicate a preference for retaining the traditional episcopal order and discipline of the church, and express regret that no bishop was willing to ordain priests for evangelical congregations."[15]

At first reading the problem is that no bishop at the time of the Reformation would take the step of welcoming into his presbyterate, or into the episcopal college, anyone holding the positions of the reformers. But the underlying problem is the differing interpretation of this action and its consequences. Catholics would claim that the bishops insisted upon fidelity to church communion, which the reformers were breaking up. Lutherans would claim that if Catholic bishops would not ordain the reformers, then fidelity to the authentic tradition outweighed the preservation of succession; pastors would have to assume the responsibility of handing on the ministry of pastoring to their successors.

The chief doctrinal disputes of the time—priesthood of all believers versus the priesthood of the ordained, as well as justification by faith versus justification through the church's sacramental ministry and the good works of believers—were serious enough, but contemporary dialogues have evidenced how much these disputes can be resolved through careful discussion on the part of faith-filled Christians.

The passions that prevented careful discussion at the time were engendered not only by doctrinal differences but also by deep-seated corruption in church office. For example, a major part of the dispute on indulgences into which Luther inserted himself in 1517 was the debacle over succession in the archbishopric of Mainz:

> The Archbishop died in 1505, and in order to save the expenses involved in electing and then in providing for a new archbishop the seat was left vacant for eight years. It was then filled in an election of extraordinary irregularity. Twenty-three-year-old Prince Albrecht Hohenzollern of Brandenburg, who was already Archbishop of Magdeburg and administrator of the diocese of Halberstadt, was elected in addition to his existing benefices. He had been under age for Magdeburg according to Canon Law, and he was still under age

---

15. "Eucharist and Ministry: A Lutheran-Roman Catholic Statement," in Empie and Murphy, eds., *Eucharist and Ministry*, 15.

for Mainz. He had had to pay a great fine to Rome in order to get approval of the former; a further great fine was payable again for approval of the latter; a fine of 21,000 ducats for the appointment, and one of 10,000 ducats for wrongly accumulating ecclesiastical offices. This was money lent to him by the banking house of Fugger. It was to be repaid from cash collected by means of the preaching of an Indulgence which would encourage the faithful to do the good work of subscribing to church funds. Half of the proceeds would go to the building of St. Peter's Basilica in Rome (the present building) and half to the Fuggers, as the Archbishop's repayment. [16]

While the details of the dealings over the archbishopric of Mainz were not known to all, there was enough of this and other situations in the air to scandalize the faithful who cared to think about it. This is hardly the sort of behavior that would inspire a lofty view of the episcopal office as the guarantor of communion. In addition, without going into specific historical instances it is obvious that other abuses abounded. Otherwise the Council of Trent would not have to issue a canon of reform instructing that care be taken to choose suitable candidates for the office of bishop. [17] Other canons which set about reforming the episcopal order give evidence of other serious failures on the part of bishops. Many did not preach to or teach the faithful entrusted to their care. [18] Indeed, often bishops who were appointed only for the sake of the income to be derived from the benefice failed to reside in their dioceses, never really exercising any pastoral care. [19] Intrinsically connected with this problem was the abuse of possessing more than one benefice, as we have seen with Prince Albrecht who was at the same time archbishop of Magdeburg and Mainz. [20]

It is not difficult to appreciate that abuses such as these were serious obstacles to respect for episcopal office on the part of those Christian faithful who were aware of them. It was in desperation that Luther turned to the civic rulers of the day for some help in righting the wrongs he observed, since there was no hope of getting help from the bishops, themselves caught in the mire of corruption. When, then, it came time to find successors for themselves the reformers could not expect to find bishops eager to offer their services for ordination, nor would the reformers want to be

16. John M. Todd, *Luther: A Life* (New York: Crossroad, 1982), 14–15; see also 99f.

17. *Decretum de reformatione*, sess. XXIV, can. I, in G. Alberigo et al., eds., *Conciliorum oecumenicorum decreta* (Bologna: Istituto per le Scienze Religiose, 1973), 759.

18. Ibid., can. III (p. 762 in Alberigo).

19. *Decretum de residentia episcoporum et aliorum inferiorum*, sess. VI, cap. I (pp. 681–82 in Alberigo).

20. *Decretum de reformatione*, sess. XXIV, can. XVII (pp. 769–70 in Alberigo), which is a supplement to can. XIV forbidding the purchase of an office.

drawn into the corruption of the ecclesiastical system of the time since their very protest was against the system.

However, the corruption that prevailed at the time of the Reformation no longer prevails. Contemporary bishops cannot be accused of the abuses that afflicted the episcopal office in the first decades of the sixteenth century. The situation is so different in our own time that the church is clearly at a different stage in the development of the episcopacy as the guarantor of ecclesial communion.

Nor is development at an end. Increasingly bishops are seeking to be more faithful disciples of Jesus: intensifying their spirituality, seeking theological competence, collaborating with their clergy, consulting the members of the local church entrusted to their pastoral guidance. Is not this ongoing transformation of the episcopal office an invitation to Christians who currently do not recognize the episcopal order of communion to take another look?

To recognize that the corruption of the Middle Ages has been overcome is not to imply that further transformation in the exercise of oversight by the local bishop is not necessary. For if the bishop is genuinely to be a servant of the local church even as its leader, then some sort of accountability to the church needs to be put in place. I am not suggesting new structures with all the committee work and reams of paper that would thus be generated. Accountability is also an attitude, one that the person committed to service quite naturally possesses. But accountability can be fostered as well.

For one thing it might be good to return in some way to seek the consent of the faithful in the election of the local bishop. Again, the most obvious way, by means of a vote, may not be the most desirable way. But consultation with the clergy and laity (and not only in secret) and respect for the results of the consultation would give the entire local church a greater sense of its endowment with the Holy Spirit, and it would give the bishop a greater sense of his responsibility to be accountable to the faithful. Episcopalians, Lutherans, and other churches have already and for a long time paved the way in this regard.

In another area, the episcopal order can be further transformed along the lines of inviting more participation in the life of the local church. While church documents of these latter years of the twentieth century solidly stand by the affirmation that the Holy Spirit graces all the faithful, and that every member of the faithful has something to offer the promotion of the mission of the church, so much initiative remains in the hands of the bishops, either theoretically or because of long years of institutionally promoted inertia on the part of the majority of the baptized, that the imagination needed for greater participation in matters of faith simply is not spontaneously forthcoming. The bishops need to become more convinced about the potential of every member of the church, and the bishops need to take more initiative to change structures that keep the faithful out of the active realms of church life.

The Ordained Priesthood

Chapter 3 includes a survey of the doctrinal development of the sacramental character that distinguishes the priestly character of the order of bishop, as well as of the order of presbyter, from the priestly character of the baptized. The same chapter also proposes how it is possible to employ the method of theology articulated by Bernard Lonergan to transform theological understanding of sacramental character from one that is based on metaphysical analysis to one that is based on intentionality analysis. Both the history of the doctrinal development and the transformation of the theological understanding of character into intentional categories can contribute to a historically conscious interpretation of the Second Vatican Council's much discussed statement on the two participations in the priesthood:

> Now the common priesthood of the faithful and the ministerial or hierarchical priesthood, although they differ in essence and not only in degree, are nevertheless ordered to each other; for they participate each in its own peculiar way in the one priesthood of Christ.[21]

From its specifically ecumenical perspective the Lima Document of 1982 also acknowledges two distinctive ways of sharing in the priesthood of Jesus:

> Jesus Christ is the unique priest of the new covenant. Christ's life was given as a sacrifice for all. Derivatively, the Church as a whole can be described as a priesthood. All members are called to offer their being "as a living sacrifice" and to intercede for the Church and the salvation of the world. Ordained ministers are related, as are all Christians, both to the priesthood of Christ, and to the priesthood of the Church. But they may appropriately be called priests because they fulfil a particular priestly service by strengthening and building up the royal and prophetic priesthood of the faithful through word and sacraments, through their prayers of intercession, and through their pastoral guidance of the community.[22]

---

21. *Lumen gentium*, art. 10.
22. *Baptism, Eucharist and Ministry*, 23 n. 17.

Roman Catholic doctrine on the priesthood of bishops and presbyters maintains that ordination by a bishop in communion of succession and tradition is required for authentic conferral of the character of ministerial priesthood. This requirement accords with the meaning of the church as a communion of which bishops are the guarantors, for the priest's specific role is, on the part of bishops, to exercise the ministry of oversight of word, sacrament, and care in a local church and, on the part of presbyters, to exercise that ministry for a portion of the local church. The meaning of the requirement is that the trinitarian communion of equality, diversity, and mutuality, in God and analogously in the church, includes order.

Intrinsic to the sacramental character of episcopal and presbyteral order is presidency over word and sacrament. Ecclesial communion is eminently expressed in the celebration of the Eucharist, which effectively brings the Trinity's action of redemption to bear upon the assembly of the faithful gathered for the liturgy of the Lord's Supper.[23] Since the bishop is guarantor and guide of communion, nowhere is the church more visibly present than in those eucharistic celebrations of the local church presided over by the bishop.[24] Within the smaller assemblies of the faithful for worship within the local church, ordained presbyters preside over the eucharistic liturgy.

The epiclesis of the eucharistic prayer makes clear that it is the Holy Spirit whose power effects the presence of the risen Lord at each celebration of the Lord's Supper. But the reality of communion, supported by the joint guarantors of tradition and succession, requires that the Eucharist not be presided over simply by a member of the faithful chosen from the congregation. Not anyone may use the words of Christ and invoke the Holy Spirit to bring about the saving presence of Christ. Only one of the faithful ordained to represent Christ before the assembled faithful has the ability to fulfill this role.[25]

Administration of the sacrament of penance and reconciliation also requires the agency of the ordained priest. Again, it is the local bishop who legitimates the restoration of every sinner to communion with the body of the faithful. Reconciliation is not simply a matter between the individual and God, for life with God in Christ is life carried out concretely with one's fellow Christians in ecclesial communion. And while it is commendable and

23. For a more extended development of this statement, see the Second Vatican Council, *Constitution on the Sacred Liturgy*, arts. 6, 7.

24. See *Lumen gentium*, art. 26.

25. C. J. Dumont deals with these issues of tradition, succession, and sacramental ministry at length in his criticism of the 1973 agreement-statement of the Group of Les Dombes in "Eucharistie et ministères: A propos des 'Accords des Dombes,' Essai de critique constructive," *Istina* 18 (1973): 155–207.

to be encouraged that individual Christians confess to and become reconciled with one another, still that is not the same as reconciliation with the whole church. For ecclesial communion is not simply a matter of interiority, although it is certainly that, but it is also and essentially a public communion. Sacramental order is one expression of the public dimension of ecclesial communion. Thus, the bishop and presbyters ordained by bishops preside over the sacrament of penance and reconciliation.

Character expresses the affirmation of faith that episcopal and presbyteral order in word, sacrament, and pastoring is not merely a set of functions God has established for the sake of orderly organization of the Christian people. Character expresses the faith that order, like baptismal regeneration, is relational intentionality as a way of being. It has an ontological quality. By means of conferral of the sacrament of orders and of the sacraments of baptism and confirmation, new ways of relating to the triune God and to the already baptized faithful are publicly confirmed. Moreover, they remain a permanent possibility for those who have been baptized and ordained. By the sacramental character conferred in baptism, confirmation, and ordination human subjects can follow through with new interpersonal relations with God and with their fellow human beings.

Whether in each instance the baptized or ordained subject implements her or his character, and the extent to which the character's potential is implemented, depend on further factors, both environmental and personal. Thus, some baptized persons use every means at their disposal to live out of their baptismal character in love of God and love of neighbor as vital disciples of Jesus. Other baptized persons move in and out of active faith. Others drop away altogether. Sometimes not the personal choice of the baptized, but rather the family, neighborhood, or parish environment exercises the chief influence to promote fidelity or to keep a person ignorant of baptismal opportunities and responsibilities.

The same is true of ordination. While the sacramental character of orders remains as a "characteristic" of the subject, the ordained person may not implement the order received because of a personal choice not to do so (resignation, retirement) or because of an institutional decision (suspension, excommunication). If, at some future time, the ordained Christian returns to the exercise of the ordained priesthood, there is no need for a second ordination. Confirmation of the return by the church suffices because the character to perform ordained ministry has never ceased to be present during the period of inactivity.

Why did the reformers reject the ordained priesthood as it existed in the Roman Catholic church of the sixteenth century? The judgment of the reformers was that the system of ordained priesthood was a usurpation of power that belonged only to Christ and his Holy Spirit and that the system forced the suppression of the right of all the baptized to function as a priestly people. With regard to the first judgment, it was possible to point to the granting of indulgences as a power play by the ordained ministry to control God's gracious gift of forgiveness and reconciliation. Administration of the sacraments, too, was viewed as unevangelical priestly control of the channels of grace.

The Roman church seemed to think that bishops and priests wielded the power of salvation. The preachers of indulgences, for example, functioned as ministers of the word of God who promoted this manipulative viewpoint. It was God who saved, but it was the priests who chose how and to whom to dispense God's salvation. So much did this seem to be the prevailing religious view that administration of the sacraments and quasi-sacramental rites of pilgrimages and with relics became regarded with an awe accorded magic.

In such a situation of abuse, the legitimate, instrumental agency of the church's ordained ministry became severely obscured. The entire enterprise seemed to be aberrant. And since it was so entrenched, the possibility of reformation of the ordained ministry of the Roman church was no longer deemed by the reformers to be possible. So what was called at the time "the new faith" (*die neue Glaube*) began to take shape.

On a second front the reformers judged that the Roman church denigrated the priesthood of all believers, which conferred the ability to have direct access to the mercy of God through faith in Jesus, to offer spiritual sacrifices, and to give witness to the word of God. Inordinate emphasis upon the ordained priesthood had pushed the priesthood of the faithful into desuetude. Simply baptized people of the sixteenth century could find it difficult to look upon themselves as endowed with any significant Christian dignity. To be really a Christian one had to profess vows as a religious. Even better, one would seek orders, if one were male. Nor was the order of deaconate of much value except as a stepping-stone to priesthood, since the deaconate is not a priestly order.

The reformers inveighed bitterly against this failure to take baptism seriously. In their writings they sought to restore baptism as the preeminent Christian sacrament of entrance into company with Christ, and indeed faith in the redeeming word of God as primary. The church's hierarchical organization and sacramental system was rejected as unfaithful to the gospel. The visible church itself was more modestly viewed as the organization of the new People of God. Some of the reformers viewed the church's ordained ministry as divinely willed, and some viewed it as a humanly determined office whose value was merely functional.

One of the disadvantages under which both Protestant and Catholic re-formers of the sixteenth century labored was the lack of a well-developed and generally available ecclesiology. In fact, the crisis generated by the Reformation served as the catalyst for the full-scale inauguration of theological reflection on the church. The lack of an adequate ecclesiology unfortunately limited the efforts of the reformers of either the Catholic or the Protestant camps to work out questions of ministry, and it hampered their ability to carry on any sort of fruitful dialogue with one another.

Fortunately, ecclesiology has been one of the areas most thoroughly developed by theologians in the nineteenth and twentieth centuries. As a result ecumenical dialogues among the churches are increasingly sorting out the problematic raised by the reformers in their rejection of ministerial priesthood. For their part, the bishops of the Second Vatican Council and Catholic theologians have been able to work out a more successful understanding of the doctrine of the instrumental agency of ministry and of the distinction and interrelationship between baptized and ordained ministries. Movement on both the Catholic and ecumenical fronts continues its slow but steady pace.

Contemporary Catholic response to the twofold problematic of the reformers regarding the ordained priesthood can take the following form: The primary reality to which the term "priesthood" applies is the priestly reality of the one unique high priest, Jesus. The priestly work of Christ is the radical principle of redemption and of the formation of the community of disciples. Christ is thus the head of the church. Relative to the priesthood of Jesus, the ordained priesthood is analogical. The priest is ordained to act as a sacramental instrument of the priestly work of Christ by forming and guiding the community of the faithful by means of word, sacrament, and pastoral care.

The baptized, whose life in Christ is served by the ministrations of ordained bishops and presbyters, are filled with the Holy Spirit of Jesus to be corporately and individually a priestly people. Their participation in the priesthood of Christ is not that of orders; they do not form and guide the community as ordained priests do. The baptized are commissioned to bring the sanctifying priestly power of Jesus the one high priest to bear upon the multiple situations in which human beings constitute the world: marriage and family, civil government, education, law, medicine, the arts, agriculture, the trades and professions, all the activities that occupy human beings socially and individually.

Both the ordained and the baptized participate in the priestly mission of the Lord Jesus to bring God to the world and to bring the world to encounter God, to constitute the human world in conversation and communion

with the triune God. Both are real participants in the unique priesthood of
Christ, so that the ordained as well as the baptized are instruments of Christ
in the world.

Ministry of the Bishop
of Rome to Worldwide
Ecclesial Communion

As early as the claim for the mutual guarantee of Christian fidelity by apostolic tradition and apostolic succession, there is also a claim for the
unique role of the church at Rome. When Irenaeus of Lyons offered a list of
the succession in a local church, he chose the church of Rome. In his opinion, he did not make an arbitrary choice, but chose Rome because, as he
said, the church of Rome is the greatest and most ancient church, the one
known to all, the one founded and formed by the apostles Peter and Paul.
Irenaeus goes on to insist that "it is necessary that every church, that is, the
faithful everywhere, agree with this church because of its superior origin.
In [the church of Rome] the apostolic tradition has always been preserved
for the faithful everywhere."[26]

It is not surprising from a historical perspective that the church at Rome
should assume a certain eminence in the early centuries of Christianity.
Rome was the center of the empire. Much would be happening at the political center of the world, which would invite church life to gravitate there,
too. In addition to a political eminence, however, the church of Rome took
on an evangelical superiority among the churches.[27] Irenaeus provides some
of the specifically religious reasons for Rome's ascendancy: it was believed
to be the church founded by Peter and Paul, and (for this reason?) it was a
church that could be counted on to be in touch with the apostolic tradition.

Granting a certain eminence to Rome does not mean that other local
churches thought of themselves as dependent on Rome. Other local
churches acted on their own initiative. Moreover, when disputes arose
among the churches, tension was sometimes generated between Rome and
other churches without the non-Roman churches considering themselves
to be unfaithful. Disputing churches certainly did not always accede to the
demands of the church of Rome, as, for example, in the Easter controversy
between Pope Victor and the Eastern churches. Nevertheless, there was a

---

26. *Adversus haereses*, III, 3, 2.

27. See James F. McCue, "The Roman Primacy in the Patristic Era: The Beginnings Through
Nicea," in Paul C. Empie, T. Austin Murphy, and Joseph A. Burgess, eds., *Papal Primacy and the
Universal Church*, vol. 5 of *Lutherans and Catholics in Dialogue* (Minneapolis: Augsburg, 1974), 58–
72.

unique respect for the church of Rome on the part of the other churches both East and West.

The decretals of the bishops who presided over the church of Rome at the end of the fourth century forge further the personal primacy of the Roman bishops. Siricius began what became a customary way of expressing a Petrine function for the universal ecclesial communion: "We—or rather, the blessed apostle Peter in us, who, as we trust, protects and keeps us in everything as the heirs of his government—bear the burdens of all those that are burdened."[28]

By the time of Leo I the churches recognize a universal ministry on the part of the bishop of Rome. The Council of Chalcedon (451) accepts Leo's *Tome* on the christological questions of the day with the declaration that has become famous: "This is the faith of the fathers; this is the faith of the apostles; this is the faith of all of us; Peter has spoken through Leo."[29] At the same time, the Council of Chalcedon also endorsed a certain authoritative primacy of Constantinople over the churches of the East, in some ways comparable to that of Rome in the West. Tension between Rome and Constantinople continued intermittently until the open breaks of the ninth and eleventh centuries. (Fortunately, Patriarch Athenagoras and Pope Paul VI officially began a healing process in 1965 when they rescinded the mutual excommunications that had been in effect since 1045.)

A third central moment in the movement toward the primacy of the bishop of Rome in the universal church was the papacy of Gregory I (590–604). By the time of Gregory civil authority in the Roman Empire had eroded to the extent that the bishop of Rome, patriarch of the entire western portion of the empire, had to assume not only the spiritual leadership but also civil leadership, especially in the Italian peninsula. This combination of spiritual and temporal jurisdiction quite naturally added to the sense of papal primacy. Gregory forged an accompanying theology to bolster his position, so much so that Jaroslav Pelikan writes of Gregory's tenure as "the significant turning point for the papacy."[30] Gregory expresses the Petrine ministry this way: "To all who know the Gospel it is obvious that by the voice of the Lord the care of the entire church was committed to the holy apostle and prince of all the apostles, Peter. . . ."[31]

28. Arthur Carl Piepkorn, "The Roman Primacy in the Patristic Era: From Nicea to Leo the Great," in Empie, Murphy, and Burgess, eds., *Papal Primacy and the Universal Church*, 83.

29. Ibid., 94.

30. Jaroslav Pelikan, *The Emergence of the Catholic Tradition* (100–600), vol. 1 of *The Christian Tradition: A History of the Development of Doctrine* (Chicago: University of Chicago Press, 1971), 351.

31. Ibid.

The assumption of a more active, universal ministry on the part of the bishops of Rome, however, should not be misconstrued as simply a usurpation by the bishops of Rome of a role only reluctantly conceded by the other churches. Regularly, from the beginnings of a recognition of Rome's unique place among the local churches, a special role was accorded the bishops of Rome by other churches and by theologians. One thinks in this regard of the instance of Irenaeus in the *Adversus haereses*, quoted above, and of Cyprian of Carthage (bishop from 251–258). Cyprian may not have favored a primacy of teaching or of jurisdiction on the part of the Roman see, and he had no hesitation to take strong exception to Bishop Stephen of Rome on the matter of rebaptism of Christians baptized outside the communion of churches, but he also maintained that the unity of the churches was somehow tied in to the role of Peter. In fact, Cyprian's own relations with the church of Rome caused him to agonize over the matter of Roman primacy and of episcopal authority and how the two were related.[32]

In some way Cyprian's dilemma has continued through subsequent centuries. There has been both wholehearted acceptance and complete rejection of a ministry to the universal church on the part of the bishop of Rome. Even those who accept a unique Petrine ministry find themselves sometimes uneasy about and in tension with the decisions of the Roman see and sometimes with the style with which various popes have exercised their ministry to all the churches. The two most notable conflicts in which Roman authority was much at issue were the complete breakdown of unity between the eastern and western portions of the church in 1054 and the tumultuous parting of the ways between the reformers and the Roman church in the sixteenth century.

There is, of course, a danger in being too simplistic in seeking an underlying cause of complex events such as those culminating in the mutual excommunications of 1054 and in the bitter separations of the sixteenth century. Having stated the need for caution I hazard the suggestion that the underlying issue that vexed Christians (including Roman Catholics) then and now who have had trouble with Roman primacy is the issue of power. Does the Roman see possess the power to decide for the universal church? If so, are there unacceptable ways, as well as inappropriate ways, for the Roman see to exercise its power?

The history of the relationship between the local churches and the church of Rome seems to give evidence that, after the development of the church in the early centuries to the point of recognition of primacy on

---

32. See Peter Hinchliff, *Cyprian of Carthage and the Unity of the Christian Church* (London: Chapman, 1974), 106–12.

the part of the bishop of Rome, the issue of unacceptable and inappropriate ways of exercising its ministry was more often the concern. Quite naturally, as Christians of other local churches considered themselves to be injured by Rome's unacceptable or inappropriate uses of its unique position in the ecclesial communion, more radical questions about the very reality of a primacy arose.

Three problems predominate among the unacceptable uses of papal power. The first is excessive centralization. The history of the effort to position all power in the church in the bishop of Rome began, not unjustifiably, with Gregory I, but then reached its zenith, far more excessively, in the popes of the eleventh century, most notably Gregory VII, and in the popes of the thirteenth century, most notably Innocent III. While the scandal of lay investiture plagued the eleventh century and disarray relating to the Albigensian heresy troubled the thirteenth century, these were not sufficient cause for the bishops of Rome to disregard the local churches in their search for order.

The diminishment of the diocesan bishops to surrogates of the Roman pope weakened rather than strengthened ecclesial communion because centralization leads to uniformity. But ecclesial communion ought to be analogous with the communion of the divine Trinity and that is a communion whose characteristics are equality, diversity, and mutuality. Diocesan bishops need to be free, as equals, to represent the diversity of their local church as well as to promote the unity to be enjoyed among all the churches. Moreover, the see of Rome might have used its power in the age of the imperial papacy to promote rather than preempt mutual encouragement and correction among local churches in a region. No doubt it can be argued that reformist popes with high ideals, such as Gregory VII, found the local churches to be so corrupt that there was no other route for the popes to take than to assert their authority in the strongest possible way. But then one must lament the general state of decline that allowed wealth and civil power to accumulate in the hands of church officials from the time of Emperor Constantine, and lament as well the way in which the Roman popes were co-opted into this unfortunate process by their own centralizing efforts.

Acknowledging that hindsight is easier than foresight, we move on to the second problem of power that has afflicted the Petrine ministry, that of the way in which Rome has often imposed its judgments and decisions upon the churches and upon individual Christians. Serious dialogue in the direction of truth has too often been left aside in favor of unilateral action. Vital ecclesial communion becomes lost in backroom politics, intrigue, harshness, and fear. Often, it is true, Rome's actions have been consonant with the prevailing zeitgeist. Still, should not the primatial see as the "presidency of charity" not be expected to deal with problems in any age in a way that awakens observers to note: See these Christians, how they love one another!?

Memories of the *auto da fe*, of the treatment of Galileo at the hands of the Roman curia, and of curial punishment of Congar and Rahner, Küng and Boff in the twentieth century stay alive and cause uneasiness for a long time. Even national hierarchies sometimes chafe at the summariness with which the primatial see intervenes in the regional church. The reasons for calling an individual or a church to task may be just, but the manner may be harshly incommunicative.

A third area in which papal power has suffered abuse is in the incompetence and downright corruption of some of its subjects. Umbrella categories such as incompetence and corruption cover a wide range of types: the rashness of Boniface VIII (1294–1303), the moral turpitude of Alexander VI (1492–1503), the military preoccupations of Julius II (1503–1513), the love of grandeur and military might of Urban VIII (1623–1644), the weakness of Pius VI (1775–1799).

On the other hand, it should be noted that it is frequently difficult to determine the objectivity of determinations against this or that pope. For the perceptions of critics can easily be swayed by ideology, bad feelings generated by dealings with the pope in question, and lack of knowledge of the circumstances prompting a pope's attitude or decisions. It is regularly the case that no matter who exercises authority on any level, others find reason to criticize.

Recent ecumenical dialogues between the Roman Catholic church and the Orthodox, Anglican, and Lutheran churches have begun to recover an ecumenical appreciation for the unique place of the bishop of Rome in ecclesial communion. The Lutheran–Roman Catholic dialogue in the United States has been the catalyst for a recovery of the Petrine traditions of the New Testament. Some consensus on the special place of Peter among the Twelve and in the New Testament churches is beginning to emerge.[33] The summary statement on Peter of the participants in the Lutheran–Roman Catholic dialogue in the United States is useful to quote here:

> Among the companions of Jesus, he is given the greatest prominence in the New Testament accounts of the origins of the church. He is spoken of in the Gospels in terms relating him to the founding of the church, to strengthening

---

33. Notable is the careful study, Raymond E. Brown, Karl P. Donfried, and John Reumann, eds., *Peter in the New Testament* (Minneapolis: Augsburg, 1973).

his brethren, to feeding the sheep of Christ. He is a prominent figure in some of the Pauline letters, in Acts, and for two of the Catholic Epistles—a fact which suggests that he was associated with a wide-ranging ministry. Subsequent church history made him the image of a pastor caring for the universal church. And so, although we are aware of the danger of attributing to the church in the New Testament times a modern style or model of universality, we have found it appropriate to speak of a "Petrine function," using this term to describe *a particular form of Ministry exercised by a person, officeholder, or local church with reference to the church as a whole.* This Petrine function of the Ministry serves to promote or preserve the oneness of the church by symbolizing unity, and by facilitating communication, mutual assistance or correction, and collaboration in the church's mission.[34]

Cautious acceptance of the primacy of the church of Rome in a recovered Christian unity is then tendered:

The bishop of Rome, whom Roman Catholics regard as entrusted by the will of Christ with this responsibility [for the universal church], and who has exercised his Ministry in forms that have changed significantly over the centuries, can in the future function in ways which are better adapted to meet both the universal and regional needs of the church in the complex environment of modern times.[35]

The Anglican–Roman Catholic dialogue has also taken up the issue of papal primacy. The statement bringing to a close more than ten years of interchurch dialogue and officially received by Archbishop Donald Runcie of Canterbury and Pope John Paul II addresses the issue thus:

If God's will for the unity in love and truth of the whole Christian community is to be fulfilled, this general pattern of the complementary primatial and conciliar aspects of *episcope* serving the *koinonia* of the churches needs to be realized at the universal level. The only see which makes any claim to universal primacy and which has exercised and still exercises such *episcope* is the see of Rome, the city where Peter and Paul died.

It seems appropriate that in any future union a universal primacy such as has been described should be held by that see.[36]

What kind of Catholic position can be taken on papal primacy that is appropriate in such a positive ecumenical environment? First, Catholics

---

34. Common Statement of "Differing Attitudes Toward Papal Primacy" in Empie, Murphy, and Burgess, eds., *Papal Primacy and the Universal Church*, 11–12.

35. Ibid., 22.

36. Anglican–Roman Catholic International Commission, *The Final Report* (Washington: USCC, 1982), 64.

must be clear on our view of the why and what of the primacy of the bishop of Rome. Catholics are convinced that the universal ministry of the bishop of Rome is not simply a convenient organizational arrangement for a world-wide church. The presidency over all the local churches by the bishop of the apostolic see is rather a consistent development of the New Testament formation of the church which has taken place under the guidance of the Holy Spirit.

Apart from presiding over his own local church in word, sacrament, and pastoral care, the bishop of Rome has the responsibility of looking out for the communion in truth and love of all the local churches worldwide. It is the Petrine responsibility of confirming the disciples of Jesus so that all remain faithful.

The bishop of Rome does not exercise his universal ministry alone or in isolation. Each bishop has been ordained to be responsible for the health of the whole church, a responsibility exercised collegially as an expression of ecclesial communion. As bishop, the bishop of Rome is a member of the episcopal college. But as bishop *of Rome* the pope is head of the episcopal college. The college acts with and under the bishop of Rome.

It is not the prerogative of the bishop of Rome to usurp the responsibility of the local bishop to preside in word, sacrament, and care over the local church. The bishop of Rome can, however, criticize and correct, as indeed the bishop of another church might criticize and correct the bishop of Rome. Juridically, however, the bishop of Rome is not subject to any other bishop or even to the college of bishops, whereas other bishops are subject to the bishop of Rome in the sense that he has a decisive authority to promote unity and peace in the church as the bishop who presides over the catholic communion.

At the same time the pope's authority is not an absolute authority. One of the bishop-participants intervened at the First Vatican Council to remark, "The power of the supreme pontiff is limited by natural and divine law. It is limited by the precepts and teachings of Jesus Christ our Lord. It is limited by the common good of the church. It is limited by the voice of conscience. It is limited by right reason and by common sense. It is limited by the rule of faith and discipline, etc. . . . . But it cannot be limited or restricted by the bishops, either individually or corporately, either in council or out of council."[37]

Ecclesial communion needs the Petrine ministry because communion is an intense bond that cannot function only in spirit but must find expression in a visible, corporate way. An episcopal college without a head is inade-

---

37. Quoted by Patrick J. Burns in "Communion, Councils, and Collegiality: Some Catholic Reflections," in Empie, Murphy, and Burgess, eds., *Papal Primacy and the Universal Church*, 169.

quate to confirm the communion. If there were no specifically instituted head, one of the bishops would have to arise spontaneously to assume the function on a worldwide level of confirmation, convocation of the other bishops, mutual exchanges through letters and visits. But would such a spontaneous "presidency" provide an emotional appeal for the unity of all the faithful? And when such an energetic bishop were not forthcoming would the unity of the churches begin to fade?

On the other hand, a universal ministry on the part of the bishop of Rome has evoked as much hostility as reverence. Why has the papacy recurrently become such a force for disunity? We have noted the problems connected with power, and others could be brought forward as well. It is clear that the universal ministry carries with it the danger of overstepping its bounds so that damage is done to the integrity of local churches or individual Christians. Papal primacy is a ministry to be exercised with great delicacy if the ecclesial qualities of equality, diversity, and mutuality are to be kept in balance.

Recently Pope John Paul II noted that the exercise of the Petrine ministry has taken various forms throughout the history of the Christian church. He went on to claim that new forms, suitable to our own time, can be worked out for the exercise of papal primacy with a view to promoting the more unified Christianity that is sought in this ecumenical age. The pope made his remarks on December 6, 1987, at a celebration of the Eucharist in the Vatican basilica in the presence of the patriarch of Constantinople, Dimitrios I, who was in Rome for a week-long meeting with the pope.

In the course of the first centuries of our history, we each followed our own path, even while maintaining our communion of faith and sacramental life in spite of the difficulties which have arisen in our relations. During that period it was recognized that the See of Rome had not only a primacy of honour, but also a real responsibility to preside in charity, in the words of St. Ignatius of Antioch, and to foster the preservation of communion among all the Churches. I am aware that, for a great variety of reasons and against the will of all concerned, what should have been a service sometimes manifested itself in a very different light. But, as you know, it is out of a desire to obey the will of Christ truly that I recognize as Bishop of Rome, I am called to exercise that ministry. Thus, in view of this perfect communion which we wish to reestablish, I insistently pray the Holy Spirit to shower his light upon us, enlightening all the pastors and theologians of our Churches, that we may seek—together, of course—the forms in which this ministry may accomplish a service of love recognized by all concerned. [38]

38. *L'Osservatore Romano* (English language edition), Dec. 21–28, 1987, 8.

The pope's openness to the possibility of changes in the style of papal presidency over the churches takes on special meaning in the light of the historical reality that the centralization of so many kinds of power in the pope and his curia is a phenomenon of the second thousand years of the church's existence. During the first thousand years the local churches and the collegial assembly of bishops in synods and ecumenical councils took the initiative in matters of church life.[39] Practically speaking the First Vatican Council brought the second thousand years' tradition to a climax by concentrating on the pope's powers. In the wake of that council the diocesan bishops were, in the common view, little more than surrogates of the pope. But the Second Vatican Council, without in any way denying the prerogatives of papal primacy, teaches that bishops, presbyters, deacons, and the baptized faithful also are full subjects of church life, with specific contributions to make on their own initiative.[40]

Reenvisioning the way that papal primacy functions so that fears and hostility can be overcome does not seem to be such an impossible task. The key seems to be twofold: humility and communication. Humility insofar as the servant of unity and peace in the ecclesial communion is in a privileged position to stand in respect and reverence of the rich and diverse contributions of Christians the world over to the life of the communion. Since the 1920s when Pope Pius XI welcomed the cultural diversity of the church by the appointments of native bishops in Asia and Africa, bishops of Rome have increasingly endorsed, praised, and promoted the diverse gifts of the People of God.

On the level of communication, ways of consulting bishops, theologians, and lay people were introduced by the Second Vatican Council. The Synod of Bishops, the International Theological Commission, the Pontifical Council on the Laity are all meant to develop consultation and communication within the worldwide communion of the church. But the impression is often given that the agenda of those groups is closed, and that participants are limited to those least likely to be critical. Broader consultation and communication among the world's Christians, including those who have ideas that are uncongenial to the pope and the Roman curia, would foster the sense that the president of the church is ready to hear, discuss, and consider all sides of issues facing the church.

It does not seem that people resent the fact that ultimately the bishop of

---

39. See Hermann J. Pottmeyer's distinction of the first thousand years from the second thousand as providing two different forms of papal primacy in "Continuità e innovazione nell'ecclesiologia del Vaticano II," in G. Alberigo, ed., *L'ecclesiologia del Vaticano II: Dinamismi e Prospettive* (Bologna: Dehoniane, 1981), 71–95.

40. Ibid., 88–91.

Rome confirms definitive interpretations of Christian meaning and makes decisions about definitive Christian practice, for the church is not a democracy. But some of the principles of democracy, most especially the sense that each church member can expect to be heard, can valuably be incorporated into church life. Christians of good will who represent every point of view should be welcomed into the organs of consultation.

Mutual Recognition of Ministries

What must Christians involved in the ecumenical dialogue be prepared to accept and to concede in order to enact a mutual recognition of ministries? First we need to spend enough time with each other in as many different situations as possible (e.g., the pope's imaginative suggestion that he go skiing with the kings of Sweden and Norway), pray with each other as often as possible, study each other's patterns of discipleship thoroughly, cooperate in already acceptable ways in the church's mission so that we come to respect, and even stand in awe of, one another's commitment to Christ Jesus. This, after all, is the heart of Christianity, without which there is no unity worth pursuing. Yves Congar states it with eminent clarity:

> The substance and truth of the unity of the church is made up in and by Jesus Christ. All the images by which the New Testament expresses it convey this. The New Testament speaks of the church as a building, a vine, a flock, a bride, a body, always in relationship to Jesus Christ. But the Christ is only the cornerstone of a single construction; he is only the stem of a single vine, the shepherd of a single flock, the husband of a single wife, the head of a single body which is organically one. . . . The unity of living reference to Christ forms the basis for the existence of a Christian communion between the churches, encompassing them all, by virtue of which ecumenism is possible and even necessary.[41]

It is a truism, of course, to lay down as the first principle of mutual recognition of ministry that the partners in conversation be in touch with each other's commitment to Christ. However, it can easily happen that this first principle be so taken for granted that the partners actually forget it once the conversation begins, and become distracted by lesser, more contested, realities. Thus, unnecessary demands might be made.

Once the conversation partners are in touch with the commitment of each other to Christ, and once that mutual commitment is continually

41. Congar, *Diversity and Communion,* 11–12.

understood and affirmed in mind and reverenced in heart, a sense of genuine communion takes over the discussion. The partners realize that ecclesial communion is already present. Thus, they become even more determined to actualize unity and peace as far as the gospel is understood to demand it.

A second realization follows from the first: the Holy Spirit continues to work in each of the ecclesial communities, bringing about their present fidelity to the gospel and promoting whatever fidelity is lacking. Those churches presently engaged in ecumenical dialogue surely acknowledge both the commitment to Christ of the other churches with which they are engaged in conversation and also the continued activity of the Holy Spirit in those churches. But, again, when does acknowledgement of these two fundamental realities translate into practical recognition on the part of the separated ecclesial communities?

The Holy Spirit has continued to work without interruption in the separate ecclesial communities since 1054 and the sixteenth century. Otherwise how would faith in Christ and fidelity to Christ's gospel remain alive? Specifically, the divisions within Christianity, unfortunate as they continue to be, may have served the excellent purpose of keeping alive dimensions of Christian communion that would have been severely repressed if separation had not taken place.

The Eastern Orthodox, Anglicans, and Lutherans have been especially successful in preserving ecclesial communion through the college of bishops. Preservation of the ministry of the bishop not only on behalf of the local church but also on behalf of the communion of churches was not an insignificant cause of the schism between East and West. Excessive centralization of decision-making power in the bishop of Rome fed into general Western disdain for Eastern church customs. Would not the Eastern churches have lost important dimensions of their local autonomy if the schism had not taken place? The Eastern Orthodox and their uniate sister churches have managed to keep alive for the benefit of the entire ecumenical church a particular and ancient way of living out collegiality.

While the strictly religious, sixteenth-century origins of the Anglican communion seem to me to be of questionable tenability, the idea of an English branch of the worldwide communion of churches parallels the idea of a branch of the church attentive to the needs of German-speaking Christians as promoted by Luther and other reformers in the German lands. It is not a matter of an English church or a German church, but of an urgent diversity that could meet the particular needs of preaching the gospel of Jesus in situations of emerging nationalisms. The Roman church was not prepared to deal with diversity in unity in the early sixteenth century. Preoccupations with centralization, moral corruption, political maneuvering—all were applications of power that led Rome to insist upon imposing its uniform order upon local churches much in need of expressing diversity. Have not Lutherans and Anglicans, with their episcopal order of local church government, and responding to particular cultural expressions, been doing the universal church a service, comparable to that of the Eastern Orthodox churches, of keeping alive important aspects of the autonomy of the local churches? In addition, Martin Luther performed the long-needed task of bringing back into ecclesial affirmation and decisions the active priestly dignity of every Christian disciple.

Congregational churches have also revived and kept alive ministerial elements of ecclesial communion that had fallen into desuetude. Ecclesial communities of the Reformed tradition and Methodists bring us back to appreciation of the life of each portion of God's people, the individual congregation or parish, which functions as the small community of word, sacrament, and care in the urban and village neighborhood and in the countryside.

The so-called Free churches, such as Baptists, Mennonites, Pentecostals, and fundamentalists, have vigorously maintained the freedom of individuals to act upon the inspiration of the Holy Spirit. They remind the rest of the church, especially at historical moments when institutionalization becomes particularly stodgy and weighty, that the Holy Spirit promotes new initiatives not only during the New Testament time when prophets and evangelists arose spontaneously, but also at each later time in the life of the church. These groupings of Christians have also kept alive another element of communion, namely, the free responsibility of conscience enjoyed by each baptized member of the body of Christ. This has been especially salutary at times when personal responsibility was in danger of becoming lost in the overwhelming communalism of hierarchically centered Christianity.

At the same time the strong organizing activities that prevail even in the Free churches are an indication that eccesial communion demands order. God is at work redeeming the world in Christ and by the power of the Holy Spirit in quite human ways. The order of the divine communion, which has entered into human history in the missions of the Word and of the Spirit, is expressed both invisibly and visibly in the order of church life. The particular aspect of ministry that Catholicism has kept alive during the years of schism and separation is that of order, both episcopal and presbyteral, including the dimension of sacramental, ordained priesthood, all gathered into a worldwide unity ensured by the ministry of papal primacy.

At critical times within the progress of Christian history separation has seemed to many to be the only way to ensure the preservation of some essential dimension of communion. Unfortunately, preservation of whatever dimension was at stake meant the breakdown of communion. As temporary measures these ruptures may have been necessary, as I have just sketched. But now restoration of communion is in the forefront of Christian projects among many of the separated ecclesial communities. Every ministerial dimension of Christian discipleship currently promoted by the several ecclesial communities should and can be retained in a unified Christian church. Thus, no one of the separated communities needs to give up dimensions it has struggled so valiantly to preserve. It would be necessary, on the other hand, for each community to adopt the essential dimensions of communion preserved by the other communities.

When, then, will churches in dialogue know that the time is ripe for mutual recognition of ministries? I suggest three steps.

1. The first is to continue patiently with the interchurch dialogues taking place on national and international levels. Perhaps the common statements emerging from the dialogues need to become more frank about just what agreement has been achieved and what needs to be done. The Faith and Order Commission's *Baptism, Eucharist and Ministry* (BEM) paper is a fine example of a text that is forthright in its request of the several churches to reconsider where they might accede to what has been preserved in the other churches. Also helpful in this regard are the reception documents of the many churches who have responded so willingly to BEM. However, BEM seems to have glossed over enduring rankling differences. And the responses generally reiterate positions of difference without much sense of rapprochement. As a result, the responses of the churches that have received the document give the impression that many ecclesial communities sense that they are being called upon to give up what they deem to be essential.

Perhaps the Faith and Order Commission might attempt to lay out an entire plan of worldwide communion that frankly takes into account the particular dimensions of communion preserved in each church according to the way in which that church deems it to be essential. In other words, the text would not simply encourage mutual recognition of ministries while inviting the separate ecclesial communities to continue on their way in much the same patterns that have so far characterized their ministry. The text would point out more directly where each type of ecclesial community would have to adopt essential dimensions preserved by other communities. Reception by the several ecclesial communities could then be awaited, on the basis of which work could begin on a fresh draft of a plan for worldwide communion.

From the perspective of the discussion of this chapter, areas that would need to be addressed include the establishment of a type of oversight by bishops such that lines of authority in the individual ecclesial communities could be mutually recognized by the several communities, although it would not be necessary that authority be exercised in precisely the same way within each ecclesial community.

In another area, the Eucharist would be acknowledged by all as a central sacramental celebration of Christian faith, although doctrines of sacrifice and real presence would not need to be identical. However, doctrines of the Eucharist on the part of the uniting ecclesial communities would have to be mutually acceptable, since there would be occasional intercommunion. The uniting statement in this area might be: You claim more/less than we claim, but at least we do not find your claim inimical to evangelical faith.

In the matter of papal primacy, ecclesial communities would have to find a suitable doctrine and structure enabling acknowledgment of a universal authority of the bishop of Rome. Structurally, it would be necessary to develop a procedure by which the pope could be elected by representatives of all the uniting ecclesial communities. Furthermore, to allow the election of an ecumenical pope, it would probably be necessary for the pope elected only by the Roman Catholic College of Cardinals to resign.

2. Once churches are satisfied that the dimensions of ministry they consider essential are ready to be adopted by the other churches seeking unity, and once the churches have decided to take the courageous step to include in their church order the essential dimensions of ministry of the other ecclesial communities, it will be possible to take the second step, namely, to arrange a mutual recognition of ministries. It will be important to bring along both leaders and members of the uniting ecclesial communities to the point of agreement since such a major step toward reunion will require the wholehearted commitment of a significant majority of the ordained and the baptized in even the smallest parishes and congregations if it is to be successfully implemented.

At the same time, no judgment needs to be passed upon the ministries exercised by the other churches at any time prior to the moment of mutual agreement. Questions about the validity of another church's sacraments or orders during the period of separation will be rendered unnecessary by the achievement of agreement upon a transformed ecclesial order that acknowledges what all come to agree to be the essential components of Christian ministry.

In any case, the past cannot be altered. Each ecclesial community has judged and decided honestly and sincerely before God. But mutual recognition will not be based upon the decisions made separately in the past. It will take into account what each ecclesial community has kept alive of the order of ecclesial communion, but a newly forged, agreed-upon form of order will be the basis of mutual recognition.

3. Assuming that the dimensions of ecclesial communion laid out in the previous pages will somehow be present in a transformed, interchurch Christian ministry, mutual recognition will include the Catholic sense of order. From the moment of mutual recognition all the ecclesial communities will adopt episcopal leadership of the local church and order as the sacrament that renders bishops priestly presiders over word, sacrament, and care in the local church. Thus, the third step toward mutually recognized ministry on the part of the uniting churches would be to accept the already established and accepted leaders in each community as bishops, who would henceforth ordain bishops and presbyters, and who would be present at the ordination of one another's bishops to demonstrate episcopal collegiality. These bishops would in turn be recognized by the bishop of Rome and would also acknowledge the primacy of the see of Rome, transformed, as Pope John Paul II invites, into a suitable form "in which this ministry may accomplish a service of love recognized by all concerned."[42]

Because of the highly extraordinary circumstances of a moment of reunion it seems that the church would have the power to waive some kind of sacramental ordination of the newly recognized bishops. Universal acknowledgment and common prayer together at the Eucharist would be sufficient to reinstitute the succession within the local church of each ecclesial community. The real point would be to acknowledge each church's fidelity to the tradition and thus to continue the succession from the moment of that acknowledgment and of the simultaneous recognition of a universally accepted ecclesial order, the restoration of full communion.

42. *Lumen gentium*, art. 8.

Chapter Six

INCULTURATING MINISTRY IN THE UNITED STATES

THE ELEMENT OF INCULTURATION OF MINISTRY HAS BEEN introduced in chapter 1 as a methodological presupposition of contemporary Christian ministry. The argument is that ministry, as one dimension of church, is an extension of the incarnation of the divine Word in human history. Just as the Word could only become incarnate in a particular culture, so church and ministry can become incarnate only by insertion into the individual cultures that the gospel of the incarnate Word addresses and transforms.

The issues of ministry that have been addressed thus far in the present study have cultural aspects to them. Questions about the ministry of the baptized and the ordained and the relationship that exists between them, questions of women in ministry and of mutual recognition of ministries among the separated ecclesial communities would not have been addressed at all in some earlier cultures and are addressed as they are in the present study partially because of the influence of contemporary culture. However, each of the issues discussed thus far is without doubt a question of theological significance for the worldwide church, made up of members of so many national and regional groups, each characterized by different languages and customs.

The present chapter sets out to investigate how the transcultural reality of Christian ministry as the activity of word, sacrament, and pastoral leadership and care has become specifically inculturated in the particularity of the Catholic church within the North American culture of the United States. In the following pages the distinct and peculiar is studied, not as superior to the distinct inculturations of ministry in France or England,

Zimbabwe or South Korea, but simply as distinct. Such study yields a specific understanding of Christian ministry that is theological, in that its concern is instances of inculturation, and historical, in that its concern is a particular people at particular places and times.

The method of proceeding includes several steps. First, ministry of word, sacrament, and pastoral leadership and care are taken to be the fundamental tasks of the church in every place and at every time. Second, it is recognized that what changes is the cultural context within which the fundamental tasks are implemented. Thus, the context needs to be determined. In the present instance influential elements of the cultural context of the United States in the republican era, the age of immigration, and the present late-twentieth century era are highlighted. Third, the context is shown to yield themes that give a particular shape to the ministerial tasks. Thus, with regard to each era the present chapter first lines up contextual factors yielded by the culture; second, it lists ministerial themes forthcoming from the cultural factors; third, it describes the particular shape that ministry of word, sacrament, and pastoral care take under the influence of the themes emergent in the culture. The result of the study is an understanding of the penetration of the gospel into American culture. The chief benefit of the study is recognition that the success of ministry is not unrelated to the extent to which it appropriates and transforms the cultures it enters.

Ministry in the Republican Era of the United States

For our purposes the study of ministry in the republican era of the United States is restricted to the years of the American ministry of the first bishop in the United States, John Carroll of Baltimore, who returned from Belgium and England after the suppression of the Jesuits in 1773 and continued actively as priest and bishop until his death in 1815. Two characteristics dominate the context of the inculturation of Catholic Christianity in the emerging nation of the United States of America. The first has to do with the constitutive elements of the new nation, the second with the fortunes of the papacy at the end of the eighteenth century.

The American republic is a product of political ideas spawned by the Enlightenment, especially as they were developing in nineteenth-century England and France. [1] There was close rapport between the founders of the

1. John Courtney Murray has suggested that, more remotely, elements of the spirit of American polity can be traced to ideas of the common good and public consensus developed by Thomas Aquinas. See his *We Hold These Truthes* (Garden City, N. Y.: Doubleday, 1964), 102–25, 280–317, and *passim.*

American republic and the intellectual and political ferment that led to the French Revolution. At the same time, the founders of the republic were landed gentry of British extraction. The resulting combination meant that political revolutionary theory was tempered by the British sensitivity to law and orderly government. Thus a military revolution was undertaken to overthrow British rule because it was perceived to have failed to take into consideration the just needs and concerns of the American settlers. But the revolution did not become a bloodbath as did the French revolution. "Liberty, fraternity, equality" could just as well have been the slogan of the American revolution. But the spirit of the new American political entity in the republican era, while it did not completely overcome religious and ethnic bias among the settlers from Europe, and while it related to native Americans with a strange mixture of respect and disregard, and baldly ignored the basic human rights of black people, nevertheless did not strike out on an anarchic and violent vendetta against now this and now that group within the society.

Catholics, under the leadership of John Carroll, confidently strove to take their place in the new republic. It was a new instance of the inculturation of the Catholic tradition of Christianity:

> American Catholicism has European origins. But it also has a peculiarly American history, continuously in contact with the ideas of democracy, due process of law, representative government, religious pluralism, activism, pragmatism, and all the characteristics of this land which for so many years knew limitless frontiers, rapidly growing industry, and an aggressive, adventurous population.[2]

A second influential characteristic of the context in which ministry became inculturated in the new American republic was the extreme state of the papacy. The pontificates of both Pius VI (1775–1799) and Pius VII (1800–1823) coincided with the nationalist movements in Europe and the United States, in which the meddling of foreign governments was rejected. In addition, when Rome was occupied by French forces in 1798 Pius VI came under their control and was held prisoner until the time of his death. Pius VII dealt more directly with Napoleon, whose fortunes rose rapidly. The Pope resisted manipulation by the emperor and this led to Pius's imprisonment by the emperor from 1809 to 1814, during which time Pius, in protest, refused to exercise his authority.

Coming as these papal imprisonments did in the early years of the Amer-

---

2. James Hennesey, *American Catholics: A History of the Roman Catholic Community in the United States* (New York: Oxford, 1981), 4.

ican republic, Rome could not exert either interest or intervention of any significance in the formation of the church in the United States nor could John Carroll look much for suggestions and direction from Rome. Moreover, because of the prickly sensitivity to foreign influence on the part of the citizens of the newly independent nation, Carroll considered it necessary to make very clear that intervention on the part of Rome in the ecclesiastical affairs of the Catholic church in the United States was undesirable.

Within this context Catholics, especially English-speaking settlers of the thirteen original colonies and their descendants, although they were not heartily welcomed in every instance by their compatriots, generally felt at home in the new nation. Not experiencing the antipapal and anticlerical sentiment that characterized France and England during the same period, and beneficiaries instead of a tolerance for religious diversity that was unheard of in their past, Catholics assessed their possibilities positively: they could practice their Catholic faith without interference and they could contribute as enfranchised citizens to the civic life of the nation.

John Carroll was comfortable among his fellow religionists of different Christian denominations, even as he defended the particular truth and value of Catholicism.[3] His attitude is notable in a treatise he penned in response to a statement published by a priest and fellow ex-Jesuit, Charles Wharton. Wharton's 1784 *Letter to the Roman Catholics of Worcester* (in England, not Massachusetts) explained why he had chosen to disavow the Catholic faith. Carroll replied with *An Address to the Roman Catholics of the United States of America by a Catholic Clergyman.*[4]

Throughout his letter Carroll draws careful distinctions that show him to be quite respectful of Christians of persuasions other than Catholic. It is true, Carroll writes, that the leaders of the Christian people sometimes forbid their congregations to read texts that can be deleterious to their faith. At the same time, "in the course of his [Wharton's] theological studies, was he himself ever denied access to the writings of our adversaries? Were not the works of Luther, Calvin and Besa, of Hooker, Tillotson and Stillingfleet, and all the other champions of the protestant cause, open to his inspection?" It is true that "they are in the *communion of the church*, who are united in the profession of her faith, and participation of her sacraments, through the ministry, and government of her lawful pastors. But the *members of the catholic church* are all those, who with a sincere heart seek true religion, and are in

3. James Hennesey, "Catholicism in an American Environment: The Early Years," *Theological Studies* 50 (1989): 663–66.
4. John Carroll, "An Address to Roman Catholics of the United States by a Catholic Clergyman," in Thomas O'Brien Hanley, ed., *The John Carroll Papers* (Notre Dame, Ind.: University of Notre Dame Press, 1976), 1: 82–144.

an unfeigned disposition to embrace the truth, whenever they find it. Now it never was our doctrine, that salvation can be obtained only by the former. . . ." It is true that the church condemns heresy, but heresy is "not merely a mistaken opinion in a matter of faith, but an obstinate adherence to that opinion. . . . Hence they [Catholic theologians] infer, that he is no heretic, who, though he hold false opinions in matters of faith, yet remains in an habitual disposition to renounce these opinions, whenever he discovers them to be contrary to the doctrines of Jesus Christ."

In a similar vein Catholics in the pre-Revolutionary American colonies had caught the spirit of the age of Enlightenment. Autonomy, expressed as freedom from the interference of outside governments, would not be tolerated in the new society taking shape on the mid-Atlantic shores of North America. Relative to the government of their religious affairs, Catholics wanted to be sure that Rome would not act to upset their fragile religious freedom in the new world. Appointing a bishop could be just the move to bring on the upset. Later, after a native Episcopalian bishop had been appointed without creating any stir, Catholics felt easier about having their own bishop. Ultimately, the clergy were invited to elect the man who would become the first native bishop in the United States. They chose John Carroll, and he was confirmed by Rome in 1789.

It was a formidable task to have to establish the means of ministry for Catholics inhabiting the rapidly expanding territories of the United States. There were few ordained ministers, and many of these defied a corporate approach to the administration of the church. Some priests who made it to the United States had proven to be misfits in Europe, and turned out to be no better suited to ministry in the United States. There were also the tensions that arise as different ethnic groups try to form a single community. The particular circumstances of Native Americans and of African slaves, as Carroll calls them, also received the attention of the newly established local church.

In a situation demanding the first organization of the church such as that faced in the republican era it is no surprise that the ministry of pastoral governance and care should loom large. In cooperation with the Catholics for whom he was bishop, John Carroll had to arrange for the regular administration of word and sacrament for a far-flung congregation. He did not have many priests with whom to work. To complicate matters he was often unable to confirm his decisions regarding parish disputes or the nomination of bishops for the new dioceses he determined needed to be created because of Pope Pius VII's long imprisonment. Carroll's correspondence and pastoral letters witness to his worry and chagrin over the inability of the Apostolic See to function during the period of 1808–14.

The rapid growth of both the United States and of the number of Catholics the new country led to the establishment of several new dioceses in
1808: Boston, Philadelphia, Bardstown, and New York (although New York
remained vacant for a time). Baltimore became the metropolitan see and
John Carroll the archbishop. The new bishops immediately faced problems
of staffing their dioceses with sufficient priests. For this reason, Bishop Stephen Badin of Bardstown traveled to France immediately after his episcopal
ordination to solicit recruits. The bishops also needed financial backing for
the organization of the church in the United States, but it was not until the
second decade of the nineteenth century that organized charitable societies
in France and Germany began to help fund the church in pioneer and Native American territories.[5] Consequently, parishes often struggled to support their enterprises, including the pastor. The stipend system was important for priestly subsistence. Still, Archbishop Carroll was able to plan a
cathedral in Baltimore and gain for his project the services of the premier
American architect of the day, Benjamin Latrobe, the architect of the Capi-
tol in Washington.

Caring for the Native Americans presented special problems. The Jesuits
had evangelized in upper Canada and New York state and the Franciscans
had done the same in the southwest and California. But once the thirteen
colonies became the United States the situation changed. For one thing, as
the westward expansion moved forward, the new U.S. government had to
determine how to relate to the native peoples. The church moved along the
same lines as the government, as is evidenced by a letter of Bishop Carroll
to George Washington in 1792. The bishop notes that Washington and
Congress have determined that the U.S. is to conduct itself "with the mild
principles of religion and philanthropy." Carroll wants to inform the president that the Catholic church, through its presence in Kaskaskia in Illinois
territory, will make contact with the indigenous population for the purpose
of "disseminating the principles of Christianity among the natives of the
Western territory." Carroll also asks Congress for some financial support for
the mission.[6] Later history reveals that priests, such as Benjamin Marie Petit,
not only Christianized the Native Americans but also became defenders of
their human rights when the government forgot George Washington's principle.[7]

Of course, Carroll was a member of his American culture, which means
that he approved of the westward expansion of the American frontier with-

5. See Hennesey, *American Catholics*, 112.
6. Hanley, *John Carroll Papers*, 2: 24–25.
7. See Hennesey, *American Catholics*, 130f.

out taking into account the rights of the natives to the land they occupied. Along with most (all?) of his fellow citizens whose roots were in Europe, Carroll was capable of calling the Native Americans "savages" and, reasonably, he worried about attacks upon missionaries working on the frontier.[8] Still, Carroll's concern for the Native Americans as human beings the equal of the Europeans is evidenced in his correspondence with native communities. In a letter to the Native Americans of Maine Carroll writes, "I promised to you last year, that I would immediately endeavour to procure a pastor for your souls, to give to your children the holy rites of baptism, to administer to yourselves the sacrament of reconciliation, & exercise all the other functions of ministry."[9]

Pastoral care of black people, almost all of whom were slaves, posed another challenge to the newly formed American church. In this matter, as with the Native Americans, the Catholic church was not a leader in promoting the civil rights of black people. Even as the battle became pitched in the period just prior to the Civil War, there was hardly a Catholic voice of prominence raised in opposition to slavery. Part of the reason for this may be that many of the abolitionists were also anti-Catholic, making it at least awkward for Catholics to join the abolitionist movement.[10] Nevertheless, it is noteworthy that the First Council of Baltimore in 1852, so soon before the Civil War, made no mention of slavery.

In view of these mid-nineteenth century attitudes, it is heartening to observe that in the earlier republican period, when slavery was an unquestioned given, Carroll and some of his fellow Catholics were not insensitive to the issue of slavery. Carroll emphatically notes that he owned no slaves at all.[11] However, Catholics and Catholic institutions owned slaves. But slaves were invited to Christian faith, worshiped with the entire household, and celebrated the sacraments just as other Catholics. In fact, the resolutions of the first diocesan synod of Baltimore recognize that slaves should not be denied the sacraments even if they cannot have the benefits of religious education to a desired degree.[12]

Further insight into the attitudes of Carroll and like-minded Catholics regarding the situation of the slaves is revealed in correspondence between the bishop and a parish priest, John Thayer. Thayer is so dismayed with the ill-treatment of the slaves owned by one or more of his parishioners that he

8. See Carroll's 1792 letter to the congregation at Vincennes in Hanley, *John Carroll Papers*, 2:55.

9. Ibid., 58.

10. See Hennesey, *American Catholics*, 145.

11. Hanley, *John Carroll Papers*, 3:239.

12. Ibid., 1:530.

wants to leave the service of that parish. Carroll responds by offering the following counsel:

> While you confine yourself within the bounds of solid doctrine, you may act freely, & unrestrained by any ecclesiastical interference, in remedying the abuses of slavery; and when you have done your duty, if all the good effect possible & desirable does not ensue from your endeavours, you must bear that, as every pastor must bear the many disorders, which will subsist in spite of his most zealous exertions. . . . I am as far from being easy in my mind at many things I see, and know, relating to the treatment & manners of the Negroes. I do the best I can to correct the evils I see; and then recur to those principles, which, I suppose, influenced the many eminent & holy missioners in S. America & Asia, where slavery equally exists.[13]

Ministry of the word was a matter of great concern to Carroll and the first American bishops who served alongside him. Poor preaching was apparently a problem of considerable proportions. Part of the problem was congregations of different ethnic and language groups; part was the lack of moral integrity and spiritual development on the part of the clergy.[14] Under the best of circumstances, outstanding preachers are rare. Unfortunately, in the church of the New World, far from the intellectual and cultural centers of Europe, when an outstanding preacher did appear upon the scene, that talent was sometimes diluted by serious problems in other areas. Such was the case with William Hogan, the pastor of St. Mary's in Philadelphia, who was a fine preacher but used his apparently considerable powers of persuasion to turn the congregation against the bishop.

Among worthy sermons extant from the republican era are a number of Carroll's on a variety of topics: sacramental and doctrinal themes, liturgical festivals, and miscellaneous topics such as the duties of parents, American independence, a jubilee year, and an appeal for school funds. Present-day students of ministry of the word in the republican era are treated to an outstanding instance of high-caliber Christian teaching in Carroll's response to Charles Wharton's resignation from Catholic faith and priestly ministry. The response, which is similar to a treatise, is theologically intelligent, dialogical, and urbane.[15]

Complete academic education was one way in which the church could develop a more adequate instruction in the faith. John Carroll expended

---

13. Ibid., 2: 122–23.
14. See Hennesey, *American Catholics*, 75–76, 94.
15. The address appears in Hanley, *John Carroll Papers*, 1: 82–144.

considerable energy to arrange the establishment of Georgetown College as a school for Catholic males—once established, the student body included a large number of Protestants as well—hoping that many of its graduates would continue on to study for the priesthood. To educate priests for service in the United States, Carroll contracted with the Sulpicians to organize St. Mary's Seminary in Baltimore. His concern was to produce a native clergy, "men accustomed to our climate, and acquainted with the tempers, manners, and government of the people, to whom they are to dispense the ministry of salvation."[16]

The early Catholic bishops were also concerned about the education of women. Carroll had hoped that the Carmelite nuns would be willing to enter into the active apostolate of the education of young women, but when they would not give up their contemplative life, he welcomed the Visitation sisters in their establishment of a school near Georgetown.[17] Carroll also welcomed the considerable efforts of Elizabeth Ann Seton, and encouraged others to assist her with her educational establishments, for, Carroll commented, Seton is surely a saint. Stephen Badin also welcomed several congregations of sisters to his new diocese of Kentucky to devote themselves to the educational apostolate. The bishops knew that rectification of the lamentable lack of knowledge of the faith on the part of the Catholic population could not be left to chance or even to the ministry of the clergy, who were without both time and expertise. Schools were the answer.

On the other hand, the teaching ministry of priests was not discounted. The first diocesan synod several times instructs priests to exercise their responsibility to catechize candidates for the sacraments before they are actually conferred. The synod, for example, lists the doctrines of Christian faith that those petitioning for the sacrament of marriage should know.[18] The same synod sets down the order of divine services and instructs that during Sunday mass, after the reading of the Gospel in the vernacular, "there should be a sermon, such that the hearers shall be instructed to correct their faults, and encouraged to the perfection of the Christian life." In the afternoon on Sundays a service of vespers ought to be celebrated and "afterwards there should be catechetical instruction."[19]

Nor were priests and other catechists left to their own devices in the proposal of Catholic doctrine and devotion to their congregations. Carroll

16. Quoted in Jay P. Dolan, *The American Catholic Experience: A History from Colonial Times to the Present* (Garden City, N.Y.: Doubleday, 1985), 107.
17. On the Carmelite nuns, see Hanley, *John Carroll Papers,* 2:32.
18. Ibid., 1:530.
19. Ibid., 531.

himself adapted English and French catechisms several times. The Carroll catechism went through several printings and exercised influence on catechetics in the United States long after his death.[20]

Sacramental ministry, both liturgical and devotional, took shape in the new nation much as it did in the European culture in which it originated. In parishes with a resident pastor Sunday morning mass and Sunday afternoon vespers were celebrated. What distinguished sacramental ministry in the United States from its European counterpart is the openness with which Americans of other religious persuasions were comfortable, if not with Catholic piety itself, at least with the nonthreatening character of Catholic worship. Thus, they felt free to attend Catholic churches occasionally, as at a 1774 Sunday vesper service in Philadelphia's St. Mary's Church attended by George Washington and John Adams.[21]

Bishop Carroll promoted the use among Catholics of all the devotional aids to Catholic spirituality. His sermons and instructions encourage eucharistic devotion, the rosary and litanies, fasting and abstinence. But the heart of Carroll's sacramental ministry was liturgical. Sunday morning mass and Sunday afternoon Vespers were the foundation. Beyond that, Carroll even encouraged the laity in the recitation of the Divine Office.[22] Carroll's episcopal colleagues equally promoted these devotional aids. But the spirit with which the promotion was advanced differed. On Carroll's part Catholic Christianity, while distinct from other forms, particularly Protestant piety, was not inimical to them. He often preached to mixed congregations, and, as we have seen, possessed a profoundly open-minded view toward religious plurality. So his encouragement of a Catholic piety was in the service of Christian living, not Catholic sectarianism. Moreover, Carroll taught moderation. In promulgating the laws of fast for the season of Lent or in preparation for Holy Communion, Carroll was careful to temper the legislation with provision for those living in rural areas, for whom travel over long distances or heavy manual labor in the fields without nourishment would work a hardship.

Far more rigorous in attitude was Bishop Stephen Badin of Bardstown. He and his collaborator Charles Nerinckx came from a Jansenist background, bringing with them "a grim 18th-century French spirituality."[23]

20. Charles J. Carmody, "The 'Carroll Catechism'—A Primary Component of the American Catholic Catechetical Tradition," in Timothy Walch, ed., *Early American Catholicism, 1634–1820* (New York: Garland, 1988), 313–22.

21. See Adams's description of the service in Hennesey, *American Catholics*, 62.

22. See Joseph P. Chinnici, *Living Stones: The History and Structure of Catholic Spiritual Life in the United States* (New York: Macmillan, 1989), 26.

23. Hennesey, *American Catholics*, 82. See also Dolan, *American Catholic Experience*, 121.

They insisted upon a rigorous piety for the Catholics of their territory. Badin demanded strict adherence to church legislation regarding fasting, and one priest working in Badin's diocese complained to Bishop Carroll in a letter that Catholics were being unjustly deprived of receiving Holy Communion. He wrote, "Young people are not admitted without a solemn promise of not dancing *on any occasion whatever*, which few will promise & fewer still can keep. All priests that allow of dancing are publicly condemned to Hell."[24]

In summary, ministry in the United States during the years of John Carroll's career offered the same word, sacrament, and pastoral governance and care that are the staples of Christian ministry. But there are differences peculiar to the new situation. It is clearly Roman Catholicism, but with Enlightenment qualities. Most especially, political attitudes of the emerging United States of America are integrated, consciously by many of its practitioners including, first of all, the metropolitan archbishop, into the Christian ministry of this time and this place. Anglo- and French-Catholics of the republican era were pleased to be a part of the uniquely distinctive enterprise of American democratic government and they considered that the insertion of Catholic Christianity into the American republic was a fresh opportunity for the faith. That is what makes the Catholic church and its ministry during the republican era a new instance of the incarnation of gospel truth and values.

Ministry during the Age of Immigration

Plans for a relatively placid future on the part of the original leaders of the Catholic church in the United States were profoundly upset by the turn of events in the church's fortunes that began around 1820 with the first wave of Irish immigration. From then, until the National Origins Act of 1924 imposed strict limitations upon immigration, literally millions of individuals and families made their way to the United States from foreign countries. They came freely, if not always eagerly, in the hope that they could discover and create a better future for themselves or, at least, for their children. Among the immigrants were huge numbers of Roman Catholics, so many that the church went from being a small minority in a heavily Protestant nation to becoming by 1850 the largest single religious group in the country. James Hennesey has stated dramatically but without exaggeration: "Immigration transformed American Catholicism."[25]

24. Quoted in Chinnici, *Living Stones*, 29.
25. Hennesey, *American Catholics*, 173.

To appreciate the particular shape that Catholic ministry took during the roughly one hundred years of the age of immigration, two contextualizing elements and four themes need to be highlighted. The first contextualizing element is that Catholic immigrants poured relentlessly into the territory of the United States, most through Ellis Island, but also from French Canada, across the Rio Grande from Mexico, and, later in the twentieth century, into New York and Miami from Cuba and Puerto Rico. Each group of immigrants brought with it a distinct ethnic identity which included religious beliefs, customs, styles of worship, and social sensibilities. So different were the cultures of each group of immigrants from the others, including the different groupings of Roman Catholics, that it is not possible to speak in general of Catholic immigrants without also taking into account their differences. [26]

The second reality contextualizing ministry in the age of immigration is the nativist reaction of the Anglo-Protestants who had founded the republic and who dominated the sociopolitical, economic, and religious landscape of the United States. Nativists found everything foreign repulsive and a threat to the common good of the fragile nation that had so recently been created: non-Protestant religions such as Catholicism and Judaism; languages other than English; races other than white.

The particular threat Catholics seemed to pose was their profession of allegiance to a foreign power, the temporal head of a European state, who ruled both his political territories and the Roman Catholic church in the style of an autocratic monarch. Moreover, Catholics celebrated sacraments, and especially the sacrifice of the mass, which many Protestants considered to be blasphemous, and Catholics seemed to engage in superstitious devotion to the saints. Catholics, nativists thought, rejected the Bible as the Word of God. Alongside these threats, the immigrants of all backgrounds were arriving on the shores of the United States in such numbers that they were likely to gain economic and political power at the expense of the citizens already in place.

It should be added that, while nativism is mainly a Protestant phenomenon, there were nativist tendencies among Catholics as well. Anglo-Catholics resented the Irish Catholics when they first started immigrating to the United States because the Anglos deemed the Irish, with their virulent anti-Protestantism and peasant manners, to be a threat to the acceptance the modest and nonaggressive Anglo-Catholics had won for Catholi-

---

26. See the descriptions in Harold J. Abramson, *Ethnic Diversity in Catholic America* (New York: John Wiley & Sons, 1973); and James S. Olson, *Catholic Immigrants in America* (Chicago: Nelson-Hall, 1987) of the different qualities of ethnic identity of Catholics from Ireland, French Canada, Italy, central and eastern Europe, Mexico, Cuba, and Puerto Rico.

cism in the republican era.[27] Later in the nineteenth century, Irish Catholics came to dominate the Catholic church in the United States. They resented those Catholics from cultures different from their own who resisted rapid assimilation into the uniformity that the Irish bishops and priests sought to create in the United States.

Four themes recur as we study ministry during the age of immigration. The dominant theme is the maintenance of ethnocultural identity in a strange new environment. A function of preserving this sort of identity was more self-conscious practice of the Catholic faith on the part of the new immigrants. For most of the Catholic immigrants settling in the United States their Catholicism was integral to their ethnic identity. Thus, to preserve ethnic identity it was necessary for the immigrants to maintain and even enhance their Catholic faith. The Irish and the French Canadians were staunchly Catholic, for example, because it was their religious tradition and because it was a way to stand up against the proselytizing efforts of the Protestants who were out to Anglicize them by Protestantizing them. German Catholics taking refuge from the Protestantizing campaign (*Kulturkampf*) in Germany fought to preserve their ethnic and religious identity as an integral whole. While there were variations with other immigrant groups, a common factor was the integration of ethnic identity and the Catholic faith. To maintain the one, the other had to be maintained as well.

A second theme that recurs in the ministry of the age of immigration is concern about the unity of the Roman Catholic faith in the New World. With so many cultural distinctions separating the various immigrant groups that kept arriving on the American shores wave after wave, and despite their common commitment to the Roman Catholic faith, it is not surprising that factions arose within the church in the United States. In this situation there was a constant concern on the part of the hierarchy: how was the one Roman Catholic church to find expression in the new nation when so many different ways of being Catholic characterized the different ethnic groups?

A third theme is the promotion of Catholicism's rightful place alongside the other religions and Christian denominations of Americans. Fear that Catholics might be intimidated or persuaded to become Protestants, or that Catholicism, especially when it was a minority religion, might simply be swallowed up by the larger reality of the nation whose ethos was Protestant, kept Catholics vigilant to every move of Protestant evangelization as well as to the threat of religious indifference.

Bishops, intellectuals, and politicians knew that they were dealing with

---

27. Creole Catholics in Louisiana also espoused nativism against recent immigrants. See Hennesey, *American Catholics*, 119.

a major issue when it came to the viability of the Catholic church in a nation grounded upon democratic social construction and religious plurality, a maximum of individual freedom, and a capitalist economy. These values are not compatible in an unqualified way with Catholicism. The church is hierarchical and hardly democratic. Concerning religious plurality, Catholics possessed a trenchant view of theirs as the uniquely true church of Jesus Christ. This attitude did not lead them to look kindly upon the endless proliferation of denominations and sects that characterize Christianity in the United States. Individual freedoms were surrendered to the higher reality of the church community, as was the quest for economic success and advantage; both renunciations could be interpreted to be the antithesis of the American way of life. Somehow the American nation and the Roman Catholic church did not seem to make good bedfellows.

The final theme influencing ministry in the age of immigration is the converse of the third theme. It is the appropriation by the Catholic church in the United States of values of the American ethos and the polity created from that ethos. Inevitably tension and conflict accompanied this effort at appropriation, again since the values of the American nation seemed so often to be contrary to the values of Catholicism. But just as John Carroll and the Catholics of the republican era had been convinced that Catholicism could benefit from its insertion into the American polity and even thrive in the new nation, so prominent Catholics of the era of immigration shared that conviction and promoted both Catholicism and the American arrangement of the sociopolitical order.

For example, John England, nominated to be bishop of Charleston in 1820, "promoted the lay-trustee concept and made it an integral part of local church government. Viewing such a republican form of government as a harmonious blend of American and Roman Catholic traditions, England sought to achieve a situation in which, he said, 'the laity are empowered to cooperate but not to dominate.' "[28] Thus, according to England, democracy could have a positive influence upon the organization of the Catholic church without overturning the structures of hierarchical authority. England's approach was not to prevail, however, for most American bishops of the nineteenth century did not have the open-minded mentality or the patience, or perhaps the ability, to maintain both their authority as leaders of the local church and a cooperative attitude toward the laity. Lay trusteeism was gradually dismantled, but not without great conflict.

Another leader who tried to relate Catholicism and American values in a

---

28. Dolan, *American Catholic Experience*, 166. See also Hennesey, "Catholicism in an American Environment," 668–69.

positive way was John Ireland, archbishop of St. Paul (bishop from 1875–1918). Ireland's conviction about the possibility of a happy relationship between the church and the republic is unmistakable:

> I love too deeply the Catholic Church and the American republic not to be ever ready to labor that the relations of the one with the other be not misunderstood. It is true, the choicest field which providence offers in the world today to the occupancy of the Church is this republic, and she welcomes with delight the signs of the times that indicate a glorious future for her beneath the starry banner. But it is true, also, the surest safeguards for her own life and prosperity the republic will find in the teachings of the Catholic Church, and the more America acknowledges those teachings, the more durable will her civil institutions be made. [29]

Ireland favored the assimilation of Catholic immigrants into the American mainstream rather than the establishment of long-term separated communities. Attendance by Catholics at the common or public schools was Ireland's vehicle for assimilation. [30] Ireland was not naive about the Protestant character of the public schools. [31] But he was of the opinion that Protestant influence could be overcome, and that Catholic involvement in the public school system would integrate Catholics in a wholesome way into the American nation.

While all four themes sketched above were not consciously or explicitly implemented in each instance of ministry during the age of immigration in the United States, none of them was ever too far from the surface, for they were all preoccupying concerns of a rapidly growing Catholic church taking shape in an environment never before experienced. Keeping this phenomenon as well as the four themes and two contextualizing elements in mind, the three types of ministry are now considered.

As it did in the republican era, so in the age of immigration ministry of pastoral leadership loomed large. During many of the years of both periods the Catholic church was about the business of establishing itself in the United States. If the two eras are viewed as a chronological continuum, the entire period must be characterized as in flux. Structuring the ways that the ministries of word, sacrament, and care could be implemented effectively was not finally settled upon until the end of the nineteenth century. Differences appeared mainly among the different ethnic groups, especially

---

29. Quoted in Marvin R. O'Connell, "John Ireland," in Gerald P. Fogarty, ed., *Patterns of Episcopal Leadership* (New York: Macmillan, 1989), 139.

30. Ibid., 146.

31. Hennesey, *American Catholics*, 186.

between the dominant Irish Catholics and Catholics of other ethnic groups. Clashes generated by the conflicts between Catholics and nativists were also frequent.

One area that became the setting for frequent clashes was the parish. In some form parishes had been part of the organizational structure of the Catholic church since the fourth century, but in the United States the immigrating groups found that banding together in parishes provided them with an ideal structure for preserving both their religious faith and the ethnic identity so much interwoven with their faith. When large numbers of Irish immigrants first came to the United States in the 1840s, new parishes were established in the midst of the areas where they settled, mostly in the cities, providing a place for the members to maintain close contact with their fellow expatriates through both worship and socializing.

Anyone whose experience of parish is limited to territorial parishes would expect that when freshly arrived immigrants of ethnic backgrounds other than Irish, for example, the Germans, arrived in the United States and settled near an already existing parish church, the newcomers would simply attach themselves to the parish in the area. This was not, of course, the way in which parish life developed in the United States.

Although they were Roman Catholics too, the newcomers felt like aliens: they spoke and often appeared different; they could not warm to the devotions or lack of devotions prevailing in the parish; popular feast days and the customs by which to celebrate important religious moments were not shared; temperaments varied widely. The already established parishes were so stamped with the ethnic identity of the Irish who built the parish that the Germans could not adapt. Moreover, the Irish were not able to overcome the obstacles and make the Germans feel welcome, since they were just as much limited by their culture. A comfortable fit between the two simply could not be arranged. It was far easier for the Germans to form their own parish. And so it was with the French Canadians, the Italians, and every other group that came to the United States during the nineteenth and early twentieth centuries. National parishes were established to accommodate the ethnic particularities of the immigrant groups.

At the center of the parochial structure was the pastor. Not only religiously but socially as well, the priest was the leader of the community. This was especially true in Irish, French Canadian, and eastern European parishes, less so in German parishes, and even less in Italian and Hispanic parishes.[32] German Catholics preferred to have the lay people work closely

---

32. Olson, *Catholic Immigrants*, 22–25 on the Irish, p. 50 on the French Canadians, p. 54 on the Germans, p. 74 on the eastern Europeans, p. 86 on the Italians, p. 151 on the Mexicans.

with the priest. Northern Italians respected the priest's role in the community, but southern Italians often resented the priest because he was too different from the members of the congregation: a landholder (in the old country) and celibate. Hispanics respected the priest but since their practice of religion was less sacramental in orientation and more directly connected with their patron saints, the priest's role did not loom large.

While each of these cultures was transposed with its peculiar old-world attitude toward the priest, the groups that arrived earlier and tended to dominate the unfolding of the church in America set the pattern for the priest's role.[33] Most especially, the Irish set the tone for the priest's role as the center of authority in the parish. Eventually the lay trustee system of the German parishes yielded to the autocracy of the pastor of the parish and the bishop of the diocese. Efforts to bring the Italians to a more priest-centered Catholic faith also succeeded to a great extent. But the same has not been true of Hispanics, no doubt, at least in part, because there is not a large corps of Hispanic clergy.

While parishes were the supporting structure for the faith life of Catholics in the neighborhood or village, the unifying element of Catholicism in the nation was the network of dioceses, the number of which continued to grow throughout the age of immigration. Diocesan bishops kept in regular and relatively close contact with each other through correspondence and travel, but most of all through meetings of the entire hierarchy of the United States. In a remarkable display of collegiality, the American hierarchy met in regional or national council thirty-four times between 1829 and 1900. This "process became the voice of American Catholicism."[34]

Moreover, the hierarchy showed that they were in charge. The most outstanding example, perhaps, is the suppression of the parochial power of the lay trustees. The hierarchy also gained control over the assignment of priests. This was a struggle to achieve, since often ethnic immigrants would arrange for a priest to come from Europe to pastor the parish the lay people had themselves established and paid for.

Since the Irish had the advantage of being the first immigrants to arrive and the even greater advantage of speaking English, their influence outweighed that of other ethnic groups. Irish bishops made up the greatest single bloc in the American hierarchy. Thus, it is no surprise to read Jay Dolan's conclusion that "the Irish tradition of an authoritarian clergy and a

---

33. Ann Taves has stressed centralizing and institutionalizing influences of certain devotional practices that require the ministry of the priest, e.g., the granting of apostolic indulgences. See her *The Household of Faith: Roman Catholic Devotions in Mid-Nineteenth Century America* (Notre Dame, Ind.: University of Notre Dame Press, 1986), 96.

34. Olson, *Catholic Immigrants*, 197–98.

deferential laity had become the normative model in the United States" by the turn of the century.[35]

The Romanization of the American church was another route to unifying the widely diverse ethnic immigrants flooding into the country. Since all the Roman Catholic immigrants belonged to the supranational Catholic church united around the bishop of Rome, it became an especially valuable strategy for unification to stress the Roman connection. The Vatican sought this stress first of all, not least because the age of immigration in the United States coincided with the ultramontanist movement in Europe.[36] While there was opposition from some quarters (Cardinal James Gibbons, Archbishop John Ireland, Bishop John Keane, Fr. Dennis O'Connell) to what seemed to be misunderstandings on the part of the Vatican of the reality of the church in the United States, there was never any doubt about the American church's loyalty to Rome. And the condemnation of Americanism in 1899 solidified the Roman connection as the predominant unifying force of the Catholic church in the United States.[37]

Ministry of the word was especially distinguished on two fronts during the immigrant era: parish missions and parochial schools. Missions had become popular in Europe during the post-Tridentine period as a way to bolster the faith of Catholics sorely tried by the religious conflicts generated by the Protestant Reformation. Missions became equally popular as a way to bolster the faith of Catholics in the United States during the nineteenth century.

The early nineteenth century brought with it a second religious enlightenment in Protestant circles in the United States, paralleling the first great enlightenment of the eighteenth century. Revival meetings were the rage among Protestants. Beginning in the 1850s parish missions became the Catholic equivalent of the Protestant revival meetings. Tactics and expected outcomes of both the Protestant and Catholic varieties were comparable.[38] Parish missions functioned as a way to counter the proselytizing efforts of Protestants, to reenforce the faith of immigrants in the midst of the confusion of the entirely new circumstances of their lives, and to generate a Catholic faith that had not been so strong in the Old World to begin with.

Dolan has noted that "the principal aim of the mission was individual

35. Dolan, *American Catholic Experience*, 172. See also Jay P. Dolan, *The Immigrant Church: New York's Irish and German Catholics, 1815–1865* (Baltimore: Johns Hopkins University Press, 1975), 165.

36. Marvin R. O'Connell has written of this period: "Never before had the papacy's prestige among Catholics stood higher, never before had the theoretical right of the pope to 'universal jurisdiction' been more effectively exercised" ("John Ireland," 144).

37. Fogarty, *Patterns of Episcopal Leadership*, 87.

38. Dolan, *Immigrant Church*, 156–58.

conversion."[39] To engender individual conversion the mission was highly personalistic and experiential.[40] The practical route to conversion was a personal experience of the restorative gift of God's grace leading to sacramental confession of sins and absolution from the priest. On this basis of forgiveness of their sins Catholics would begin to attend mass regularly on Sundays, or, if they were already in the habit of Sunday mass, they would now attend with deeper devotion.

The parish mission's strong emphasis on regular reception of the sacrament of penance and weekly participation in Sunday mass as the way to grow in the graces gained by conversion had an effect beyond the religious well-being of the person converted. Since the sacraments were administered by ordained priests at the parish, and since the parish was a constituent element of the diocesan and worldwide Roman Catholic church, the parish missions served to enhance the institutional strength of the Catholic church in the United States and its fidelity to the Roman See.[41]

Besides personal renewal of faith and participation in the church's sacramental life, the parish mission promoted moral living. Of special concern to Christians of all sorts in the United States throughout the nineteenth century was temperance. Excessive drinking was considered to be the evil root of the breakup of families, indigence, and religious indifference, whereas temperate adults avoided taverns, stayed at home, and thus fulfilled their family responsibilities faithfully. Moreover, the temperate person (men were the chief targets of the concern for temperance) was diligent about his job and careful to save from his earnings, thus providing better for his family's present and future. Finally, the temperate person was more alert to his religious duties, and thus was more assured of salvation.

A second area of emphatic focus of ministry of the word in the age of immigration was the establishment of the parochial school system. As formal education took root, and children were more and more required to be educated, immigrants sought education for their children as well. However, large numbers of Catholics judged that the public or common schools in their neighborhoods or locales were destructive of Catholic faith. The schools promoted Protestant Christianity, at least simply because the American ethos was Protestant, but also because schools and their teachers sometimes deliberately set out to woo Catholic students from their faith to the profession of Protestantism. Unwilling to subject their children to such as-

39. Ibid., 153.

40. Jay P. Dolan, *Catholic Revivalism: The American Experience, 1830–1900* (Notre Dame, Ind.: University of Notre Dame Press, 1978), xviii.

41. Again, this result parallels the European experience of mission; ibid., 32. See also Olson, *Catholic Immigrants*, 196ff.

saults upon their faith, and also eager to preserve their ethnic distinction, Catholics in many instances chose to establish their own schools.

By the turn of the century, a vast network of parochial schools had been established throughout the country, promoted certainly by favorable decisions at the Councils of Baltimore, especially in 1852 (the first to encourage the establishment of parochial schools) and 1884 (the council that decreed that every parish was to establish a parochial school).[42] At the same time, because of the burdens of funding the schools, as well as the difficulty of finding adequate personnel, enthusiasm for the parochial school was not universal on the part of parents, pastors, or bishops.

Besides the more practical considerations of funding and personnel, there were other reasons that parochial schools were not universally favored, with the result that the school system never did include all, or even a majority, of Catholic children. Probably of major significance, although it would be difficult to document, is that in the nineteenth century as now, many Catholic parents were simply not interested in sending their children to parochial schools. Indifference might not be the only factor here. Improving the status of their children within their new American homeland might be another.

Despite the fact that some were not altogether in favor of them, and that funding was difficult, and that never more than half the Catholic schoolchildren were educated in them, the parochial schools became a major vehicle for handing on the faith in the immigrant church. Catechism lessons and participation in liturgy and devotions were included in the daily scholastic routine. Loyalty to the church was fostered by means of the strong presence of clergy and religious in the administration and on the teaching staff. Pride in the school that had provided one's education became indistinguishable from pride in one's Catholic faith. What was true for parochial elementary schools was also true for parochial and private Catholic high schools, colleges, and universities. As the church in America entered the twentieth century, ministry of the word was implemented on a massive scale by the nuns, priests, and brothers teaching in the vast Catholic school system.

What characterized the ministry of sacrament in the age of immigration? Sacramental worship was structured according to the reforms decreed by the Council of Trent. Moreover, depending on the success of parish missions in various places, regular participation in the sacrament of penance and regular attendance at mass on Sundays became more common for Catholics than it had often been in the land of origin. Despite the uniform-

---

42. Dolan, *American Catholic Experience*, 275.

ity of the liturgy, including the same Latin language, however, Catholics of one ethnic background were generally not comfortable worshiping in churches that ministered mainly to Catholics of another background. It was a matter of language and style. The Irish were more quiet, while the Germans liked to sing. Italians paid more attention to their saints. Each communicated in a different language.

Devotions were important for every ethnic group, but they too varied from one group to another. While the Corpus Christi procession was important for the Germans, the Italians celebrated a *festa* each year in honor of the local patron, for example, Our Lady of Mount Carmel on July 16 or St. Anthony on June 13, or any of several others according to the town or region in Italy from which the immigrants hailed. The Poles had their distinctive religious customs too: "They built a replica of Christ's tomb on Good Friday and filled Easter baskets with food blessed on Holy Saturday. On Christmas Eve they celebrated Wigilja supper, sang 'koledy' Polish carols, and distributed 'Oplatki' wafers to friends and relatives. Following funerals they held a 'Stypa' feast and celebrated a 'Poprawiny' the day after a wedding."[43]

The religious practice of all the immigrants, including those who rarely celebrated the sacraments, was rich with ethnic-oriented devotions. The array of devotions provided a bond among the members of the ethnic group, even as it separated each group, not only from Americans of other religious persuasions, but from Catholics of other ethnic identities. Still, as has been pointed out, "modernization, acculturation and assimilation have been inexorable" among the immigrant groups, "constantly working to transform the minority values and loyalties and bring them in line with those of the larger society."[44] Appreciating the inexorability of this process and remembering the past of ministry in the United States, we now shift our attention to ministry in the contemporary United States.

Word, Sacrament, and Pastoral Care at the End of the Twentieth Century in America

During the first six decades of the twentieth century Catholicism in the United States was especially characterized by the self-confidence of institutional success and an attitude of superiority. The efforts of nineteenth-century ministry to establish a stable and enduring way of Catholic life

---

43. Olson, *Catholic Immigrants in America*, 116–17.
44. Ibid., 171.

seemed to have paid off. On the church front the hierarchy was clearly in control and yet the laity also had a sense of their dignity and necessity in the church. On the civic front Catholicism was increasingly respected as a partner in the American enterprise.

The hierarchical centralization of church authority was accomplished as the Eucharist became the heart and soul of Catholic piety in America.[45] Immigrant Catholics of every background in some way came to understand the Eucharist to be the central expression of their faith so that by 1963 weekly mass attendance on the part of Catholics reached 71 percent.[46] Since only the priest is empowered to preside at the Eucharist, a Eucharist-centered piety bolstered the priest's authority in the ecclesial community. Significantly, the priest's authority extended to the temporal and financial affairs of the parish (and of the diocese in the case of the bishop), and the Eucharist became the sacred cornerstone of the whole range of sacerdotal authority.

Strong eucharistic piety for the laity, on the other hand, served to provide a spiritual ground for their daily living as well as to enforce their loyalty to the ecclesiastical hierarchy. "Exposed as they were to the prevailing Protestant culture and necessarily preoccupied with business interests, the laity's commitment to monthly holy hour, to periodic visits to the Blessed Sacrament, and to nocturnal adoration represented their allegiance to a parochial community and their obedience to its leaders."[47]

Parish missions are a second movement of nineteenth-century Catholicism which became consolidated as well as transformed in the twentieth century. No longer parochial nor revivalistic in their spirit, the missions developed into the retreat movement. Retreat centers were established by religious orders of women and men and by dioceses. Organizations of men and women were formed whose sole purpose was the promotion of retreat opportunities especially for lay people. Joseph Chinnici notes that "the whole retreat movement, in its numerical and financial growth, its propertied base, organization, and close cooperation between laity, religious orders, and priests reflected the growth of the American Catholic community and its development, in the first half of the twentieth century, of relative stability and economic security."[48]

Connected to eucharistic piety, and almost always conducted by priests, retreats also solidified lay loyalty to the hierarchical church. Whereas, how-

45. Chinnici, *Living Stones*, 146–56.
46. Andrew M. Greeley, *The American Catholic: a Social Portrait* (New York: Basic Books, 1977), 127.
47. Chinnici, *Living Stones*, 150.
48. Ibid., 159.

ever, eucharistic piety was often understood in individualistic terms, the retreat movement was imbued with a sense of social responsibility. It awakened lay Catholics to shake off the excessively passive role into which they may have drifted (or been relegated by the hierarchy) and become more engaged in active Christian apostolic activities.

Catholic schools, institutions strongly promoted in the nineteenth century, flourished in the first half of the twentieth century. The sheer enormity of the Catholic educational enterprise is awesome in its rapid growth throughout the early decades.[49] By 1930 it became possible for Catholics in large numbers to receive their entire education, from kindergarten through graduate school, in Catholic schools. Here, as in the areas of liturgy and spiritual renewal, what was happening in the Catholic community was that "energies previously devoted to coping with religious needs of immigrants were diverted to consolidating and stabilizing institutional structures."[50] What was in process of formation was not only the Catholic faith within American culture but an American Catholic culture.

Just what form this culture should take, however, was becoming increasingly complicated, for the adversarial situation of immigrant Catholics in the Protestant nation, a situation that enabled Catholics to develop a culture set apart, began to break down increasingly in the twentieth century. Catholics began to enter the American mainstream. They committed themselves wholeheartedly to support their country's efforts in both great wars of the century.[51] They became elected representatives of government on every level, with a Catholic finally achieving the highest elected office of the United States in 1960. They found educational and business success and the financial rewards that come with it on a par with other Americans. In short, Catholics had finally become assimilated into the United States.

The self-confidence of early twentieth-century American Catholicism tended, however, to mask unsettling forces that emerged with full impact after 1960. These forces, together with the major Catholic ecclesiastical event of the century, the Second Vatican Council, function as the contextual factors for ministry in the United States at the present time. Since it is not altogether clear how much change the forces imply and how desirable such change is, polarization easily develops among people who react differently to the forces at work in church and society.

A first contextualizing factor is the increasing absorption of life processes and social arrangements by technologization, which continues at a

49. Hennesey, *American Catholics*, 237–38.

50. Ibid., 237.

51. Hennesey notes that of 3,948 conscientious objectors to military service in World War I, four were Roman Catholics (ibid., 225).

fast and furious pace. Even people who throw themselves into every fresh technological advance find themselves left behind as now this and now that breakthrough takes hold. Although its technological hegemony is presently being strongly challenged in various centers in western Europe and Japan, the technological revolution began and continues unabated in the United States. Machines do more and more of our work; gadgets fill our lives. Anyone can verify by personal experience how things produced by increasingly sophisticated technology both keep the day going smoothly and create frustration when the things fail to function. Communications around the globe are instant, provided one has a computer and an appropriate modem. Elections of politicians as much as papal presence to the faithful are profoundly influenced by communications technology. Such matters as state-of-the-art sound equipment, air conditioning, digital organs and carillons all have a part to play in contemporary liturgy, as do audiocassettes and satellite receivers in religious education and television expertise in evangelization. The technological revolution is no insignificant factor in contemporary Christian ministry.

Technological development has created a global village out of the widely diverse peoples of the earth, and this functions as a second contextualizing factor in contemporary ministry. No matter how separated geographically, people of every corner of the globe are discovering that their isolation from other groups is diminished, if not eliminated, by communications technology. No matter how distinct culturally, people find that elements of other cultures, sometimes widely differing from their own, are assimilated so that, for example, Americans cultivate a taste for foods and other goods developed in every conceivable nation, dams are built on the Senegal River in Mali by mixed teams of West Germans, French, Saudi Arabians, and Americans, and teenagers the world over hook up to Japanese-made radios, listen to British rock groups, wear American jeans, and eat McDonald's hamburgers. These, of course, are but superficial reminders of the more profound interdependence of the global economy. Whether the rich get richer, and the poor get poorer, or a more equitable standard of living accrues to all, economic order is increasingly the result of worldwide influences. Economic order relates people through travel, telecommunications, language, exchange of goods and services. As people interrelate on those levels, other levels of human development come into play as well: art and entertainment, political philosophy, social relationships in marriage and friendship, and religion. People influence and are influenced by the religious systems of others as much as by their systems of manufacture and banking, though the former influence is not so readily acknowledged as is the latter.

A third contextual factor is the advance of modernity into the Catholic self-consciousness. Modernity with its empirical method in the natural sciences and historicity in the humanities has influenced Catholicism from the time of Galileo and Descartes. But for most of the period from the seventeenth through the twentieth centuries the church and modernity were adversaries. The church decried modernity as destructive of the divine-human relationship; modernity abandoned the church as irrelevant. But gradually historical criticism found its way into biblical exegesis and the history of doctrine, church structures, liturgy, and spirituality. Even Thomism, the church's officially sanctioned philosophical system, was historically retrieved, with the discovery that the scholasticism that had governed so much Catholic doctrinal and theological formulation was decadent, that is, not faithful to the vitality of Thomas at various stages of his own thought's development. Moreover, the Kantian turn to the subject combined with Wilhelm Dilthey's discovery of the historicity of human reflection could not be ignored by the church's intellectuals and pastors.

Modernity had received a more positive hearing from some Catholic scholars at each stage of its unfolding, and was more insistently demanding a hearing from Catholics throughout the first decades of the twentieth century, but it rushed into the church as if a dam had burst when Pope John XXIII invited communication with modernity (*aggiornamento*) at the end of the 1950s. However, since modernity had been held at bay for so long, its reception at long last was engineered with such a mixture of critical and uncritical appreciation that the faithful of every role and stripe were cast into uncharted waters of change that allowed no one, from the pope to the neophyte Catholic, the advantage of steering a serene course.

The Second Vatican Council stands as a fourth major contextualizing factor of contemporary Catholic ministry in the United States. Neither Pope John XXIII nor the Second Vatican Council he convoked was the most significant causes of the onrush of modernity into the church, for the causes were much more profoundly within the collective consciousness and subconsciousness of a Catholicism that could no longer prevent nearly four centuries of human history from touching the church, especially when its members were otherwise living in the midst of that history. The Second Vatican Council did, however, function as the officially sanctioned process by which the institution permitted itself to adopt an open stance toward much that is characteristic of modernity. Moreover, because technology afforded the possibility of rapid, global communication, and because the democracies developed since the late-eighteenth century had created the new reality of millions of educated Catholics, the questions debated at the Council became debated by Catholics, and other interested persons, throughout the world.

In several areas the Council reviewed the church's tradition in the light of the contributions of modernity, appropriated some of those contributions into the tradition, and revised its theological and ministerial directions. For one thing the Council took historical criticism seriously in its decrees on how the church would receive and study the biblical Word of God and on the renewal of the liturgy. It joined a historically minded ecclesiology to the retrieval of biblical images to teach a doctrine of the church that celebrated the share in Christ's priesthood enjoyed by all the baptized, began to revive the collegial role of bishops that had prevailed during the first thousand years of Christianity, and promoted an active laity more explicitly than had even been suggested in previous church documents. It reversed the church's post-Reformation defensiveness against Protestantism and even more timeworn belittlement of Judaism and other religions and welcomed dialogue and, to a limited degree, partnership with all the great world religions. The Council went on to eschew any past inquisitorial attitudes to true and false religion, instead paying homage to the rights of persons in the matter of religious conviction. Finally, in the conciliar document on the church in the world, the Council led the church away from the virulent attacks on modernity that had characterized the previous three centuries, and attempted a balanced review of what was positive and what was negative in modernity.

It was a mind-boggling array of initiatives for the Roman Catholic church to take at a time when a mind-boggling array of new scientific, political, and technological initiatives were in the process of coming together in worldwide society. It should surprise no one, therefore, that twenty-five years after the close of the Council the church and its ministry would still be in an unsettled state, which is exactly where we find ourselves. The Council itself is now reviewed with more balanced criticism, its initiatives appreciated but against the backdrop of subsequent events. Moreover, technology, international interdependence, and the knowledge explosion continue to reshape the worldview of diverse members of the church in diverse ways. Thus, while we can report on how ministry is being accomplished within contemporary American culture, we have no illusions that what we are reporting is a static state of affairs. For many current problems are not being addressed by the present way of doing ministry, and new issues keep looming on the horizon.

Within this unstable context five themes dominate contemporary Catholic ministry of word, sacrament, and pastoring in the United States. To my mind the theme most profoundly affecting church life at the present time is the shift from uniformity of thought and action to a diversity that at times becomes individualistic. Certainly during the early decades of the century, at least after the modernist crisis of the first decade, Catholicism in America was perceived to be a uniform, if not rigidly undoubted, set of beliefs and practices. Catholics themselves considered that all were in agreement on the essentials, whatever differences might exist regarding certain particulars of theology or ecclesiastical strategies. Then, after the Council, priests and religious abandoned their vows in great numbers, married couples more readily divorced, the membership on the left and on the right felt comfortable dissenting from papal teaching. Such externally visible moves revealed a great deal of rethinking of the meaning of their Catholic faith on the part of ordained and baptized Catholics alike.

That wave after wave of such unprecedented action could wash up on the shores of ecclesiastical life so suddenly, although there was no official warrant for much of this sort of action in the Second Vatican Council's teaching, is evidence that the uniformity that had seemed so solidly in place during the early years of the century was actually no more than a veneer.

Astute observers of the theological ferment, the restrictive measures of the Holy Office, activist journals such as *America* and *Commonweal*, and the university scene would have been able to note that uniformity was hardly a characteristic of American Catholicism even before the Council.[52] They could have called for a more serious search for the actual unity of the Catholic tradition. But apparently there were very few astute observers, or at least they were not paid much attention. More obvious was a self-confident rallying round the papal flag. When the Council signaled a more open attitude, instead of reasoned reflection and debate ensuing, it was more like the lid being blown off a pressure cooker. Turmoil in church life has not abated in the years since the Council; there is no sign that it is likely to calm down soon.

The transition from seeming uniformity to a wide range of diversity within the Catholic church in the United States has had tremendous impact upon ministry. From Catholic to Catholic, and therefore from parish to parish and even from diocese to diocese, theologies and strategies can differ widely. The Catholic church in the United States has been the locus of much experimentation by people of every stripe. Sometimes the effort to respect differences has resulted in the extreme of individualism in which the corporate reality of the church has been lost altogether. But by and large American Catholics have maintained a sense of belonging to the one, holy,

---

52. With regard to the university scene, e.g., Philip Gleason reports that even before 1960 at Notre Dame University the goal of a curriculum integrated by Thomism was considered to be outdated and impossible of achievement. See Philip Gleason, *Keeping the Faith: American Catholicism Past and Present* (Notre Dame, Ind.: University of Notre Dame Press, 1987), 268 n. 58.

catholic, and apostolic church even as the Catholic church in the U.S. continues to join the rest of the universal church to work out just what *belonging* entails.

Distinct from the diversity that characterizes Catholic life at the present time, but complementing it, is a second theme that exerts a great deal of influence on contemporary ministry in the U.S., namely, the freedom of U.S. Catholics to doubt. This freedom to doubt replaces the premodern sense that to have faith means to be, and, God willing, to feel, absolutely certain about the tenets of faith and one's trust in God. We are dealing here with a clearly postmodern phenomenon. Philip Gleason writes, "On the speculative plane, the great problem was to reconcile the dogmas of faith with the findings of modern science, biblical scholarship, comparative religion, history, philosophy, and psychology."[53]

But it is not simply a postmodern problem. Doubt belongs essentially to faith. Gleason quotes Garry Wills in this regard: "Doubt is the test. Faith is rooted in it, as life in death. Faith, unless it is mere credulity, . . . is a series of encounters with doubt, perpetual little resurrections; cynicisms met and transcended, never evaded. . . . The only way is the long way, through indirection, doubt, and a faith that survives its own death daily."[54]

Since doubt is unsettling, and everyone, if possible, would prefer the serenity of certitude, unfortunate reactions to doubt can develop. For some, doubt seems to be a failure of faith. They become convinced that they have lost their faith, and so they abandon the church, either thinking themselves guilty for not having made the effort to keep their faith alive or thinking the whole enterprise of faith and church outmoded in an age when faith is no longer necessary or possible. Others become frightened by the uncertainty they observe in their fellow Catholics and consider it a threat to themselves. They search frantically for a new way to be secure. Since uncertainty has now become a characteristic of Catholicism in a way that had not been so in recent memory, such people feel compelled to seek a secure Christian faith elsewhere, sometimes in the emotion-as-conviction of Pentecostal denominations or in the certainties of fundamentalist denominations. For those who stay with the struggle in the Catholic communion, there is often enough the anguish and dismay that comes with wondering about the quality of personal fidelity or about what is essential to Catholic Christianity. The doubt of committed Catholics is a theme that shows itself in contemporary ministry.

Two themes of contemporary ministry in the United States come more

53. Ibid., 160.
54. Ibid., 154.

directly from the Second Vatican Council: shifts in the identity and roles of ordained and baptized Catholics and the appropriation by American Catholics of the values and disvalues of American culture. With regard to the first theme it would be too strong a claim to assert that there has been a general reorganization of ministerial roles now that the church has officially recognized that the baptized have a significantly active role to play in the church's mission. But there is no doubt that the pattern of ministry is undergoing thorough reexamination, entirely justifiable in the light of the theology taught by Vatican II. If the church remains faithful to the ecclesiology of *Lumen gentium*, the outcome of the present reexamination will yield greater balance between the roles of the baptized and the ordained. But because reexamination of the patterns of ministry is still in process, and continues to include both critical and uncritical reflection and decisions, the ministry of both the ordained and the baptized is in both healthy and unhealthy flux.

Still, some consensus has been reached. The priest is no longer looked upon as the sole agent of ministry. Designated and more spontaneous ministries on the part of the baptized are being recognized and implemented, although, as we discussed in chapter 2, what roles call for the nomenclature of ministry is a matter of dispute in some circles. A broader range of activities inspired by Christian faith is being accepted as genuinely ministerial; ministry is not limited to ecclesiastical activities. The role of women in ministry is also becoming gradually better appreciated and promoted, although it still lags lamentably. In general, every baptized Christian is believed to be graced with charisms the church is learning to welcome if the baptized person is ready to exercise them on behalf of the common good.

A theme that has influenced ministry in the United States since the beginning of the nation is the issue of the relationship of the Catholic ethos and the American ethos. This theme functions in contemporary ministry in terms of a friendliness of American Catholics to particularly American qualities such as individual freedom, democratic government, and justice for those who live on the margins of society, deprived of significant participation in the good things life offers to so many other people. Happy as they are to be a part of the American commonwealth, contemporary Catholics also find themselves drawn in by the less noble qualities of the American ethos: greed for things, superficial religiosity, excessive competition.

The more immediate sources of the current view of America's opportunities and dangers for Catholic faith are two, the political and economic success of Catholics in America and the Second Vatican Council's Declaration on Religious Liberty (*Dignitatis Humanae*). Largely engineered by American theologian John Courtney Murray, the declaration places the Catholic church squarely in the camp of those who advocate religious liberty for individuals and within nations. After centuries in which the Roman Catholic faith (and others) had been imposed upon the citizenry as the state religion, the American experiment of disestablishment was now endorsed by the universal church because the theory, which John Courtney Murray was able to trace to the reflection of Thomas Aquinas, was shown to be practicable in the success of Catholicism in the United States, whose national constitution guarantees the right of individuals to choose their own religious worldview and practice.

At about the same time as the Council, American Catholics were attaining a high point in their political and financial success in the United States. Catholics no longer need think of themselves as the oppressed minority in the Protestant nation, at least not on the basis of their Catholicism. They can share in all the benefits of the good life that the United States has to offer. On the other hand, perhaps Catholics, together with their fellow Christian compatriots, have become so assimilated that there is danger of losing the values of Christian faith: recognition that to be human is to be a creature, sinful and redeemed; evangelical simplicity; the communion of rich and poor alike; concern for justice to the marginalized. [55]

Functioning alongside of and even pervading each of the four themes highlighted above is a fifth theme: the desirability of constituting the church as a community. Theologically, the theme of community was struck in *Lumen gentium*'s choice of its predominant image of the church as the People of God. The drafting committee of the dogmatic constitution explained its choice of People of God as the principal image, preferable to the other possible image, the Mystical Body. [56] While Mystical Body also functions as an image of unity, it begins with the diversity of the members of the body, which then become organically united into a single body. But People of God functions first as an image of a great assembly united in a common faith, and then includes the diversity of roles exercised by individuals. The Council wanted to stress that God first calls the world's scattered individuals into a people whose unity is constituted by God's gracious love. The order of the chapters of *Lumen gentium* supports this rationale by placing the chapter discussing the image of the People of God before the chapters developing the teaching on the diversity of roles in the church. [57]

55. For differing perspectives on the desirable appropriation of the American ethos by the Catholic ethos, see Dennis P. McCann, *New Experiment in Democracy: The Challenge for American Catholicism* (Kansas City: Sheed & Ward, 1987); George Weigel, "Is America Bourgeois?" *Crisis* 4 (Oct. 1986): 5–10; and David L. Shindler, "Is America Bourgeois?," *Communio* 14 (1987): 262–90.

56. See my "The Priest, Prophet and King Trilogy, Elements of Its Meaning in *Lumen Gentium* and for Today," *Eglise et Théologie* 19 (1988): 184.

57. Ibid., 183.

Since the Council, efforts have been made in word, sacrament, and care to promote the community life of the church. Because the individual character of the Christian's relationship with God and the individual responsibility to overcome sin and attain heaven had perhaps been exaggerated in the period since the Enlightenment, the Council's emphasis upon the communitarian character of church life responded to a need in the consciousness of Catholics that had been untapped for too long, and a longing for community burst into the open. Promoted by church ministry since the Council, the church as community has also recently been recognized to be in need of balance with individual responsibility. The theology of communion, as promoted at the 1985 Extraordinary Synod of Bishops, is seen as one way to foster a balanced ecclesiology.

Taking into account the contextualizing factors and the five themes, we outline, first, ministry of sacrament, then of word, and finally of pastoral care and leadership.

American Catholics moved quickly after the Second Vatican Council to implement the church's directives to renew the administration of the sacraments.[58] As the most frequently celebrated sacramental liturgy, the Eucharist received immediate attention and lively reaction. The altar was positioned to be free-standing, placed near the congregation, and the altar rail removed, in service of bringing the priest and the congregation closer together and into a more relational style of worship. The baptized entered the sanctuary to proclaim the biblical readings and assist the presider with the distribution of communion to the congregation. Congregational singing began to be strongly promoted. Moving the furniture for worship, developing diversified roles at liturgy, and inviting universal responsiveness during liturgy all gave external expression to the Council's call for "full participation" in the liturgy. The sacrifice of the mass was to be clearly an assembly of the faithful around the tables of Word and Eucharist. Ironically, just at the moment that eucharistic renewal seems to be generally in place, and the church is ready to move to the next step of rendering the renewal more profound, the number of priest-presiders is declining drastically. Will the Catholic church have to find an alternative Sunday liturgical ministry to eucharistic presidency?

Perhaps the greatest achievement of the last twenty-five years in the United States in the area of ministry of sacrament is that worship is generally no longer perceived as the effort of individuals to work out their personal salvation without regard to their sisters and brothers of faith. Catho-

---

58. An informative list of changes that have been introduced into American Catholic life since the Second Vatican Council appears in *A Shepherd's Care: Reflections on the Changing Role of Pastor*, prepared by the Priestly Life and Ministry Committee of the National Conference of Catholic Bishops (Washington: USCC, 1987), 5–30.

lics sense and many know that the baptized are called to form a community of faith where each is alert to the others, where salvation is pursued by all working together, not only for the church's members but for all the world's people. The need of the moment, noted increasingly in church documents of the last several years, is for the renewal of Catholic worship to move beyond the arrangement of the furniture and even beyond a superficial communitarian spirit to a depth of communion with one another in the life of the triune God, even as we celebrate diversity of roles, temperament, and culture among the People of God. It is a matter of the achievement of a total ecclesial consciousness.

The prodigious efforts to renew the church's communal worship over the last few decades are accompanied not only by more enthusiastic participation in liturgy by many who attend, but also by declining numbers of American Catholics at Sunday mass. If the liturgy seems not to address their specific needs, or if the style of the celebration is unsuited to their mood or temperament, Catholics in sizeable percentage opt to neglect liturgy often or altogether. Partially this is due to the phenomenon of Catholics finding their voices and their feet in the post–Vatican II church. Congregants do not hesitate to criticize what they do not like about their parish, its priest(s), and the local celebration of worship. It seems partially due also to the American spirit of individual freedom, without any attendant commitment to the common good.

Ministry of the word also takes new shapes under the influence of the themes that have been noted. It is recognized that preaching the gospel in the United States at the present time requires sensitivity to the diverse receptivities of America's diverse Catholics. [59] There are also efforts to make preaching ecumenically sensitive. For example, as a start, several churches, including the Roman Catholic, have adopted a common lectionary for Sunday worship. If Christians of different denominations hear the same Scriptures proclaimed and preached on Sundays, they may thus find themselves in dialogue more about their common faith. In another area, as Catholics become more self-determining in their choice of which parish to attend or whether to drop out of practice of the faith altogether or to enroll in another denomination, preachers begin to recognize their responsibility to address the issues of faith as profoundly and honestly as they are able. Evangelization has become a significant word in the late twentieth century in the United States, and a major dimension of its use is reaching out to Cath-

---

59. See, e.g., Priestly Life and Ministry Committee of the National Conference of Catholic Bishops, *Fulfilled in Your Hearing: The Homily in the Sunday Assembly* (Washington: USCC, 1982), 22.

olics who have been alienated from their church or from Christian faith altogether. More subtly, preachers recognize that those who faithfully fill the pews at Sunday Eucharist can be suffering through their own doubts and are in need of a word that is sympathetic, convincing, and encouraging.

The Second Vatican Council's constitutions on liturgy and on divine revelation revived a challenge that had been issued several centuries earlier by the Council of Trent, namely, that Catholic preaching be improved. Specifically, Vatican II called for preaching at liturgy to be homiletic: a reflection upon the Scriptures of the day exhorting the congregation to fidelity to the Christian way of life. More biblically grounded and locally oriented homilies mean a departure from the more doctrinal and generic sermons of previous generations. The Council's explicit reflection upon the evangelizing mission of the church not only to territories that have not yet heard the gospel message, but also in the midst of well-established churches whose fervor has grown cold, has also proved to be a challenge to liturgical preaching. It reminds preachers that the gospel message is always new, that faith can never be taken for granted, that there is always further faith development to be achieved.

Renewal programs that have burgeoned in the United States during the later decades of the twentieth century are also instances of acceptance of the challenge of ongoing, indeed, continual evangelization. Contemporary renewal programs are a continuation in the present time of the missions that flourished in immigrant America. Now, however, the stress is not exclusively upon personal renewal but upon the development of Christian communities that accept responsibility for the salvation of their fellow human beings both inside the church and in the broader society. In the late 1960s the Better World Movement (*Il Movimento per un Mundo Migliore*), founded after World War II in Italy, became a popular vehicle for parish renewal in some dioceses in the United States. More generally implemented, and still being promoted, was the *Cursillo* ("little course in Christianity"), a weekend program of evangelization and community building. The parish process of RE-NEW has also been popular in the United States. Contemporary renewal programs invite more active involvement on the part of the participants, rather than simply a passive presence at lengthy sermons. It is anticipated that in their aftermath more parishioners will become actively engaged in the parish catechetical, liturgical, or social apostolates, and join support groups that gather for personal prayer or Bible reading and mutual reflection.

Distinct in its approach from other renewal programs is the charismatic renewal, which swept through the Catholic church in the United States in the years immediately following the Council and continues to be strong throughout the country. Frequently directed by lay leaders, the charismatic renewal is structured around weekly prayer meetings in which participants voice their needs and concerns and are strengthened by the prayer of the entire group. Prophetic utterances, teachings by the leaders or invited guests, healing services, and at least occasional celebrations of the Eucharist during prayer meetings also characterize the program of the charismatic renewal. True to the contemporary preoccupation with building community, participants in charismatic renewal groups frequently form tightly knit bonds among themselves. A tendency to drift into individualistic Christian fundamentalism, however, sometimes besets charismatic renewal communities because their intense, personal interpretations of events can create a sense of being directed by the Holy Spirit apart from the wider church community.

Each of the renewal movements includes extensive participation of the nonordained members in leadership roles. Often the groups are characterized by a strongly democratic government. Sharing responsibility among the ordained and the baptized is a natural response to Vatican II's teaching on collaboration in the church's mission. Increasing inclusion of lay women and men in the catechetical enterprise of parishes has also become common since the Council. Again, this is a function of the universal responsibility of all baptized adults for the church's mission, although the continually decreasing number of religious and ordained in the United States during the last several years is also a factor in inviting more lay participation in catechesis.

A serious problem the church has had to face since the Council is the poor preparation of lay people for their increased responsibility in the church. If one's religious education is limited to studying the catechism until about age thirteen and listening to the homily at Sunday mass, not much by way of an adult appreciation of the Catholic faith can be expected. To respond to this lack of training, adult education programs arose in great numbers in parishes across the country in the years following the Council and they continue, although it seems to a lesser extent, in the present. It is difficult, perhaps impossible, to assess the quality of parish-based adult education. Moreover, education in this manner never reaches large percentages of American Catholic adults. The challenge of inviting Catholics to lifelong development in the faith remains to a great extent unmet.

A model of adult faith development that is enjoying increasing use, however, is the Rite of Christian Initiation of Adults (RCIA). Modeled by the catechumenate and mystagogy of the early centuries of Christianity, the RCIA is primarily intended for adults who seek admission into the church.

The program has, nevertheless, been found to be adaptable for adults and adolescents who have been Catholics since infancy. A structured community context for faith development that remains permanently in place enables adults to move through stages of development at their own pace. There is room for times of doubt and uncertainty, for less and more sophisticated approaches to church life, for different emphases on prayer, Bible study, doctrinal and theological reflection, spirituality, and social action. Because, however, the RCIA is an ambitious undertaking, requiring an active approach to faith development on the part of a large number of parishioners, many parishes shy away from introducing it. Long-established patterns of more passive and less expressive and reflective parish life are not easily abandoned.

Books, audiocassettes, and audiovisual cassettes have also become extensively used in contemporary ministry of the word. Because of the ecumenical atmosphere in the church Catholics do not limit themselves to publications by Catholic authors but quite freely avail themselves of other Christian authors as well. Generally this is a good fruit of the ecumenical age, but it does lead to confusion at times about distinct beliefs maintained by the Catholic church.

Even more influential than printed material and individual cassettes is the mass medium of television. Protestant evangelists have vast followings, including Catholics. With a few exceptions, notably Mother Angelica (EWTN) and the cooperative venture of the Interfaith Television Network (VISN), Catholics have been slow to get into televangelism. Of late, the nation's bishops have supported a Catholic television ministry, but it continues to flounder. A tentative explanation I tender is that Catholic ministry is intrinsically connected with church community and sacraments (whose objective is communion), and one cannot participate in sacramental communion while sitting in one's living room watching television. Television is more suited to an exclusively word-oriented ministry (whose objective is conversation). But within the Catholic ethos ministry of the word cannot be implemented in an exclusive way; it is profoundly united to sacramental communion.

As we move from the veneer of uniformity that had to some extent characterized Catholic intellectual life, reflection, writing, and teaching during the earlier decades of the twentieth century, to a more open-ended and less absolutist intellectual climate in the later decades, we can expect fear, charges, and countercharges, as well as experiments to test how far a church, one of whose marks is unity, can live with debate and disagreement. Because Catholic intellectual life deals with understanding convictions of faith and even with establishing beliefs, we cannot simply treat conversations and debates among Catholics as the recreation of a salon society. It is a matter of ministry of the word of God.

The contemporary atmosphere of debate began before the Second Vatican Council as biblical scholars and historians sought critical understanding of Catholic doctrines using the resources of modern scholarship. During the Council bishops themselves engaged in debate with one another. In itself there was nothing at all surprising about the fact of factions among bishops. What was new is that few Catholics had prior experience of serious disagreements among bishops because few remembered the debates that permeated the First Vatican Council and all the great ecumenical councils.

After the Council, Pope Paul VI's publication of the encyclical *Humanae Vitae* (1968) elicited public statements of disagreement from theologians relative to its teaching against artificial contraception, as well as massive disagreement in practice by millions of Catholic married couples. The debate moved from disagreement about particular doctrines and theology to debate about disagreement itself. To some it was to be expected that an educated Catholic membership, including bishops, lay people, and theologians, should engage in conversation that would regularly erupt into debate and disagreement. The likelihood of such disagreement recurring seemed to set the stage for new procedures to work out a unified Catholic position on the burning questions of faith and morals. It is not that the bishops no longer possess the role of the pastoral magisterium, or that the pope is not the final arbiter of Catholic belief and practice; it is just that a way has to be found to accept the contribution of all faithful and reflective Catholics who choose to enter the discussion.

Other Catholics strongly disagree with the more participatory approach to Catholic intellectual life and to the process of arriving at doctrinal positions. In their view there is a radical distinction between the teaching and the learning church. Learners only learn and never contribute to the process of arriving at the doctrines to be taught. Teachers, on the other hand, are assured of the guidance of the Holy Spirit without consultation of the wider church membership. From this perspective debate and disagreement are instances of disloyalty to the leaders of the church and infidelity to the church's doctrine.

At the present time no solution to these opposing points of view has been discovered. Charges and countercharges continue to fly. American bishops and theologians are at work, however, to discover a process of conversation among themselves. They also seek to defuse some of the tension-filled atmosphere by recognizing that the perception of serious disagreement among bishops, theologians, and lay people on various sides of issues is overdrawn. Addressing the annual meeting of the Catholic Theological Society of America in 1989, Archbishop John L. May, then president of the National Conference of Catholic Bishops, stressed the collaboration that has existed between American bishops and theologians and recognized a "developing cooperation" which appreciates "both the teaching authority of bishops and the indispensable service of theologians."[60]

Alongside ministry of sacrament and of word, ministry of care is undergoing significant change in the United States in the late twentieth century. Once again the Second Vatican Council is significant, along with the confidence American Catholics have found as citizens of the American republic. During the immigrant era Catholics founded hospitals, orphanages, and homes for working women and men, not in the first instance because they were spontaneously motivated by Christian charity and compassion, but because some Protestant institutions which already existed induced those Catholics for whom they cared in their institutions to give up their Catholic faith. Catholics determined that they would have to found their own institutions of care for their own people.[61] Thus, Catholics who on their own were more concerned about their personal salvation and not so much concerned about society's marginalized members, even if they were Catholic, became concerned when it appeared that Catholics cared for in Protestant-controlled institutions would lose their faith.

As Catholic institutions of care for the sick and the homeless became well-established and took in people of other faiths as well, a genuine commitment to the needy developed among American Catholics. Religious congregations dedicated to care were welcomed and became major institution-builders. Organizations for church members, such as the St. Vincent de Paul Society, a parish-based program of outreach to the needy, became widespread. Throughout the age of immigration and the first decades of the twentieth century, however, the focus of care for the sick, the unemployed, orphans, working women and men, and families and individuals displaced by war was on the products of social systems.

It was only after the Second Vatican Council that the causes of social displacement and unrest began to elicit the concern of Catholics in a major way. Questions about systemic social sin emerged. Think tanks to study possible remedies for social ills were established. Lobbying of legislatures to address the causes of unemployment, poverty, and disease became a Catholic enterprise. Efforts like these were a natural outcome to serious

---

60. John L. May, "Theologians and a Climate of Fear," *Origins* 19 (June 22, 1989): 88.
61. Dolan, *Immigrant Church*, 121–40.

reception of the Council's pastoral constitution on the church in the modern world with its concentrated look at social and political realities of the twentieth century. In addition, now that they had found their way into the American mainstream, Catholics felt more comfortable as a public church. The episcopal leadership of the church in America, through their national conference, committed themselves to a more public agenda.

The bishops set up lobbying machinery in Washington. They issued public statements about major moral issues in American society—issues such as the Vietnam War, housing for the poor, racism, abortion, the death penalty. In the 1970s the bishops used the occasion of the bicentennial of the American Revolution to insert the Catholic church into the debate on American public policy. In the 1980s national pastoral letters on peace and the economy generated response from the White House, newspaper editorials across the country, and international attention. Catholic ministry of pastoral care has clearly entered an era in which the church is a major public institution in the United States.

Ministry of pastoral care as leadership within the church is also undergoing significant change in the American church at the present time. Again, the stimulus can be traced back to the Second Vatican Council as well as to the American ethos. The Second Vatican Council called for more consultation in the government of the church. On the diocesan level this has translated into the establishment of diocesan pastoral councils and in the parish of parish councils. Committees of clergy and laity regarding a wide range of concerns flourish.

Americans are a democratic-minded people and so American Catholics are entirely comfortable with the implementation of participatory models of church governance. In fact, American Catholics tend to expect that decisions within the church will be arrived at in a democratic way, with each member of the diocesan or parish council being awarded one vote when it comes to the time of decision. It is no easy matter for American Catholics to be consulted and then to await the decision of the hierarch in charge, either bishop or pastor.

But the church is not a democracy. Oft-quoted article 21 of *Lumen gentium* teaches that the bishop's consecration into the fullness of the sacrament of orders is the foundation of the teaching and governing offices. The article goes on to indicate that the same consecration is the sacramental source of power to continue Christ's work by any member of the Body of Christ. The local bishop thus presides over the incorporation of others in his diocese into active participation in the mission of the church through baptism and confirmation. The bishop is the focus of order in the church.

Still, the American bishops seem to be recognizing that unless the members within their jurisdiction, baptized and ordained alike, have a sense that they are respected as adult members of the community whose input into present functioning and future directions is valued, church community will flounder and could ebb away. Many bishops are dedicated in their ministry of leadership to wide consultation with members of their diocese and shared responsibility. Even those who are not recognize that the days in which the ordained are active while the baptized are passive are over. They too seek some ways in which to broaden the ministry of leadership.

This may be an appropriate place to bring to a close this discussion of ministry in the United States. It is evidently not an exhaustive discussion. To the extent that it has been successful, however, it has delineated the meaning of the inculturation of ministry within a particular culture. I trust that the discussion communicates how the universal Christian ministry of word, sacrament, and care is particularized as it becomes incarnate within each culture.

Chapter Seven

THE INTERIOR FORMATION OF THE CHRISTIAN MINISTER

CHAPTERS 2 AND 3 DISCUSSED HOW THE GRACE OF GOD works through the sacraments of baptism, confirmation, and order to bring about a transformation in the orientation of their recipients toward God. This transformation is permanent because God's grace is not withdrawn and the spiritual subject never falls out of existence. The transformation is named a character in each of the three instances.

By baptism and confirmation the effects of Christ's saving life, death, and resurrection become personally applied to countless women and men, inserting them into the community of the divine persons. In addition, each baptized person is gifted with particular charisms to be used to promote communion and conversation throughout the church and wider society as well.

Order is totally oriented to service of the community. The recipient of the sacrament is ordained to exercise the ministry of leadership of word, sacrament, and pastoral guidance of the local church or a portion thereof.

The impression could be created that public conferral of the three sacraments is all that is required for them to accomplish their purpose in humanity. If that were the case, we would be dealing with metaphysical claims that not only would have no ascertainable grounding in human consciousness, and therefore be only extrinsically effective, but we would also be setting ourselves up for accusations of mystification rather than theology. Thus, the present chapter argues that the public ceremonies of baptism, confirmation, and order confirm, stabilize, and advance conscious events which are individually verifiable as persons appropriate their interiority and publicly verifiable in the actions of baptized, confirmed, and ordained persons. For by their fruits you shall know them.

However, the foremost purpose of the present chapter is not to ground metaphysical, theological claims in verifiable, conscious events, important as such grounding is. It is rather to emphasize that without appropriation of their interiority by the subjects of the characters of baptism, confirmation, and order, the privileges and demands themselves of the sacraments are likely to remain merely external. What is needed is the opposite, namely, for baptized and ordained persons to be self-conscious ministers of the gospel. Then they are well aware of the riches in which they participate, and well motivated to distribute them generously.

Thus, the present chapter examines the actual consciousness of Christian ministers. A first section makes the claim that two images preside over the consciousness of authentically Christian ministers. I name them the attitudes of communion and service. They could also be named orientations residing in the subject who desires to be a faithful minister of the gospel of Jesus. In the present discussion, then, communion and service are not categories with a defined content, although as they have entered into the heritage of Christian theology they have also been formulated into categories.

A second section starts with the claim that the attitudes of communion and service are susceptible of authentic or unauthentic implementation. Authentic implementation requires that Christian ministers be subjects pursuing self-transcendence. Consistent self-transcendence is pursued through conversion in six dimensions of subjectivity: Christian, religious, intellectual, moral, affective, and psychic.

Following descriptions of the conversions, the chapter stays with the dynamism of the basic structure of subjects pursuing self-transcendence to examine in terms of intentionality what ministry is about. Thus, the objective of ministry specified in previous chapters as communion and conversation is here recognized, within the context of the structure of subjectivity, to be a number of occurrences of the communicative function of meaning, through a wide range of carriers of meaning, in which the church community and its individual members, as privileged collaborators with the missions of the divine Trinity, promote healing and creating in human affairs.

Core Attitudes:
Communion and Service

Specifying the self-consciousness of baptized and ordained Christians is the formation of attitudes of communion and service. The two attitudes reenforce each other, although they are distinct from one another. The person who meets Jesus and hears his word and that of the church awakens to a longing for communion with the triune God through the ministry of Jesus himself. Sometimes the longing is sensed more tangibly in a desire to share fellowship with like-minded Christians at worship, in service projects, and in friendship. Fellowship of this sort can be powerfully sustaining. But its limitations are felt too, not so much in a negative way, as in a longing for more profound communion, for which even the best human fellowship merely prepares but never achieves.

Sometimes the longing is for more immediate communion with God. Unless and until the discipline of prayer advances, conscious communion with the triune God remains elusive too, although it beckons persistently. Even those who taste communion convincingly find that the experience is more a glimpse that sustains than an uninterrupted presence. The longing for communion must ultimately be fulfilled in some other life than the present.

Still, the need to express that transcendent longing for communion is what generates the search for communion on the part of the members of the church among themselves. In some way, we sense, we are best when we strive to create bonds among ourselves that mirror the bonds that exist among the persons of God. Diversity among equals, mutual interdependence, order in our relationships: these trinitarian-based concerns have moved in and out of the church's consciousness throughout the history of Christianity. Is not the reason that longing for communion is inextricably rooted in the Christian subjectivity an endowment of the character of the sacraments of Baptism, Confirmation, and Order? From little groups gathered for morning worship or for evening Bible study to base communities, from parishes to the local church to the church universal Christians strive for communion.

Balancing the several elements of communion seems never to have been accomplished existentially at any moment in the history of Christianity, and this is no doubt the reason for the disappointment, acrimony, separation, and efforts at reunion that recur continually. Nor, it seems, will there be any lasting satisfaction until we are gathered up once and for all into the divine communion.

But our whole being cries out for us never to give up our efforts to create the sort of ecclesial communion that faithfully expresses in its own limited way the communion of the triune God. Not only that but we long to have some influence upon creating dialogue and communion throughout worldwide society. And when instances of communion and dialogue materialize, even in small ways, we feel exhilaration and a freeing of our spirits.

Besides longing for communion, the self-consciousness of the baptized and the ordained includes the desire to be of service. Undoubtedly, selfishness and complacency also characterize Christians as much as other persons, just as desire to be of service characterizes persons of good will, whatever faith they profess. Indeed, it can be argued that, along with communion, service is one of those deep human attitudes, residing at least in the subliminal consciousness of every human person. In their noblest manifestations the great religions draw these attitudes into consciousness. Sometimes they emerge in individuals without any ostensible outside influence to elicit them. Among the world religions, Christianity, through the gospel of Jesus, not only draws the attitudes of communion and service into consciousness but explicitly relates them to the paschal mystery of the Lord's passage.

Thus, when the Christian appropriates the attitude of service it is within the context of the service of Jesus. Jesus reminds his disciples that "I am among you as one who serves" (Luke 22:27), and "The son of man came not to be served, but to serve, and to give his life as ransom for many" (Mark 10:45). As Jesus' self-consciousness is selfless, eager to assist the well-being of others, so his followers.

It has been noted that to move from being a fleeting longing to a consistent one, communion requires the discipline of years of prayer. Service, too, requires discipline if it is to be consistent rather than a sporadic attitude. The discipline promoting a long-standing attitude of service is that of responding to people in need repeatedly from instance to instance. By acting on the momentary impulse of generosity or the promptings of duty, subjects learn to value the attitude of service, and to seek to respond to it more consistently and out of love.

While the formation of attitudes of communion and service is at the heart of the self-consciousness of baptized and ordained Christians, both communion and service are readily tied into multiple meanings and manifestations. The centuries have been witness to the truth that equally committed Christians can have quite different views about the implementation of both attitudes. Church order and ministry that are the fruit of genuine communion and service are created by subjects who are sufficiently developed to seek what is true, good, beautiful, and loving. They are capable of eschewing what is false, valueless, ugly, and hateful. To seek the former and avoid the latter is a matter of increasing self-transcendence. Freedom for self-transcendence is a function of the process of conversion of human subjectivity. To the several dimensions of conversion we now turn our attention, not only focusing on each dimension but indicating its role in authentic ministry.

Conversion

Aspects of the conversion of human subjectivity have already been discussed in chapter 1. But there conversion was assessed as methodologically significant for doing theology. In the present chapter our concern is rather with the formation of the interiority of the Christian minister, most especially the development of authentic attitudes of communion and service. Here, then, we consider once again Christian conversion, as well as religious, intellectual, and moral conversion. In addition, affective and psychic conversions are probed. The six are different dimensions of the transformation of individual subjects along the path of ever more advanced self-transcendence.

In common parlance all these dimensions of human subjectivity are not included among the references of conversion. When dealing with human subjectivity, conversion commonly refers to the movement of a person from being unengaged or only peripherally engaged in religion, or from being involved in a "false" religion to embracing the "true faith." On the part of Christians the language of conversion is originally biblical, naming the passage from sin to grace, from a life doomed to damnation to one blessed with the assurance of salvation. But conversion can be understood more broadly. It can be applied existentially, when the passage is from unauthentic to authentic self-determination. It can be applied in Marxist terms of reference to the movement from false to true consciousness.

Bernard Lonergan's application of the term to the self-transcending transformations of human subjects in several areas of their subjectivity is the meaning of conversion employed here. The specifically Judeo-Christian reference of the term is included, but three dimensions of subjectivity are determined to be especially susceptible of conversion, namely, the religious, in a more generalized sense than simply the Judeo-Christian tradition, the intellectual, and the moral. A further two areas of conversion have been drawn out of implications in Lonergan's writings by two of his students, Robert Doran (psychic conversion) and Walter Conn (affective conversion).

In this broader meaning, conversion names the process of radical change in a subject's orientation, whereby one's horizon on reality shifts to include dimensions that had previously been unknown or known only in an informational way. The transformation that is conversion effects a self-engaged involvement of the subject in a more complete grasp of reality in its several dimensions. When a subject undergoes conversion, then, she or he becomes ever more existentially engaged by what is true, good, beautiful, and loving in reality in all its dimensions.

If it is to be a lasting achievement rather than a passing glimpse, conversion is gradual, advancing slowly, securing now this and now that new gain, as well as suffering false starts and enduring painful lapses and recoveries. Gradual though it is, conversion, in any one of the areas, is not imperceptible. The subject feels the tension of transformation as it catches on to the demands of self-transcendence. Within the process moments of a leap forward can stand out.

Christian Conversion

Christian conversion means that a subject has met the Jesus of history who has become the Christ of faith, and been so attracted by his person and message that the subject is entirely engaged by the Lord. A person may be introduced to the Lord by parents or a friend, by the fellowship of a Christian community, by reading the New Testament, or by observing a disciple of Jesus. But the meeting itself is personal. The subject is aware of coming under the influence of Jesus who lives as the risen Lord. It is not unlike the engagement that takes place in other situations where one person comes under the influence of another.

From being attracted to the Lord, the subject finds the gospel message increasingly convincing. One hears or reads or observes, and wants to know more. Sometimes quite quickly, but more often gradually, the person forms a commitment to the Lord and the good news. The commitment, too, can move from being peripheral to more central to total. Poring over the Scriptures to take on the mind and heart that were in Christ Jesus becomes a priority for the subject undergoing Christian conversion. One longs to spend time in prayer with the Lord. One seeks to know the implications of faith in Jesus, both in terms of knowledge and in terms of action.

As persons become engaged with the Lord, attitudes of communion and service assume greater significance. Communion and service mean what Jesus means by them, and what the New Testament describes them to be. The subject becomes eager to live by those attitudes in the way that Jesus lived by them and taught them to others. Communion is appreciated as the indwelling of the Lord Jesus, along with the Father and the Spirit, as is described, for example, in the Johannine Book of Glory or in Pauline texts of self-emptying in such a way that Christ takes over one's subjectivity. Service is implemented in obedience to Yahweh and on behalf of one's sisters and brothers in imitation of Jesus, the *Ebed Yahweh*, as described in Mark 10:45 or Luke 22:27. The converted subject is fed by these biblical texts, pondered over and over, as the very word of the Lord addressed to her or him.

Subjects of Christian conversion also find their whole worldview being reshaped. Whatever worldview had been theirs before their meeting with the Lord, it now is dismantled and replaced with a worldview shaped by the message of the gospel. Since the gospel, for all its simplicity, does not yield a worldview without long and careful reflection, Christian converts spend years under the tutelage of faith, prayer, study, ministry, the heritage of the Christian tradition, and the living witness of other members of the community. Thus, while Christian conversion is often remembered in terms of outstanding outer events and inner movements, its actuality is a gradual process of self-transcending transformation by which the subject is thoroughly engaged in relationship with the Lord Jesus. Think of descriptions of key moments of change recounted about or by outstanding Christians such as Paul of Tarsus, Martin Luther, and John Wesley. Think also of descriptions of gradual movement toward and consolidation of key moments in the lives of Augustine, Francis of Assisi, and Thomas Merton. Whatever variations among the outstanding moments of and the slow process toward Christian conversion, in the end no one and nothing else is more significant in the person's life.

Obviously, Christian conversion is the specific conversion that underlies Christian ministry. Only the person living out of engagement with the Lord Jesus can also become committed to Christian ministry. For this reason, sustained formation from the first moment of Christian conversion is essential to Christian ministry.

I contend, however, that Christian conversion is not a sufficient formation of the interiority of Christian ministers. Interpreting the meaning of Christian discipleship and the Christian gospel, determining how to worship, or choosing which actions to pursue have all admitted such opposing expressions of Christianity that even internecine warfare, both physical and spiritual, has resulted. Demagoguery, slaughter of innocent victims, and domestic strife have all been perpetrated in the name of the gospel of Christ. Chapter and verse of the New Testament have been cited in favor of such behavior. To move beyond such truncated and even destructive interpretations of Christianity, subjects must form themselves according to all the dimensions of human self-transcendence. Then, in their subjectivity, they become authentic filters through which the gospel can be faithfully mediated. We proceed now to examine those dimensions.

Religious Conversion

Religious conversion takes place when a subject moves from ignorance or rejection to wholehearted acceptance of the human spirit's opening to the infinite. It is not just that the content is infinite, ultimately God. The human subject itself has a dimension to its subjectivity that opens onto the infinite. This dimension becomes activated when the subject becomes aware of itself being drawn beyond this-worldly concerns of whatever sort. It is being stretched to embrace something more. [1]

Christianity provides one constellation of spirit that gives expression to the something more. But so do Hinduism, Buddhism, Judaism, Islam, and other manifestations of the other-worldly dimension of human subjectivity. Whereas sometimes Christians in their conviction about the truth of their way have rejected entirely other constellations of spirit, religiously converted subjects recognize that the other ways are to be respected, and their adherents to be engaged in conversation because, while not stepping away from the truth claims of Christianity, the Christian who is also religiously converted recognizes that other ways of the spirit authentically embrace the something more as well.

How may such a claim be made? To answer most simply, religiously converted subjects value mystery. They sense, if they do not know, that it is too facile to name God on the presumption that any human mind could comprehend what the name signifies. To some, then, it seems better not to attempt to name mystery at all. Instead they seek simply to allow full sway to that which breaks out of all the boundaries of human consciousness. They know with the poet, Rainer Maria Rilke, that we people of faith often build a wall between God and ourselves, and that

> The wall is builded of your images.
> They stand before you hiding you like names, And when that light within me blazes high that in my inmost soul I know you by, the radiance is squandered on their frames.
> And then my senses, which too soon grow lame, exiled from you, must go their homeless ways. [2]

Christians are among those who name God, and Christian ministers regularly speak of God with and to the people they serve. Christian ministers should be persons who have undergone religious conversion, lest they reduce God to an object under their control. Lonergan writes what becomes sobering advice for Christian ministers:

> On what I have called the primary and fundamental meaning of the name, God, God is not an object. For that meaning is the term of an orientation to

---

1. The whole of chap. 4 of Bernard Lonergan's *Method in Theology* (New York: Herder & Herder, 1972) deals with aspects of the issue of religious conversion. See also Bernard Lonergan, "Religious Commitment," in Joseph Papin, ed., *The Pilgrim People: A New Vision With Hope* (Villanova, Pa.: Villanova University Press, 1970).

2. Rainer Maria Rilke, *Poems from the Book of Hours*, trans. Babette Deutsch (New York: New Directions, 1941), 13.

transcendent mystery. Such an orientation, while it is the climax of the self-transcending process of raising questions, none the less is not properly a matter of raising and answering questions. So far from lying within the world mediated by meaning, it is the principle that can draw people out of that world and into the cloud of unknowing.[3]

Religious conversion also keeps ministers alert to the dangers of speaking to people about God as if God were comprehensible in human terms. One of religion's historical disservices is to confirm people in their assumptions that somehow there is no genuine mystery in life, that every question is resolvable. The result is bitterness or frustration "when bad things happen to good people" who have expected something more manageable from life.[4] Transcendent wisdom eludes them. Often, unfortunately, those who might administer a more profound vision of faith are not themselves religiously converted, and thus cannot offer a more adequate religious perspective.

Religious conversion confirms the truth of the apophatic way of theology. It shows that it is not just a way of theology, but a way of religious living that is not expendable even for Christians.

Simultaneously, acknowledging mystery as the most proper name for God does not eliminate the need, insofar as we are able, to develop a doctrine of God, to affirm the triune God of Christian faith, or to seek specific determinations of the will of God. But it alerts us that our most adequate doctrinal expressions and our best determinations of the will of God, while they approach the mystery, never comprehend it. We are in love with, committed to, mystery that is at the same time real, personal, and present, and never within our grasp.

Moral Conversion

Subjects whose attitudes of longing to enter into communion and desire to be of service are formed by Jesus and his gospel, and by the tug and pull of mystery, become aware that they are losing enthusiasm for pursuing mere self-interest. Their own feelings and projects no longer dominate their actions. They sense themselves seeking to do what is good in itself no matter what the scale of difficulty. They rearrange the priority of their values according to the directives of Jesus' gospel, the relativizing power of mystery, the needs of other persons who are valued as worthy of reverence and love. Such subjects are undergoing moral conversion.

3. Lonergan, *Method in Theology,* 342.
4. I am quoting, of course, the title of Harold Kushner's popular book (New York: Avon, 1981).

It is necessary to be more specific. Human persons are endowed with an evaluative power. Every possibility is not looked upon as equally of value. Pursuit of physical, emotional, and mental health is a value. Developing one's intellectual capacities and the social graces, and establishing relationships of love and intimacy are more significant. Respecting the dignity of every human person is fundamental to all human values. Pursuing these values not just for one's convenience but for their own objective worth shifts a subject's priorities. When one's motivation, additionally, becomes religious and Christian, yet another element of value comes into play, inviting the subject to further self-transcendence.

Sometimes a person pursues a value with modest interest; at other times one becomes preoccupied in the pursuit of a value or set of values. It happens that a subject may be so committed to the pursuit of a particular value that he or she is willing to surrender life rather than compromise the commitment to the person, idea, or practical objective.

For Christians moral conversion is most often expressed in terms of the gospel. The dictates of the commandments of the Torah and the new law of Jesus inform the conscience of subjects who have undergone Christian conversion. When the ultimacy of the universe, its divine ground, and human subjects is felt and judged to be mysterious, then religious consciousness informs morality as well. But the change of subjectivity that can be named moral conversion is not itself a function of either Christian or religious conversion. It is rather a shift of evaluative orientation from primary concern with one's self-interest to primary concern with what is objectively good. One's decision-making capacity remains the same however it is oriented, but as the orientation shifts, the type of decisions shifts as well, and the person becomes an authentic moral subject.

There exist stages through which a person might pass in the process of moral self-transcendence. Lawrence Kohlberg's three major stages of moral development provide one convincing articulation of the process of moral conversion. Kohlberg names the first stage of moral judgment preconventional because it relies on responses of reward and punishment. The second stage, that of conventional conformity, consists in behaving in such a way as to receive approval as a "good" person; at this stage goodness is determined by one's peers or the authorities in a person's life. The third stage is that of postconventional or autonomous morality, in which the subject has appropriated her or his own conscience in a thoughtful and responsible way.[5] For Kohlberg the third level of moral judgment is "characterized by a major thrust toward autonomous moral principles which have validity and

---

5. See Walter E. Conn, *Conscience: Development and Self-Transcendence* (Birmingham, Ala.: Religious Education Press, 1981), 63–64, 91ff.

application apart from [the] authority of groups or persons who hold them and apart from the individual's identification with those persons or groups."[6]

Christian ministers are not necessarily morally converted. They may use the language of service, and claim to be concerned with the promotion of divine-human communion and dialogue within the church and wider society. However, what passes, for example, as the ministry of Christian leadership may be nothing more than a self-serving promotion of a leader's ego, an immoral bias. Jim Jones of Jonestown, Guyana, stands as an extreme example of a Christian who undertook the ministry of leadership without commensurate moral conversion, thus becoming an egomaniacal demagogue. He demonstrates what can happen when (presumed) conversion occurs within one dimension of subjectivity while other dimensions are neglected. Since Christians who engage in ministry do so as entire subjects, they serve out of the developed and underdeveloped subjectivity that is theirs in its several dimensions.

Christian ministers whose moral subjectivity has developed only to the stage of preconventional or conventional moral judgments and decisions may easily misjudge a prospective course of action, and influence the recipients of their ministry to do the same. If a minister's determination of what is genuine Christian service is interpreted solely by the minister's feelings that something is right or what the minister's peers think or what authority is understood to direct, but without committed orientation by the minister to do what is good simply because it is good, divine-human communion and conversation may not be served at all, but thwarted. Together with Christian and religious conversion, therefore, moral conversion is necessary for authentic Christian ministers.

Intellectual Conversion

Commitment to the good is one thing, knowing what the good is, another. The human act of knowing has undergone great scrutiny in Western intellectual civilization. Questions about the very possibility of knowing have been raised and pursued. While we are able to get through many areas of our living without raising the question of knowledge, dealing with life's ultimate questions becomes more problematical if one ignores the question of knowledge itself. Not only is this the case because contemporary women and men often reject the religious realm as nonexistent or irrelevant, but also because there are so many contrary claims, even among religionists, of the meaning of the religious realm and of the Christian gospel. The ques-

6. Ibid., 95.

tion is asked: Whose interpretations are correct? To answer that question, we must deal with the underlying question of knowledge itself.

As a subject becomes engaged by the knowledge of knowledge, the one question begins to distinguish itself into three: inquisitiveness about the specific operations involved in knowing, about why that process is knowing, and about what one knows when one faithfully implements the process.[7] As the questions are answered, one begins to recognize that the assumptions about knowledge that have been latently guiding one's pursuit of knowledge in this or that area may have been mistaken, especially if one's assumption was that knowledge is somehow a matter of observation. A shift of mentality then takes place, the shift that can be named intellectual conversion: now one has experienced, understood more precisely, and made a judgment about what operations of consciousness are involved in coming to know; it begins to dawn why the combination of these operations constitutes knowledge; it becomes evident that a subject really can come to know both the self and the world in which the subject lives, and this evidence liberates one to live in the vast universe of being.

Intellectual conversion is a great effort because the demand to pursue the question of the meaning of knowledge from beginning to end is rigorous. The landscape of Western intellectual history is dotted with outstanding figures who have raised the question and sought its answer. Plato concludes in the *Meno* that knowledge is memory. Aristotle and his medieval pupil, Thomas Aquinas, understand that the issue revolves around two questions: What is it? and Is it so? Descartes's *Discourse on Method* begins on the basis of universal doubt. The British empiricists advise us not to wander from sensible experience. Kant recognizes that, whatever its ability or lack thereof to know things as they are, knowledge is the fruit of subjectivity. Hegel finds a solution in absolute spirit. By means of each of these thinkers the question of knowledge has been asked and the history of Western epistemology has made progress toward a satisfyingly complete answer. In my estimation, however, only Bernard Lonergan has plucked the fruit of the earlier efforts and ripened it into an adequate articulation of the correspondence between subjectivity and objectivity, including a careful account of the methodical way in which to implement the subjective operations that can yield knowledge of the real.[8]

---

7. See Fred Lawrence's clear exposition of the meaning of the questions in "On the Relationship between Transcendental and Hermeneutical Approaches to Theology" *Horizons* 16 (1989): 344.

8. Most helpful, despite its difficulty, is Bernard Lonergan's 1957 book, *Insight: A Study of Human Understanding* (London: Longmans, Green). However, Lonergan's articles and books published during the twenty-year period after its appearance provide indispensable enlargements upon the argument of *Insight*. Subsequent attempts have been made to interpret Lonergan for

Perhaps in eras when there seemed to be no outstanding questions about Christian doctrine, theology, and practice (if, indeed, such eras existed), it was not necessary for Christian ministers to know what it is to think critically and to be committed to doing so. On the other hand, many unfortunate disputes within the Christian church would likely have been avoided if intellectual conversion had been more commonplace.

In any case, it is not responsible for Christian ministers, baptized and ordained alike, to ignore or avoid intellectual conversion in the present circumstances of the onrush of modernity, ecumenical engagement, and global threats and opportunities. The resolution of major issues of Christian ministry, such as those discussed in the preceding chapters, demands that the questions be addressed by intellectually converted Christians, if we are not to make the situation worse rather than better. Even when dealing with individual Christians in their day-to-day living, facile prepackaged answers are not sufficient. Bringing the Christian tradition to bear upon the complicated lives of contemporary Christians, individually and in their local ecclesial communities, requires self-transcending Christian ministers with a developed critical ability.

The greatest danger threatening Christian ministry by avoidance of intellectual conversion may be the general bias that the world's work, including ministry, can be accomplished far more adequately by people who do not trouble themselves with questions of the method of mind. To many, such questions seem speculative and elitist; better just to get on with the work at hand. Is it not irresponsible, however, simply to assume what the work at hand is and what our goals are in its accomplishment without examining whether we know objectively what is at issue and what is to be done? To move beyond assumptions that we think, speak, and act the truth, it is imperative to make the exigent efforts to know what it is to understand, make reasonable judgments, and decide responsibly.

Affective Conversion

Affect denotes the feelings of subjects as they relate to values, either when the values are persons or when they are attached to ideas or activities that

---

audiences not eager to plunge into the Socratic maieutic of *Insight*. Salutary in its accessibility is Tad Dunne, *Lonergan and Spirituality: Towards a Spiritual Integration* (Chicago: Loyola University Press, 1985). Valuable as well is Vernon Gregson, ed., *The Desires of the Human Heart: An Introduction to the Theology of Bernard Lonergan* (New York: Paulist, 1988). Both books include treatments not only of intellectual conversion, but also of moral and religious conversions. No doubt more ways to invite and guide people to intellectual conversion need to be developed that can bypass the actual study of the difficult writings of Lonergan. But the project Lonergan counsels and the procedures he developed to accomplish it remain the paradigm of intellectual conversion.

make the human world. Some subjects express their affect freely; others suppress it; most choose how much to express in different situations. "A person is affectively self-transcendent, Lonergan points out, when the isolation of the individual is broken and he or she spontaneously acts not just for self but for others as well."[9]

It is important here to distinguish between emotions and feelings. Emotions come and go; they are not reliable. Today a person's emotions may be warm and full of enthusiasm, tomorrow gloomy and lonely; one day a person is agitated, the next day tranquil. Emotions are influenced by diet, sleep, health, the weather. They are moods caused by the physical state of the subject. They are not necessarily related to the deliberate intentions of the subject.

Feelings are specifically acts of the subject, related to the subject's intentionality. Lonergan describes feelings as intentional responses to value.[10] They reenforce and express the subject's commitment to values, whether the values reside in ideas, activities, projects, or, most especially, persons. Emotionally one may feel repulsion at the sight of a disfigured person, but one's feelings of reverence for the valuable person lead one to embrace the person. Emotionally one may feel exhausted, but one's love for a crying child leads to a sleepless night of attentiveness to the child.

Why is affect an area of subjectivity that is of importance for ministry? As with any effort that is long-term and cannot rely simply on passing emotional enthusiasm, ministry relies heavily on affect for sustained devotion, dedication, and commitment. One's feelings need to be engaged. How many times do ministers who have passed beyond the initial emotion of their ministry find themselves bored, while the recipients of their ministry experience surliness or apathy on the part of the minister? The reason often is that initial emotions cannot carry one through years of ministry, day after day. But convictions about the meaning of ministry and care for the recipients of ministry are affective responses to value that do not wax and wane according to moods, but remain in place as moods wax and wane. This kind of commitment leads the minister away from the increasing superficiality that would characterize mere emotional involvement to increasingly profound appreciation of the divine meaning of ministerial activities.

Affect is central to ministry from another perspective. Ministry is oriented to people, always an invitation for persons to enter into communion and conversation with the divine community and with one another. Affect

9. Walter E. Conn, "Affective Conversion: The Transformation of Desire," in Timothy P. Fallon, and Philip Boo Riley, eds., *Religion and Culture: Essays in Honor of Bernard Lonergan, S. J.* (Albany, N.Y.: State University of New York Press, 1987), 261.

10. Lonergan, *Method in Theology*, 30–34.

is what enables persons genuinely to be in contact with other persons. As such, affective conversion is indispensable to authentic service. If a minister has no feelings of respect, reverence, awe, wonder, and love of other human beings, in the concrete and not in the abstract, and not first because of their intelligence, wit, or comeliness, but simply because they are human, it is difficult to imagine that such a minister's ministry could be effective. Ministers need not be extroverts, but they need to love people.

Moreover, ministry happens within the church as the community of faithful disciples. Community cannot survive long without a great deal of positive, expressed affect on the part of its members. The shared meanings of the gospel of Jesus the Christ are the foundation of Christian community, but commitment without affect is harsh and sterile. It cannot survive any more than a marriage can survive without affect. Members of Christian parishes and other communities who insist upon privatizing their feelings prevent the community from coalescing. Pastors of Christian communities are especially significant, for affective leadership welcomes people into the circle of common feeling. Leadership that is not affective may be honest and correct, but it does not make people feel at home.

Church and ministry are, of course, institutionalizations of human meaning, and happily so, for their institutionalization enables the continuity from generation to generation of the contributions of church and ministry to human affairs. But the same dynamic that enables survival can also lead to somewhat mechanical repetition of ministerial activities. Both the agents and recipients of ministry can too easily become subjects of routine. But communion and conversation, the objectives of ministry, are full of feeling, and the ministries that promote them depend to a significant degree upon feeling if they are to be effective.

Ministers stand in need of affective conversion to different degrees and for different reasons. Some whose family and childhood backgrounds have been less than wholesome suffer from suppressed affect or aberrant affect. Either they relate to other subjects out of the truncated subjectivity of distant or remote contact with people, cool and unapproachable, or they relate inappropriately, effusive or angry or solicitous in exaggerated or uncalled-for ways.

Other ministers need affective conversion simply because the ministerial relationship is unique among human relationships. Not a business association, nor an instance of superficial acquaintance, nor an exclusive relationship such as marriage, the ministerial relationship calls for an education of feelings so that they engage the minister in a genuinely caring, indeed loving, contact with the people whom she or he serves, but with the freedom that propels both minister and recipient into intimacy with the divine community rather than primarily among themselves. Conversion of this sort requires the gift of divine grace, understanding of the ministerial relationship, and much effort.

Psychic Conversion

In Western civilization the twentieth century is shot through with the development of the discipline of psychology, psychological commentary on passing events, and the application of a wide range of psychological therapies. Late-twentieth-century ministry benefits from the advance of psychology. So much is this the case that we can claim a need for psychic conversion for the sake of more effective Christian ministry. In support of this claim I raise three questions: What do we mean by the psyche? What would psychic conversion be? Why is it necessary for Christian ministers?

Understood within the meaning of subjectivity that is operative in these pages, the affective, moral, intellectual, and religious are not distinct compartments or faculties of the human subject. They are simply the subject implementing the operations of consciousness according to a specific pattern. The same is true of the psyche. It is not a distinct compartment of the human subject, but rather a specific pattern of the conscious operations of the subject.

At least according to depth psychology, the psyche denotes the unconscious depths of the human subject. In the present understanding, however, the psyche is a dimension of subjectivity, expressive in feelings and images, and in this way influential upon the conscious operations of the subject. Here, then, psyche refers not to the unconscious, although its roots are in the unconscious actions of the physicochemical, biological, and sensitive components of the person, more specifically in neural demands, but to these unconscious actions as they coalesce into subliminally conscious feelings and images. It denotes elements of a subject's interiority that influence the conscious activities, but have not yet themselves been adverted to, understood, reflected upon, and deliberated about. Thus, they are somehow present to consciousness and quite influential, but not appropriated.

How to tap into those subliminally conscious energies, understand their origins and routes, and achieve some kind of self-direction over them is the project of psychic conversion. It is the shift from manipulation by one's subliminal energies to appropriation of them through attention to the data of the energies, understanding and reasoning about their meaning, and responsible deliberation about how to direct them within one's life. [11] As such,

---

11. For a more complete way of expressing the meaning of psychic conversion, see Robert M. Doran, *Psychic Conversion and Theological Foundations: Toward a Reorientation of the Human Sciences*

psychic conversion joins the others described above as a fundamental instance of self-transcendence of the human subject. Psychic conversion is the conjunction of befriending the psyche through awareness with the application of intellectually converted subjectivity to the befriended psyche.

Because so many educated persons have yet to acknowledge the presence of a psychic dimension to their subjectivity, the means of attending to its patterns of operations can seem strange. Recall and reporting of dreams, spontaneous drawing and sculpting with clay, and imaginary interaction with figures evoked in guided waking imagination all bring to imagination subliminally conscious energies. Activities such as these are techniques by which the subject can attend to the data of subliminal consciousness. Of course, as noted, attending to the data is only the start; beyond that, the subject must seek to understand how the subliminal energies are influencing one's feelings, thoughts, judgments, and decisions, all of which, in turn, influence relationships and activities, and indeed one's underlying worldview. Finally, evaluative judgments and decisions need to be made so that the psychic dimension is integrated with the other dimensions of the subject.

The value of psychic conversion for Christian ministers flows from the fact that psychic energy is such an important element of human subjectivity and from the meaning of psychic conversion. Ministers as much as other human subjects are influenced in their thinking and feeling, decisions and actions by their subliminal consciousness. Unless subjects are psychically converted, the energies of subliminal consciousness remain powerful but misunderstood and unknown in their true meaning. Their power can be such as to distort the best-intentioned ministry, prolonging the evil of sinful orientations and structures, thus tearing down rather than building up the Body of Christ. Psychic energy that distorts ministerial intentions can lead to bizarre projects, such as those reported sometimes in newspapers.

What, for example, of the male pastor who relates inappropriately to his female parishioners? The reason may lie in his failure to appropriate his psyche intelligently, reasonably, and responsibly. The pastoral leader who unconsciously and compulsively manipulates and even humiliates his or her collaborators possibly suffers from entanglements of feelings (as intentional responses to values) which could be unentangled by critical psychic self-appropriation. Ministers who are workaholic, or suffering from other symp-

---

(Chico, Calif.: Scholars Press, 1981), 141–43, and, more recently, Doran's "Psychic Conversion and Lonergan's Hermeneutics," in Sean E. McEvenue and Ben F. Meyer, eds., *Lonergan's Hermeneutics: Its Development and Application* (Washington, D.C.: Catholic University of America Press, 1989), 178–92.

toms brought on by stress, or simply feeling listless and apathetic in their ministry may be in need of psychic conversion. Even minor but irritating eccentricities on the part of ministers can sometimes be relieved through thorough contact with the psyche, putting both minister and recipients more at ease.

Growing into Self-transcendence

Human subjects do not compartmentalize their lives so that they pursue the conversions in some sequence, such that once one is accomplished they launch into the next. There is no predetermined order to the call to conversion. The invitation to conversion appears to be quite coincidental. When the invitation is accepted, a person may concentrate on self-transcendence in one dimension of subjectivity. But such concentration does not exclude other areas, for each dimension is part of the entire subject. Thus, self-transcendence in one area invites it in others as well. The goal is the development of whole persons, wise, loving, good, and beautiful individuals. In turn, well-developed Christian individuals become ministers who authentically assist their fellow human beings to enter into communion and conversation with the transcendent yet intimate God.

Describing the conversions and acknowledging their interdependence is one thing; yielding to the dynamism of our subjectivity as gifted by divine grace so that we develop as self-transcending subjects is another. What are the ways to conversion? There are those we plan and those we do not plan. Both are deliberate in that even the ways we do not plan are influential upon conversion only if the subject is open to the power of unexpected events. The blossoming of a friendship, the death of a loved one, a spontaneous insight, a difficult illness are unplanned events that can generate new instances of self-transcendence.

But what about planned ways of development? It is possible to be deliberate about preparing for and responding to conversion. First, I would distinguish prayer as the single most important sustained effort in the development of Christian and religious conversion. In prayer one regularly encounters the living Lord Jesus, hears the words of the gospel as the Lord's Spirit-filled address to oneself, and fleetingly senses communion with the divine community. In the public prayer of Christian worship, persons come together to give witness to their faith, receive encouragement from the faith of others, and enter into the bonds of the community of disciples. Christian prayer draws subjects out of their self-centeredness into communion with the divine persons, which in turn leads to eagerness to be of service to church and world.

Prayer also promotes religious conversion by drawing the subject into the realm of ineffable mystery. We recognize that communion and dialogue with the divine persons are not the same as with the human persons with whom we are intimate. We may not objectify just what is happening until after years of prayer, if even then. [12] But we experience ourselves being drawn beyond what can be named and described. By this experience we not only are more at home with mystery ourselves, but we are more ready to recognize as soul partners the devotees of other religious faiths.

As Christians develop intimate communion with the divine persons they grow in their affective subjectivity as well. In love with God, they become alert to the beloved. Giving up their own concerns in love for the other becomes an increasingly congenial way to feel. It becomes a pleasure to think less of oneself and more of others. In this way prayer also promotes affective conversion relative to other human beings, who become more appreciated as beloved creatures of God, each uniquely created by God, each uniquely loveable.

People of prayer find, too, that they are invited to moral conversion. Their priority of values changes. Love of God takes precedence. From authentic love of God flows love of one's neighbor. The former supports the latter. Values such as the dignity of each human person and the pursuit of a just civilization through law, education, art, and the economy are enhanced relative to love of God because their meaning is more fully appreciated. Other values such as social relationships and physical well-being may become less or more important according to how they relate to love of God and neighbor. Thus, religious values become the criterion for all evaluation, not suppressing but contextualizing other values. In the light of religious values the truly worthwhile thing to do becomes more readily recognizable and more desirable.

Among types of prayer the examination of consciousness, which originated with Ignatius Loyola, serves particularly well to promote conversion in its several dimensions. In the examination of consciousness, the subject brings herself or himself into the presence of God, and reviews a determined period of time, usually the preceding twenty-four hours. Reviewing the instances of cooperation with the promptings of the divine Spirit that have occurred throughout the day, the subject expresses gratitude for them. Then, reviewing the instances of rejection of the divine promptings, the subject expresses sorrow. Both sorts of experience invite the subject to a clearer as well as a feeling-toned awareness of the movement of self-transcendence and its obstacles. The prayer is concluded with a view to-

12. See Lonergan, *Method in Theology*, 113.

ward the next twenty-four hours by calling upon God to assist the subject to respond faithfully.

Because the examination of consciousness considers all the inner and outer events of one's day, it provides an opportunity to bring to consciousness each dimension of subjectivity. All are welcomed as part of the totality of the subject; each is recognized to bear meaning for the individual's relationship with the divine persons. The examination of consciousness does not compartmentalize specifically religious and Christian events, but adverts to the religious and Christian meaning of the subject's dreams, intellectual puzzlement as well as the euphoria of insight, complicated human relationships, evaluation of current world events, and so on. Examination of consciousness is prayer, but it is prayer as an exercise of self-appropriation in the presence of God and with the guidance of God's Spirit.

While examination of consciousness is a concentrated effort within a few minutes of each day, reflection upon the movement of one's self-transcendence can become a discipline that extends throughout the day. The tone of the examination is beneficially incorporated, gradually, into each new activity of the subject. Subjects become increasingly more attentive to the authenticity of the operations of their consciousness. They follow through more responsibly the dynamic self-transcendence of their subjectivity. Habitual attitudes of intellectual, moral, affective, and psychic conversion assume prominence. It is the enterprise of living self-conscious lives, in the sense of self-transcendent consciousness.

I offer three instances, by way of example, in which the tone of the examination of consciousness can transfer to daily activities, rendering them occurrences of self-transcendence. The first has to do with reading newspapers or watching news programs on television, which most adults do to maintain some sense of contact with the changing events that shape contemporary worldwide society. Contact, however, can mean uncritical reading or viewing, an acceptance without question of the point of view expressed or implied. As intellectual, moral, and religious conversion become priorities for a subject, on the other hand, reading and viewing occur by means of critically honed operations of consciousness, with concern for truth, value, and religious mystery.

Dealing with the institutions of which one is a member presents a second instance. Subjects can deal with the institutional dimensions of life in the most conventional ways. Everything is assumed to be authentic: one lives as husband or wife according to the ways learned from childhood; one functions as citizen of a nation with unthinking acquiescence to the national worldview issued by the political-military-industrial alliance; one never questions whether the church is actually evangelical in the doctrines and practices it proposes. But when the conversions are in process within a subject, mindless acquiescence no longer satisfies.

Examination of one's own authentic participation in the institution, as well as examination of the authenticity of the conventional wisdom of the institution itself, begin to demand the attention of the subject. [13] Converted subjects do not become anti-institutional, for that is an unreasonable position. They become critical members of the institutions to which they belong. To take such a position renders their participation in the institution more genuine rather than less. For example, a person's affect and psyche are converted so that institutional symbols evocative of feelings of pleasure or anger are directed intelligently, reasonably, and responsibly, rather than out of subliminally conscious drives of comfortability or resentment. Or, to take another example, one's religiously converted subjectivity is sensitive to the limitations mystery imposes upon any institutional claims to adequacy in an area of human life.

Leisure, a third instance, can also be submitted to habitually converted subjectivity. Instead of claiming that when one has the opportunity to relax from one's work anything goes, converted subjects choose to be intelligent, reasonable, and responsible about how to spend their time and surplus wealth. They recognize that leisure is not empty time, but time, as all time, to respond to the dynamism of self-transcendence. They seek to involve themselves in ways that are compatible with and supportive of the Christian gospel, thus adopting attitudes of simplicity, generosity, hospitality, and good humor. They do not fail, even in their leisure, to remember those who are marginalized, and look for ways to express solidarity with them.

Of particular value in the matter of promoting conversion is the Jungian theory that the dimensions of subjectivity take shape in an unbalanced fashion in most human subjects. If the thinking function is strong, the feeling function can be eclipsed. Such a person may analyze situations remarkably cogently, but have little sense of how to evaluate or be unable to relate well to other people. If the function of observation is strong, then one may be adept at taking into account all the factors involved in a situation but be paralyzed when it comes to making judgments and decisions because there is no satisfaction that all the relevant data have yet been observed. Such people may procrastinate unreasonably.

Jung observes that in the first half of life individuals develop their strongest functions, so that these shape the personality most prominently.

---

13. Lonergan addresses these issues of major and minor authenticity in *Method in Theology,* 80. See also Lonergan's "Dialectic of Authority," in Frederick E. Crowe, ed., *A Third Collection* (New York: Paulist, 1985).

Persons seeking holistic development, however, discover that in the second half of life they are drawn to greater, as well as painful, efforts to attend to the functions that were consigned to the shadows of one's living during the first half of life. [14] Since these are truncated functions, exercises may need to be deliberately designed to foster their development.

Jung's invitation to attend to one's stronger dimensions first, but then not to neglect the weaker, offers insight into self-transcendence by conversion. At the same time as conversion happens in one dimension of the subject, development of another dimension can be neglected altogether. To avoid neglect, let each minister start where he or she is, probably with Christian conversion, and thence attend to each of the other dimensions of subjectivity. The adoption of exercises that promote conversion in various dimensions often proves helpful. For example, Christian conversion is assisted by Ignatius Loyola's *Spiritual Exercises*. In the area of psychic self-transcendence, Jung himself has designed ways to befriend the psyche, such as dream analysis and active imagination, and the more intense and long-term way of psychotherapy. Bernard Lonergan's *Insight: A Study of Human Understanding* guides readers through the very difficult process of intellectual conversion. Gradually self-transcendence in each area serves its actualization in the other areas as well.

Finally, the way of conversion is not an individualistic way. While conversion is an individual achievement, it is not a solitary pursuit. It is much assisted when individuals following through on the dynamism of self-transcendence band together into communities seeking self-transcendence in the various dimensions. Members receive guidance from those who are further along in the journey. They test with each other, by means of observation and conversation, what is authentic and what is unauthentic. They provide mutual support by feelings of care and commitment; in such an environment of acceptance, evaluation and correction can be received with loving gratitude rather than resentment.

Finding a community of individuals who support a subject's development in one or another of the dimensions of subjectivity is not such a difficult matter. But to find a community that is committed to the pursuit of all the conversions is a rare, perhaps impossible, achievement. Thus, subjects who seek to follow through with the dynamism of self-transcendence in a holistic way must become members of several communities. And they must be prepared, too, for a lonely pursuit of conversion in some areas.

---

14. Jolande Jacobi, *The Psychology of C. G. Jung* (New Haven: Yale University Press, 1975, originally 1943), 13–18.

Meaning and Ministry

The third chapter of Bernard Lonergan's *Method in Theology* treats of meaning. Meaning is what concerns human subjects. Through meaning subjects interpret the world in which they live, constitute themselves as subjects within the world, create the sort of world they decide is meaningful, and communicate to others what they themselves have found to be meaningful. These four functions of meaning recur in every stage of human history. Lonergan names them the cognitive, constitutive, effective, and communicative functions of meaning.[15] They cooperate in human subjects to create the world of human meaning.

In chapter 2 of the present work, the objective of Christian ministry was discussed from the perspective of the content of ministry. Communion and conversation were determined to be the objective of ministry. In the context of the present chapter's discussion of the structure of human subjectivity, and more specifically the structure of converted subjectivity, ministry's objective is determined more broadly to be the implementation of the communicative function of meaning. The cognitive meaning of the Christian worldview and of Christian doctrine, the constitutive meaning of the formation of Christian subjects, the effective meaning of the Christian church's influence upon society foster a further function of meaning, the enterprise of handing on or communicating to other people the meaning that has thus far been achieved. In the Christian context the communicative function of meaning is named ministry. Primarily, as we have discussed, its task is twofold: word and sacrament. In addition, pastoral leadership and care create the conditions for the success of the task.

The carriers or embodiments of meaning are several: intersubjective, artistic, symbolic, linguistic, incarnate.[16] Each functions in ministry.

The frequently mentioned "ministry of presence" is actually the last-named carrier, *incarnate meaning*. "It is the meaning of a person, of his way of life, of his words, or of his deeds."[17] To a great extent it is the way in which Jesus of Nazareth communicates meaning.

The Christian minister is the subject who has integrated the appropriation of the gospel of Jesus with one or several conversions in such a way as

15. Lonergan, *Method in Theology,* 76–79.

16. Ibid., 57–73, 78.

17. Ibid., 73. Thomas O'Meara addresses the issue of incarnate meaning when he writes in *Theology of Ministry* (New York: Paulist, 1983): "Even holy and ancient words do not ultimately explain anything as active and personal as one human being serving the presence of God in another man or woman" (p. 17).

powerfully to invite other subjects to communion and conversation simply through being in their presence. The subject who has been constituting her- or himself as Christian subject mediates this invitation by the very power of self-constitutive integration, without any deliberate effort of communication.

Ministry of presence is not a narcissistic activity in which the minister draws attention to her- or himself. That would be rather an instance of egoistic lack of conversion. Ministry of presence recognizes that in some situations the need of someone is simply to have present another person, endowed with faith, hope, and love, without concern about speech or action. The power of personal presence suffices.

Ministry is often an instance of *intersubjective meaning*, especially in situations in which individuals may identify with another person without understanding why or how the relationship occurs. "Perception, feeling, and bodily movement are involved" to create a community of feeling, fellow feeling, psychic contagion, or emotional identification.[18] Lonergan uses an example to show the distinction between community of feeling and fellow feeling: "In community worship, there is community of feeling inasmuch as worshippers are similarly concerned with God, but there is fellow-feeling inasmuch as some are moved to devotion by the prayerful attitude of others."[19]

In both instances some worshipers assist others to enter into communion and conversation with the divine persons in association with their fellow worshipers. But neither becomes aware of what is actually happening, if at all, until during or after the event. Subsequently, one may intend to move others to prayer, but then the communication can only be hoped for, not predetermined.

Related to fellow feeling is psychic contagion. The preacher moves the congregation to a response by the power of voice, gestures, and images. The devotee induces others to fast and pray by the power of suggestion. While instances of psychic contagion may be authentic, Lonergan cautions that since they are often implementations of "the mechanism of mass-excitement," they may be more likely found in the bag of tricks of "pseudo-religious leaders."[20] Similar to psychic contagion is emotional identification, found not infrequently in the ministerial context where children or teenagers become strongly attached to an adult figure who absorbs their very identity.

Since the instances of intersubjective meaning have a tenuous hold on

18. Ibid., 57.
19. Ibid., 58.
20. Ibid.

intentional meaning, their validity as authentic ministry, genuinely promoting communion and conversation with the triune God, can be determined only through careful examination. Both the agents and recipients of such ministry may be neglectful or truncated subjects, acting out of unconverted rather than converted subjectivity. Caution is in order before embracing intersubjective meaning, in Lonergan's sense, as ministerial.

Symbolic meaning is another matter. Because Christian ministry is communication whose objective is communion and conversation with divine mystery, it is shot through with symbolic meaning, meaning in which the meant is expressed by image and feeling. Since human beings cannot rise to the level of the religious except through the senses, ministry deals continually with images in the realm of the sensible, but for the purpose of lifting people beyond the sensible and leading them into the realm of spirit.

Little wonder, then, that ministers often feel themselves at loose ends; their role places them squarely in situations characterized by tension. Eric Voegelin has described this type of situation as *metaxy*, the tension between the pull in one direction of the timeless and the pull in the other direction of the time-laden.[21] Understandably enough, the original meaning and affect of the symbol can be more powerful than the transcendent meaning which it is also intended to communicate. Then the recipients of ministry must be educated in the religious meaning of symbols. Alternatively, when symbols do not transpose well from one realm of meaning to another, new religiously meaningful symbols may need to be sought.

Symbols themselves, however, cannot be replaced as carriers of meaning. For they bring the whole person into communion and conversation, "mind and body, mind and heart, heart and body."[22] While the realm of God is a realm of spirit, humanity's relationship with God needs to be communicated in image and affect. The kingdom of God Jesus preached is communicated in feeling-toned images that are concretized in human history: friendship, liberation, justice, peacemaking, hospitality. Life with God in Jesus is communicated through elemental symbols: water, food and drink, healing balm; through gesture: kneeling, standing, outstretched hands, an embrace; and through relationships: community living. Ministry serves the placement of each of these embodiments of meaning.

In itself *artistic meaning*, in its sense "as the objectification of a purely experiential pattern," is not pertinent to ministry. But when the "colors, tones, volumes, [and] movements" that are the material of art come together in the service of symbols they may contribute to the communicative meaning that

21. Eric Voegelin, "Immortality," *Harvard Theological Review* 60 (1967): 235–79.
22. Lonergan, *Method in Theology*, 67.

ministry is. Then we might speak of the meaning as applied art.[23] The most obvious instance of applied art serving religious symbolic meaning is architecture, vesture, music, painting, and sculpture that promote worship and devotion. In such cases, artists themselves may be understood indirectly to be ministers.

Ministry also interprets symbols by means of language. *Linguistic meaning* looms large in ministry because it looms large in human meaning in general. "By its embodiment in language, in a set of conventional signs, meaning finds its greatest liberation."[24] Language is at the beck and call of human subjects to express their intentions in multiple ways.

Because ministry for the most part deals with people as they live out the daily drama of their lives, its language is the discourse of ordinary or everyday language (as distinct from literary and technical language). Ministry employs this type of linguistic meaning to express humanity's meeting with the divine. Regularly, especially in teaching, preaching, and liturgical narrative, ministry's use of language is complicated by the need to translate the ordinary language of the biblical authors into the ordinary language of particular contemporary cultures. Complicating matters, too, is the more technical dogmatic and theological language that has been developed throughout the Christian centuries, and that influences the mentality of contemporary Christians because it is now inevitably a component of the entire Christian context. Sometimes, indeed, the conceptual framework as well as specific words have been adopted on the level of ordinary language. Then the question arises from many quarters: What do we mean by these words in this context? Does the "religious" language we have inherited address the religious longings of contemporary Christians within the context of their contemporary language?

Examining the carriers of meaning instructs us that as an implementation of the communicative function of meaning Christian ministry excludes no level of human being. The entire person becomes engaged, from the chemical, biological, sensitive, and psychic, to the intellectual, rational, existential, and religious. "Organic and psychic vitality have to reveal themselves to intentional consciousness and, inversely, intentional consciousness has to secure the collaboration of organism and psyche."[25] God engages the whole person, and thus every carrier of meaning is called into play to communicate the invitation to communion and conversation with mystery.

Considered from the perspective of the basic structure of human inten-

---

23. See Stephen Happel's analysis of Lonergan's work in this regard in "The Sacraments: Symbols That Redirect Our Desires," in Gregson, ed., *Desires of the Human Heart.*

24. Lonergan, *Method in Theology,* 70.

25. Ibid., 66.

tionality, communion and conversation with God stand out as the highest good that human individuals and human community might strive to achieve. The reach of self-transcending human subjects always exceeds their grasp to some extent, and even consistent effort to work toward the achievement of lofty human good requires subjects who are so much in process of conversion in every dimension that they become more or less permanently "principles of benevolence and beneficence, capable of genuine collaboration and of true love."[26] For "at the summit of the ascent from the initial infantile bundle of needs and clamors and gratifications, there are to be found the deep-set joy and solid peace, the power and the vigor, of being in love with God. In the measure that that summit is reached, then the supreme value is God, and other values are God's expression of his love in this world, in its aspirations, and in its goal."[27]

Individual Ministers in a Ministerial Church

It has already been noted that conversion occurs in individuals. Subjects of their very nature cannot hand over responsibility for conversion to the church or to any other community, for the specific subjectivity is transformed in self-transcendence by the free response of the individual. Nevertheless, as noted above, conversion is not a private affair. "The same gift can be given to many, and the many can recognize in one another a common orientation in their living and feeling, in their criteria and their goals."[28] It would seem to be the extraordinarily rare individual who could achieve self-transcendence, especially in several dimensions of subjectivity, without strong communal support. Indeed, given the trinitarian understanding of humanity created in the image of God that guides this volume, human self-transcendence requires a communal context.

Christian ministers are nurtured by the Christian community. They come out of the community; baptism into the community of disciples of Jesus stands as the foundation of Christian ministry. Ministers also spend themselves working from within the community, even when their efforts are mainly within the wider society.

These more positive statements about the church as the community that gives birth to and supports self-transcendent Christian ministers can seem to contradict other more negative readings of the church as an excessively

26. Ibid., 35.
27. Ibid., 39.
28. Ibid., 118.

bureaucratic institution that constricts the dynamic self-transcendence of individuals. Rather than welcoming the freedom and imagination of eager Christian disciples, the church organization, and not only those exercising roles of leadership, is often perceived to be reining in its members.

Evidently, institutional malaise afflicts the church as much as any other established order. Consolidating the achievements of evangelization at any historical moment in order to preserve them for succeeding generations assures stability and continuity. But the human spirit has not been created to remain fixed in some sort of stasis. Besides the consolidation of achievements that we might, with Lonergan, name integration, the operations of consciousness remain ever active, through their operators. The desire to know and to love is expressed in questions for intelligence, reflection, and deliberation.[29] As the underlying tension erupts into actual conflict, it is not a matter of the good guys doing battle with the bad guys. It is a conflict within human subjectivity, individually and communally, between self-transcendence and alienation.[30] It is a struggle that takes place within every human subject.

Institutional malaise can take on a life of its own, insofar as it becomes systematically effective but so subliminally conscious on the part of individuals that few, if any, church members are aware of the stasis that has set in. Paralleling institutional malaise is individual sinfulness. It is the refusal of the subject to pursue self-transcendence writ large into a denial of the pull of mystery itself. Sinfulness leads to alienation—unconvertedness—in all the dimensions of subjectivity, and it includes the quest for ideology and hatred of oneself and one's fellow human beings.

Both individual subjects and the communal gathering of subjects that is the church stand in need of freedom from sinfulness and malaise. Christians know that such freedom is beyond the reach of unaided human beings individually or communally. Left to ourselves we cannot persist in dynamic self-transcendence. Divine assistance, redemption, provides our one sure hope.

The privileged revelation, which grounds the Christian church, is the assurance that God is gracious to humanity. The gift of God brings the freedom of redemption to the church community and, through it, to its individual members. Thus, the church community is freed, as much as each individual, in its integrative and operative moments. If it follows the path of self-transcendence in its several dimensions, the church as the community

---

29. Lonergan discusses the tension between integrators and operators within human subjects in *Insight*, 476–77.

30. Lonergan, *Method in Theology*, 357.

of the converted possesses the wherewithal to discern when and in which ways it stands at integrative moments of consolidating achievements and at operative moments of setting out anew.

Above all, the church does not exist for its own sake. It seeks to be faithful to the dynamism of self-transcendence stirring in its members not for the sake of its own self-promotion, for self-promotion occurs when self-transcendence has come to a halt. Rather the church is a ministerial church. Its role is to be servant in the spirit of its Servant Lord. The members of the church form a community in which each can be nourished in the pursuit of converted subjectivity. Yet, it would be too narrow to stop here. Beyond the conversion of its own members, the church is responsible for being servant of the world, doing what it can to invite every segment of society to become a community of communion and conversation.

Lonergan reminds us that this project takes a good bit of creativity and healing. First, creativity. Creativity is one part of "the long, hard uphill climb" of the process of effecting a humanity formed in the image and likeness of the triune God. It is a matter of generating insights that "find new uses for existing resources."[31] The creative process is cumulative and progressive: "Growth, progress, is a matter of situations yielding insights, insights yielding policies and projects, policies and projects transforming the initial situation, and the transformed situation giving rise to further insights that correct and complement the deficiencies of previous insights."[32]

The Christian church is blessed with enormous numbers of talented people of good will (remember, every baptized person is endowed with charisms) who are committed to Jesus and his gospel. It is difficult to imagine a greater storehouse of resources. Potential for creativity abounds. The church, then, need never lose its nerve. If even less than the total percentage of the Christian people activates evangelical fervor in an atmosphere of freely welcoming insights that address the needs of the church to foster conversion among its membership and in wider society, no true, good, and beautiful option should be impossible to achieve. We can be what baptism and order call us to be.

Of course, with baptism and order come not only the power to be creative, but also the healing of creativity made necessary because of the endemic persistence of sin. Since the "wheel of progress becomes a wheel of decline when the [creative] process is distorted by bias," creativity's complement is a love that "breaks the bonds of psychological and social determin-

31. Bernard Lonergan, 'Healing and Creating in History,' in A Third Collection, ed. Crowe, 103.
32. Ibid., 105.

isms with the conviction of faith and the power of hope."[33] Eminently healing is the redemptive gift of divine love which is more powerful than the
power of sin. But it is the role of the church to appropriate the redemptive
gift and communicate it through its ministry so that alienation and ideology are overcome in a healing reconciliation that brings the dynamism of
self-transcendence to its highest expression, thus freeing the potential of
creative insight to become actualized once again with renewed vigor.

A Trinitarian Formation
of Christian Ministers

When all are in process of conversion, the dimensions of human subjectivity coalesce into a dynamic, interpersonal relationship of love with the
triune God. Affect is most profoundly reception of the love of the triune
God for humanity and, in return, love for God by human subjects whom
the Holy Spirit of Love transfixes. Psychic conversion is ultimately appreciation that subliminal consciousness is rooted in the divine time-out-of-
mind. Moral conversion commits the subject to what is most worthwhile,
namely, whatever is of God. Intellectual conversion is possession by the eros
of mind that settles for nothing less than infinite truth, nowhere more completely expressed in human form than in the divine Logos become incarnate, whom subjects meet in the freeing process of Christian conversion.
Religious conversion orients a subject in his or her total intentionality to
the mysterious source and mysterious end of all reality, the first person of
the triune God.[34]

Nowhere is the coalescence of the conversions in communion with the
triune God more intensely experienced than in prayer, both private and
public. The experience, that is, the immediacy, of prayer, however, leads to
the rest of life. It is mediated in the human affairs of those who love God.
At the heart of human affairs the word of the Holy Spirit within human
interiority combines with the word of the divine incarnation in the realm
of historical events to bring about the self-constitutive meaning that is the
church glorifying the divine source and, in turn, the communicative meaning that is ministry promoting communion and conversation.

As church and ministry take shape they are stamped in the image of the
triune God, for they are the work of persons whose lifeblood is the living

33. Ibid., 105, 106.

34. For an intriguing study of Lonergan's contribution to trinitarian theology and spirituality based on intentionality analysis, see Frederick E. Crowe, "Rethinking God-With-Us: Categories from Lonergan," *Science et Esprit* 41/2 (1989): 167–88.

God. Thus, church and ministry exhibit analogously the characteristics of the divine persons, equality, diversity, and mutuality, as well as the order of the trinitarian missions, the historical effects of the divine Source, Word, and Spirit. At the same time, because they exist in the realm of history, no concretizations of church and ministry can claim to be perfectly the image of the triune divine community. They are approximations, always suscep-tible of reshaping in changing historical circumstances. What authentic Christians are to leave in place, and what they ought to change; how they are to leave in place and how they are to change; these are issues that re-quire submission to prayer, observance, discipline, thought, and action. To meet the challenges is a noble task.

INDEX